Stratification and Inequality Series
The Center for the Study of Social Stratification and Inequality,
Global COE Program
Tohoku University, Japan
Volume 12

Inequality, Discrimination and Conflict in Japan

Stratification and Inequality Series
The Center for the Study of Social Stratification and Inequality,
Global COE Program
Tohoku University, Japan

Inequality amid Affluence: Social Stratification in Japan
Junsuke Hara and Kazuo Seiyama

Intentional Social Change: A Rational Choice Theory
Yoshimichi Sato

Constructing Civil Society in Japan: Voices of Environmental Movements
Koichi Hasegawa

Deciphering Stratification and Inequality: Japan and beyond
Yoshimichi Sato

Social Justice in Japan: Concepts, Theories and Paradigms
Ken-ichi Ohbuchi

Gender and Career in Japan
Atsuko Suzuki

Status and Stratification:
Cultural Forms in East and Southeast Asia
Mitsuhiko Shima

Globalization, Minorities and Civil Society:
Perspectives from Asian and Western Cities
Koichi Hasegawa and Naoki Yoshihara

Fluidity of Place: Globalization and the Transformation of Urban Space
Naoki Yoshihara

Japan's New Inequality: Intersection of
Employment Reforms and Welfare Arrangements
Yoshimichi Sato and Jun Imai

Minorities and Diversity
Kunihiro Kimura

Inequality, Discrimination and Conflict in Japan:
Ways to Social Justice and Cooperation
Ken-ichi Ohbuchi and Nobuko Asai

Series Editor: Yoshimichi Sato, Tohoku University
Editorial Board: Koichi Hasegawa, Ken-ichi Ohbuchi, Toshiaki Kimura, Kunihiro Kimura,
Yoshimichi Sato, Naoki Yoshihara, Mary C. Brinton, Jeffrey P. Broadbent

Stratification and Inequality Series
The Center for the Study of Social Stratification and Inequality,
Global COE Program
Tohoku University, Japan
Volume 12

Inequality, Discrimination and Conflict in Japan

Ways to Social Justice and Cooperation

Edited by

Ken-ichi Ohbuchi

and

Nobuko Asai

First published in 2011 by
Trans Pacific Press, PO Box 164, Balwyn North, Victoria 3104, Australia
Telephone: +61 (0)3 9859 1112 Fax: +61 (0)3 8911 7989
Email: tpp.mail@gmail.com
Web: http://www.transpacificpress.com

Copyright © Trans Pacific Press 2011

Designed and set by Digital Environs, Melbourne, Australia. www.digitalenvirons.com

Printed by BPA Print Group, Burwood, Victoria, Australia

Distributors

Australia and New Zealand
DA Information Services/Central Book Services
648 Whitehorse Road
Mitcham, Victoria 3132
Australia
Telephone: +61-3-9210-7777
Fax: + 61-3-9210-7788
Email: books@dadirect.com
Web: www.dadirect.com

USA and Canada
International Specialized Book Services (ISBS)
920 NE 58th Avenue, Suite 300
Portland, Oregon 97213-3786
USA
Telephone: 1-800-944-6190
Fax: 1-503-280-8832
Email: orders@isbs.com
Web: http://www.isbs.com

Asia and the Pacific
Kinokuniya Company Ltd.

Head office:
3-7-10 Shimomeguro
Meguro-ku
Tokyo 153-8504
Japan
Telephone: +81-3-6910-0531
Fax: +81-3-6420-1362
Email: bkimp@kinokuniya.co.jp
Web: www.kinokuniya.co.jp

Asia-Pacific office:
Kinokuniya Book Stores of Singapore Pte., Ltd.
391B Orchard Road #13-06/07/08
Ngee Ann City Tower B
Singapore 238874
Telephone: +65-6276-5558
Fax: +65-6276-5570
Email: SSO@kinokuniya.co.jp

All rights reserved. No production of any part of this book may take place without the written permission of Trans Pacific Press.

ISBN 978-1-920901-70-7 (Hardback)
ISBN 978-1-920901-15-8 (Paperback)

Cover image copyright: Tokkuri, used under license from PIXTA (pixta.jp).

Contents

Figures vi
Tables vii
List of Contributors viii
Preface x

Part 1: Social Stratification and the Sense of Justice

1 Culture and Fairness: Some Possible Dynamics of Cultural Variation in the Psychology of Fairness *E. Allan Lind* 3
2 Social Inequality and Sense of Fairness in Japan: Multi-Level Sense of Fairness, Social Ideals and Rationalization Mechanisms *Nobuyoshi Kawashima* 22
3 Social Class and Values in Japan *Ken-ichi Ohbuchi* 41
4 Invisible Inequality: Occupational Prestige *Yoshiya Shiotani* 65
5 Distributive Justice in Economic Theory, and the Capability Approach *Jun Matsuyama* 87

Part 2: Conflict and Cooperation in Social Relations

6 Intergroup Unfairness and Group Identification *Tomohiro Kumagai* 103
7 Maintaining the Gender Gap and Benevolent Sexism *Takehiro Yamamoto and Ken-ichi Ohbuchi* 115
8 Strategies for Coping with Discrimination: How Do Disadvantaged Group Members Explain Their Experience of Discrimination? *Nobuko Asai* 131
9 Local Cooperation and Social Inequalities *Hiroyuki Hikichi* 149
10 Pro-social Behavior and Fairness Studies: A Review and Perspective *Toshiaki Aoki* 162

Notes 179
Bibliography 182
Index 211

List of Figures

1.1	Processing fairness-relevant information	11
2.1	The effect of interaction between a belief in a just world and educational background on macro fairness	37
3.1	Difference in preference for distributive fairness criteria in Japan and the USA	43
3.2	Difference in preference for fairness criteria according to annual income	46
3.3	Difference in preference for fairness criteria according to education	47
3.4	Difference in collectivism according to annual income	52
3.5	Difference in collectivism according to education	53
3.6	Age difference in collectivism	53
3.7	Degree of support for traditional Japanese values	57
3.8	Difference in traditional values according to income	60
3.9	Difference in traditional values according to education	60
5.1	Marginal utility functions of individuals A and B	93
8.1	Mean attribution ratings as a function of the target, outcome and the population of biased people in potential interviewers	143
8.2	Cognitive strategies for coping with discrimination used by members of disadvantaged groups	147
9.1	The effect of the sense of relative deprivation in the community on community commitment and the intention to participate in community activity	161
10.1	Changes in trust of the government and intention to approve the dam construction	175
10.2	Structure of attitude formation at the commencement of negotiations	175
10.3	Structure of attitude formation after negotiations	176

List of Tables

4.1 Occupational prestige scores (from 1995 SSM Survey)   70
5.1 Utilities in different situations   89
7.1 Proportion of women in Japan's pink collar sector   120

List of Contributors

Ken-Ichi Ohbuchi
Professor, Department of Psychology, Graduate School of Arts and Letters, Tohoku University

E. Allan Lind
Professor of Management, Fuqua School of Business, Duke University

Nobuyoshi Kawashima
Graduate student, Department of Psychology, Graduate School of Arts and Letters, Tohoku University
Research Fellow, the Japan Society for the Promotion of Science

Yoshiya Shiotani
Graduate student, Department of Behavioral Science, Graduate School of Arts and Letters, Tohoku University
Research Fellow, the Japan Society for the Promotion of Science

Jun Matsuyama
Graduate student, Department of Economics, Graduate School of Economics and Management, Tohoku University

Tomohiro Kumagai
Assistant Professor, Department of Communication and Culture, Faculty of Language and Literature, Otsuma Women's University

Takehiro Yamamoto
Graduate student, Department of Psychology, Graduate School of Arts and Letters, Tohoku University

Nobuko Asai
Postdoctoral Research Fellow, the Center for the Study of Social Stratification and Inequality (CSSI), Tohoku University

Hiroyuki Hikichi
Graduate student, Department of Psychology, Graduate School of Arts and Letters, Tohoku University

Toshiaki Aoki
Associate Professor, Department of Management and Communication, Tohoku Institute of Technology

Preface

This is a book on the findings of the latest research on social conflicts and how they are settled in Japan. Most chapters are written by Japanese researchers but some are written by American researchers. Japan has walked a very unique path in post-World War II history. We are not simply referring to the miraculous economic growth from the ashes of the war. Japan has managed to avoid involvement in almost all international conflicts in the 60 years since the end of WWII. This period witnessed the Korean Conflict, Vietnam War, India-Pakistan War, Afghanistan War, Gulf War and Iraq War in Asia alone; but Japan managed to stay away from them all, not even becoming indirectly involved. Although Japan did establish the International Peace Cooperation Law (PKO Cooperation Law) in 1993, it remained extremely reserved in its application, ordering the deployment of Japan Self-Defense Forces troops to Iraq only after the Iraq War ended in 2003. Even then, the troops were sent to carefully selected noncombat zones of Iraq as stipulated in the conditions under which the Japanese Diet approved the troops' dispatch.

The post-war Constitution provides the basis for Japan's efforts to avoid involvement in international conflicts, but in the backdrop, we can also cite the Japanese citizens' strong reaction towards international conflicts, stemming from the WWII memory in which the nation as well as individual people suffered enormous losses. The nation is still recovering from the post-war mental syndrome and has exhibited intense allergic reactions to everything that reminds them of the war in any way (Hayashi, 2008). As a result, the Japanese cabinets of this period, in fear of the people's strong reaction against war, avoided official involvement in almost all international conflicts and when forced into cooperating with its ally, the US, they did so behind closed doors without letting the people know (e.g., nuclear deployment in the US military bases in Okinawa, port call of US Navy aircraft carriers carrying nuclear weapons [Kuriyama, 2010]).

The Japanese people's allergy towards conflict is not restricted to international relationships but extends to all aspects of individual social lives. People despise confrontation as a curse and pretend not to see conflicts, as if they do not exist in this world. Unity and harmony are strongly emphasized in Japanese society (Ohbuchi, 1998). During the high-growth period of Japan, Japanese companies relied on an employment system based on seniority and lifetime employment. The system emphasized equality to achieve harmony within the organization and to strengthen the sense of belonging among its employees. Economic disparities were reduced to a minimum during this period, to such an extent that everyone in the society believed that they belonged to the middle-class (Sato, 2000).

The government, in the meantime, created numerous regulations in every industry to restrict businesses. In a way, this could be viewed as an excessive attempt to prevent troubles before they even emerge, based on Japan's conflict prevention philosophy. Excessive regulations, however, had the potential risk of stagnating economic activities by favoring businesses with vested interests and preventing new entries. Fortunately enough, the distortions did not surface during the high-growth period and these political and economic structures were maintained up until the early 1990s. While enjoying domestic economic prosperity, the majority of the Japanese people remained indifferent to conflicts and injustices occurring around the world and avoided facing the issues of hostility and prejudice among social groups that lay behind such occurrences, which potentially existed in Japan as well.

However, the Japanese harmony capsule, also known as peace addiction, began to show cracks in the 1990s as Japan entered a long recession caused by the collapse of the bubble economy, followed by a complete crash in 2001 with the 9/11 terrorist attacks. The Koizumi Cabinet frantically accelerated deregulation and liberalization of economic activities in Japan, with the inevitable consequence that economic disparities have expanded and conflicts of interest among domestic groups have become clearly evident. For example, filing of new civil litigation cases doubled in 2003 compared to the 1990s. The number is currently declining but still remains at a high rate of 140 per cent of the 1990 figure (Supreme Court, 2010). To relieve the situation, the government is currently working on increasing the number of lawyers and simplifying court processes.

As we have seen, Japan, in the late 1990s, began to steer away from its previous conflict prevention principle to a new conflict resolution principle in managing society. This shift in the principle seems to be gradually permeating into the mentality of the Japanese people as well.

At the same time, the Japanese people began to face the fact that the nation does indeed have various contentious issues with other nations. The Japanese were always aware of the ill feelings that the Chinese and Koreans held towards them since WWII but generally thought that this was due to the war, and thus in the past; not because of any current conflicts. The younger generations had developed a feeling that being a target of hatred for something they had no direct involvement in was irrational, and thus dismissed the issue as emotional problems which were not directly relevant to their daily lives. However, recent territorial and trade disputes are making people aware that these issues have the potential to extend beyond emotional problems and may have substantial consequences. In other words, the Japanese people have finally become aware that they may be participants in international conflicts.

Given these domestic and international transitions as the backdrop, this book examines theoretical and empirical research on conflict resolution involving Japanese people and discusses its significance. When considering conflict issues, social justice is an important factor in discussing the cause (injustice) and the appropriateness of the solution. Thus all papers in this book approach the issue of conflict resolution using social justice as the key word. Part 1 consists of papers which analyze the disparities that are reportedly growing in modern Japan, and perceptions of injustice from the perspectives of social class, value, social principle, culture and legitimization. Part 2 includes empirical research on the Japanese people at different levels (individual, group, regional and social) pertaining to the mechanisms of the outbreak of conflicts and individual and social attempts to resolve the situations.

Ken-ichi Ohbuchi

**Part 1:
Social Stratification
and the Sense of Justice**

1 Culture and Fairness: Some Possible Dynamics of Cultural Variation in the Psychology of Fairness

E. Allan Lind

When in the 1960s and 1970s social psychologists began studying fairness judgments (e.g., Adams, 1965; Thibaut and Walker, 1975) the first experiments were done in the United States, but not long thereafter investigations of cultural variation in core fairness phenomena were undertaken (e.g., Lind, Thibaut and Walker, 1976; Lind, Erickson, Friedland and Dickenberger, 1978). As time has passed, quite a few studies in the now-substantial literature on the psychology of justice have addressed issues of cultural variation and how the psychology of fairness works in non-US contexts. This literature includes a number of different views and findings about the impact of culture on the psychology of fairness. These range from some reports contending, in essence, that fairness is not even a very important concept in some national contexts (see, e.g., Kidder and Muller's, 1991, assertion that the construct of fairness has little impact in Japan, but compare Ohbuchi, 2008c) to more common findings from empirical studies that there exist both similarities and differences in fairness phenomena across cultures (e.g., Lind, Tyler and Huo, 1997; Ohbuchi, Teshigahara, Imazai and Sugawara, 2005; Van den Bos, Brockner, Stein, Steiner, Van Yperen and Dekker, 2010). There have been a number of excellent reviews of culture-linked phenomena over the years (see, for example, Morris and Leung, 2000); most arrive at the conclusion that fairness and justice-linked phenomena are seen in all cultures but that there are some important differences in how these phenomena play out in any given culture.

The traditional approach to cross-cultural studies of fairness

The literature on the cross-cultural psychology of fairness includes many good empirical studies documenting when and how cultural differences will occur, but there is surprisingly little theory that addresses directly the origin and substance of cultural differences in the psychology of fairness. Individual reports of cultural similarities or differences are an important contribution to our science, to be sure, but it would surely be useful to find a way to deal with this substantial and growing literature in a more coherent fashion. Thus far, the theory that has been brought to bear on culture and fairness has come from outside the study of fairness. Many of the explanations offered for cultural differences use core concepts from cross-cultural social psychology or cross-cultural organizational psychology to predict and explain cultural variations in fairness phenomena. For example, Hofstede's (2001) cultural value dimensions are often used to predict or explain cultural differences in fairness judgments. Thus when Van den Bos et al. (2010) studied the impact of voice in the United States and the Netherlands the researchers predicted, on the basis of differences between these two nations on Hofstede's masculine-feminine culture dimension, that in the United States (a 'masculine' culture) those with higher performance capabilities would be more eager to exercise voice while in the Netherlands (a 'feminine' culture) those with lower performance capabilities would be more eager to exercise voice. The Van den Bos et al. (2010) studies confirmed the predictions.

This 'traditional' approach to cross-cultural studies of fairness has some potential limitations. First, because the logic must start with some international variation that has been discovered in research or theory on general cross-cultural psychology, one might suppose that there are important differences (or similarities) that are relevant to fairness processes but that are not part of these general models of psychology and culture. Thus, the logic of the Van de Bos et al. (2010) research begins with identification of the potential for differential moderation of voice effects from consideration of Hofstede's (2001) work on cultural differences between the US and the Netherlands on the masculinity-femininity dimension. But suppose that there are issue differences that are not tied to the cultural dimensions identified in Hofstede's work or to other theories of general cross-cultural psychology—how could one identify these different patterns of voice effects?

A second problem with this traditional approach is that by and large cultural features are seen as unchanging or only slowly changing. Although cross-cultural psychology works such as Hofstede's admit to the likelihood that cultures change, changes are usually seen as occurring through acculturation or culture drift processes and there is little basis in this approach for predicting relatively rapid changes in fairness ideas within any given culture. Given what we know about the psychology of fairness in individuals, though, it seems possible that fairness attitudes might change quickly within a given culture. Consider for example work on personal uncertainty and fairness judgment processes (see, e.g., Van den Bos and Lind, 2002, 2009). This literature shows that for any given individual the psychological processes involved in fairness reactions can change quite rapidly in response to stimuli that salientize personal uncertainty, with fairness phenomena showing increased vigor under conditions of uncertainty. Extended to a cultural level, might not some event that engendered widespread personal uncertainty—an event like a general economic downturn, for example—lead to a sudden upsurge in attention to fairness and in the impact of fairness-related information? Ohbuchi (2008c) offers evidence that the way Japanese think about fairness changed rather quickly, perhaps in response to changes in the national economy.

An alternative approach to cross-cultural theorizing on fairness

An alternative, more dynamic, approach to studying culture and fairness might begin with our understanding of fairness processes and the moderating factors that we know of in fairness phenomena, and move from there to an analysis of cultural variation, rather than the other way around. Following this approach, culture in any given place and at any given time could be viewed as just a set of situational and psychological conditions (albeit perhaps quite important conditions) that function as moderators in fairness phenomena. For example, instead of asking how the differences in cultural masculinity affect fairness judgments, as Van den Bos et al. (2010) did, it might be more productive to note that voice is very likely to be more important to people to the extent that it addresses issues important to the person granted voice and to their feelings of inclusion in the group. One might then note normative differences between the United States and the Netherlands in what constitute important issues. To be sure, this is precisely the argument that Van den Bos et al. (2010) advance once they use the Hofstede dimension to differentiate what might be important issues in each culture, but the critical element is that under the traditional approach the Hofstede dimension was needed first to identify the difference in voice issues.[1] Under the alternative approach suggested here, one would have looked for cultural differences in voice on issues that differ in importance across two locations whether or not these differences were linked to a distinction identified in cross-cultural psychology.

The difference between the traditional approach and the alternative approach is subtle, admittedly, but the two have important differences in their implications for research. Among the most important of these differences is the possibility in the alternative approach of seeing relatively short-term temporal changes in the dynamics of fairness. Two possible historical examples come to mind—one suggested by the uncertainty management processes described earlier and one suggested by discussions of the impact of external threats on system justification processes (Jost, Banaji and Nosek, 2004; see also Chanley, 2002; Huddy, Feldman, Capelos and Provost, 2002.)

Consider first the possibility of a culture-wide uncertainty management effect (Van den Bos and Lind, 2002, 2009) in which widespread feelings of personal uncertainty prompt greater concern with fairness issues. As noted above, it is quite possible that a strong economic downturn could engender substantial uncertainty among a great many members of the society experiencing the downturn. If each person's sensitivity to fairness increased as a result of his or her personal uncertainty, then a culture-wide increase in the incidence and strength of fairness-linked reactions would be expected. Two instances of possible short-term cultural effects of this sort are seen in Japan in the 1990s and in the United States (and possibly other countries) in the late 2000s. Ohbuchi (2008c) notes that a general population value poll conducted in 2000, after what had been described as the 'collapse of the bubble economy', showed that justice was the highest rated value, while a survey of experts eight years earlier had put justice at only 17th in the value hierarchy. Ohbuchi argues justice has always been an important issue in Japan, that the change is really one of what form of justice is being considered and how it is labeled. This is probably the case, but it is possible too that another factor in the higher ratings of justice as a value is widespread personal uncertainty prompted by very slow economic growth in the 1990s, prompting greater concerns with fairness. The extremely negative public reaction in the United States during late 2008 and 2009 to high bonuses for traders and executives in financial services firms might represent another culture-wide fairness effect. Traditionally, Americans have been very tolerant of what must often seem to the rest of the world to be outrageous individual payments in these professions. But at the time in question most Americans were experiencing substantial personal uncertainty as a result of the onset of the worst recession in years, and they may well have been sensitized to fairness issues and therefore more inclined to resent the apparently unfair overpayment of some when others were suffering deprivation. Both of these examples from recent economic history are anecdotal, in that we have no data to show that concerns with fairness was moderated by personal uncertainty, but the examples do raise the possibility of temporal effects on the culture of fairness. If we had in place some fairness-focused theories of culture and social reactions, we might also have long-term survey data to use as we study how fairness processes work to create temporal patterns in attitudes and behavior across a culture.

Another example comes from system justification theory (e.g., Jost et al., 2004), which suggests that people often rationalize away injustice in order to maintain their belief in social institutions and entities, and that this tendency to justify the system is particularly strong when the ingroup is seen as under threat. System justification processes are often invoked as an explanation for tolerance on the part of the American people in the first part of the last decade to both growing income inequality and a relaxation of legal safeguards for personal liberty (see, e.g., Chanley, 2002; Huddy et al., 2002; Jost and Hunyady, 2005). The argument is that the terrorist attacks of September 11, 2001, were widely perceived as a threat to American culture, and this led Americans to rationalize away distributive and procedural fairness concerns that might otherwise have arisen about the Bush Administration's policies in these areas. Again, the phenomenon being proposed is a temporary, society-wide expression of an individual fairness-linked psychological process.

The traditional cross-cultural approach to the psychology of fairness cannot easily explain either of these effects, nor would that approach identify differences between cultures that occur because one of these effects was playing out in one culture but not another. For example, if the system justification process just described did indeed occur, it would have led Americans to be less sensitive to social and political fairness during the early 2000s, while no such effect should have occurred, for example, among the Japanese, and this would have produced a change in relative sensitivity to fairness concerns in these two countries. This change in cross-cultural differences in sensitivity to fairness would hardly have been expected from the sorts of differences between the cultures studied in general cross-cultural social psychology, because those differences are usually based on cultural elements that do not vary much from one decade to the next. Similarly, if the speculation above about generalized personal uncertainty and the enhancement of fairness concerns in Japan and the United States in the 1990s and late 2000s, respectively, is correct, here is another cultural fairness dynamic that would not have been predicted from the traditional approach to cross-cultural fairness research. These variations in the relative size of fairness effects in the two countries at these two time periods were never studied because we had no real theory that raised the possibility of such social and economic event-based changes.

A dynamic analysis of culture and fairness

To illustrate how one might work from a general model of the psychology of fairness to an understanding of cultural variations in fairness-linked processes, I will offer an example based on two theories: Fairness Heuristic Theory (Lind, 2001; Van den Bos, Lind and Wilke, 2001), Uncertainty Management Theory (Van den Bos and Lind, 2002), and a recent chapter applying ideas from both theories to fairness and change in organizations (Tost and Lind, 2010). I first will describe the core concepts in these theories, and then I will examine how some of these concepts might be used to address similarities and differences between cultures (and across time periods).

Fairness Heuristic Theory (Lind, 2001; Van den Bos et al., 2001) argues that at its core fairness is perceived to exist when a person feels that there is balance between his or her own individual interests and those of another person or some larger social entity. In this formulation, the term 'interests' is defined broadly—it includes not only material outcomes and other components of social exchange but also the interests that individuals and groups have in maintaining their identities. People engage and identify with others because participation in some larger social entity provides advantages in material rewards and identity. Participation and engagement also bring, though, the potential for exploitation and exclusion, with all of the negative consequences that that entails. This inevitable conflict between individual and group interests is termed the 'fundamental social dilemma'. In Fairness Heuristic Theory, it is argued that it is by reference to feelings of fair or unfair treatment that people are able to resolve this dilemma on a day-to-day basis. On the one hand, the theory suggests that when there is perceived to be a proper balance of outcomes and identities, then the situation seems fair and cooperative actions are engendered (e.g., acceptance of the decisions of authorities, cooperative reactions to requests, positive feelings and contributions beyond what is strictly required). On the other hand, when the person thinks there is an imbalance of interests—when he or she believes that someone is getting more than deserved or that someone is being treated without the proper measure of dignity or respect—then the situation is unfair and the person enacts less cooperative behavior and feelings, running the gamut from performance for immediate payment only to 'vendettas' intended to harm the perceived agent of unfairness (Lind, Greenberg, Scott and Welchans, 2000).

The definition of fairness as perceived balance between individual and collective interests fits with theories of fairness going back to Adams' equity theory (1965) and continuing through the early procedural justice theory of Thibaut and Walker (1978) to my work with Tom Tyler (Lind and Tyler, 1988; Tyler and Lind, 1992) on group value and relational authority models of procedural fairness. This conception of fairness is also certainly congruent with, but distinct from, Ohbuchi's Justice-Bond Theory (2007), which goes even farther in detailing the connection between fairness judgments and felt bonds with larger social entities. The notion of fairness as a perceived balance of interests also is congruent with Folger and Cropanzano's Fairness Theory (2001) and Tyler and Blader's group engagement model (2003). The major differences among all of these theories lie in their reasoning about why and when fairness concerns are important to people, their assertions about what sort of interests are most important to balance, their analysis of how people interpret their situation and the behavior of others to discover whether interests are in balance, and their predictions about what feelings and behaviors result from perceived imbalances of interests.

When defined at such a fundamental level, fairness is almost certainly a psychological phenomenon that exists in every culture— in all societies humans are arguably concerned at least on occasion with whether their interests and the interests of others are in proper balance. Indeed, there is good evidence that fairness-like phenomena, seen as behavior that maintains a stable balance between individual and social interests, exist across a wide range of social animals including primates, canids, cetaceans, and corvids (Brosnan and de Waal, 2003; De Waal, 1996). As noted earlier, reviews of culture and fairness in human societies and organizations report variation in, but never absence of, fairness phenomena. Thus it appears that cultural differences in fairness are likely to involve questions of *how* or *when* fairness effects occur, not *whether* such effects occur. Of course, even with this assumption of universal concern with fairness there remains the need to understand the particular dynamics of how fairness phenomena will play out in any given national culture and *at any given time.*

Fairness Heuristic Theory and its successors can provide some direction to guide thinking about temporal dynamics in the interplay of culture and fairness. Specifically, these theories argue that because fairness is used as a heuristic to guide social identification and prosocial behavior, cognitive efficiency dictates that once an assessment has been formed of the fairness level of a given situation or relationship, further intensive processing of fairness-relevant information (which occurs during what is called the 'judgment phase') is abandoned and the person in question enters a state where he or she focuses on enacting the prosocial or proself behavior dictated by the judgment that the relationship is fair or unfair. In this state (during what is called the 'use phase'), incoming information and experiences are assimilated to the existing fairness impression. A number of research studies have supported this aspect of the theory. For example, Lind, Kray and Thompson (2001) showed that, as predicted by the theory, procedural fairness experiences early in an interaction with an authority figure had greater impact than did later experiences. Van den Bos et al. (2001) describe a number of studies that are in line with the theory's contention that fairness does indeed serve as a heuristic for trust and that later fairness information is assimilated to prior fairness information, even when the later information is of a different form (e.g., when procedural information follows distributive information).

Uncertainty Management Theory (Van den Bos and Lind, 2001) builds on this idea of episodic processing of fairness information by putting forward the idea that it is personal uncertainty that stimulates people to engage in strong processing of fairness information. The theory builds on a number of studies by Van den Bos and his colleagues (e.g., Van den Bos, 2001; Van den Bos, Ham, Lind, Simonis, van Essen and Rijpkema, 2008; Van den Bos, Heuven, Burger and Fernández Van Veldhuizen, 2006) that show that reminding people of personal uncertainty, or even salientizing uncertainty by providing cultural symbols of caution (such as exclamation points or flashing yellow lights), will prompt greater concern with and responsiveness to such individual fairness variables as voice or equity. Indeed there is even some evidence that the uncertainty- fairness link is 'hard-wired' into the human brain (Van den Bos et al., 2008), that both are part of a

Figure 1.1: Processing fairness-relevant information

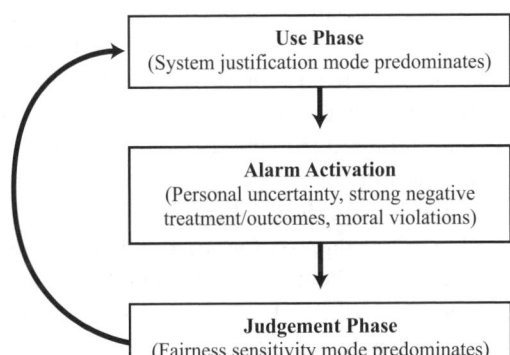

human alarm system. Especially noteworthy in the context of the current discussion is the fact that the source of the personal uncertainty need not be in the same context or relationship as the subsequent fairness effect. Experimental studies of uncertainty- or alarm-enhanced fairness effects have used unconnected uncertainty manipulations such as answering questions about one's feelings when thinking of one's own mortality (in an apparently separate experiment) or even the presence of a flashing yellow light near the point of data collection. This point is important because it suggests that the enhancement of personal uncertainty across a cultural population might increase the strength of fairness reactions even in areas unrelated to the source of the uncertainty—an epidemic illness might make people more aware of and sensitive to unfairness in their work environment, for example, or an economic downturn might stimulate fairness-based reactions in personal or political contexts.

Tost and Lind (2010) built on Fairness Heuristic Theory and Uncertainty Management Theory to explain how fairness and change might be related in organizations. One of the additions to previous theory in this new work is the incorporation of ideas from System Justification Theory (Jost, Banaji and Nosek, 2004). Figure 1.1 shows how the sequence might work in a more general cultural context than that addressed by Tost and Lind.

Use Phase fairness processes

How might these ideas be applied to predict differences in fairness phenomena across cultures? A starting point is the conception in

Fairness Heuristic Theory that psychologically fairness is the belief that individual interests (broadly defined) are in an appropriate balance with the interests of the relationship or group in question, or in social justice contexts, in an appropriate balance with the interests of society in general. Inherent in this concept of justice is the idea that there is some standard for what is an appropriate balance and that there is an interpretive process that allows the person forming the fairness judgment to decide whether the current situation matches that balance. One might suppose that part of a child's socialization would involve learning, from statements and behaviors observed, what might be the 'fair' balance for various types of relationships. In addition, there are various ideals that might guide participation in a given relationship and the attention given to each of these ideals as they are translated into signs of appropriate or inappropriate balance might vary from one situation to another or from one culture to another. For example, Ohbuchi (2007b, 2008c, this volume) has noted that although in Japan and western countries we emphasize equity, equality, and need as justice ideals because they address individual autonomy, social harmony, and social welfare respectively, there are other social ideals in other societies that might well form the basis of fairness judgments there. Thus, behavior appropriate to one's social strata, rewards for length of service, and actions in accordance with religious principles could be used to judge fairness in societies or situations that place great emphasis on social order, group stability, and religion. Since the socialized rules of fairness are those that are generally practiced in the person's society, the initial fairness belief will be positive.

In the Use Phase these initial positive fairness judgments would provoke identification with the social structure and hierarchy and, as System Justification Theory predicts, this would result in future assessments of fairness and acceptance of social structure being assimilated to this positive identification. Further, again in accordance with System Justification Theory, any external system threat would result in stronger rationalizations, pushing people to all the more strongly explain away evidence of injustice as they encounter it. In line with the primacy (Lind et al., 2001) and substitutability (Van den Bos et al, 2001) effects predicted by Fairness Heuristic Theory, new fairness information will be processed in light of strong existing fairness beliefs—the new information will be expected to match existing fairness beliefs, and any discrepancy will be discounted or ignored. People (in any culture) who are in this state may well say they care about fairness (especially if fairness is a part of the 'ideology' of the culture), but fairness-relevant experiences or information would not have great psychological power because little mental effort is being devoted to upgrading existing fairness beliefs. In this phase the flow of causality is from the perception of a social bond to a belief in fairness.

It is worth noting that external threats are not predicted to drive people out of the Use Phase. Indeed when a person (or a culture) is in this phase, external threats are predicted to provoke a 'cleansing' of discordant fairness experiences and information, whereby any suggestions of unfairness are targeted for rationalization or, if the experience is too discordant with the dominant perception of unfairness, psychological repression.

Alarm Activation

The occurrence of widespread personal uncertainty, however, would activate a radical change in how fairness judgments were generated and used. In Figure 1.1, this transition is labeled 'Alarm Activation'. Following Uncertainty Management Theory (Van den Bos and Lind, 2009), once a state of personal uncertainty or alarm is instigated, the person transitions into the 'Judgment Phase', which represents a radical alteration in how fairness information is processed and how fairness judgments are used.

It should be noted that there is a sharp distinction here between *external* threats to the social system and *personal* uncertainty. The former results in more resistance to re-evaluation of fairness in the system and the latter results in a greater inclination to re-evaluate fairness. Thus, if a person perceives his or her social system, previously perceived to be generally fair, to be under attack or to be threatened cognitively, then the person will be very unlikely to change that overall assessment of fairness. That is, on the one hand, under external threat, new fairness-linked information will have *less* impact than might be the case without threat. On the other hand, if the person is in a state of personal uncertainty that engages the human alarm system, then fairness-linked experiences and information will have *more* impact than would otherwise be the case. The flow of causality is quite different in the two situations. Under external threat, identification with the group drives fairness judgments; under personal uncertainty, fairness judgments drive identification.

These two very different processes, and the manner in which culture-wide events and perceptions might trigger one or the other, give rise to some interesting predictions (see Tost and Lind, 2010, for a discussion of similar phenomena in organizations). Because the 'flow' of causality is so different under uncertainty management and system justification processes, events or beliefs that move people from one process to another might, under specific circumstances, result in radical changes from one set of attitudes or pattern of behavior to another. Imagine, for example, a culture with substantial objective inequities or with procedures or customary interpersonal processes that are objectively unfair. As long as there is a widespread perception of threat to the social system (or as long as other factors promoting system justification processes are strong) the unfair elements of the culture will be discounted in the interest of system justification. If some or all of the members of the culture find themselves experiencing substantial personal uncertainty, though, their reactions to the 'ambient' unfairness might change substantially. As these people try to cope with their personal uncertainty, they will pay more and more attention to the fairness or unfairness that they see around them, and they may swing from being system supporters to system critics—or even revolutionaries—in a remarkably short period of time.

Of course, there are events that simultaneously raise external threat concerns and personal uncertainty, and in these circumstances it is difficult to say whether system justification or uncertainty management processes will predominate. Probably whichever psychological dynamic is most provoked by the event will predominate. This is what was suggested by the historical anecdotes mentioned above—the 9/11 attacks no doubt caused some personal uncertainty for many Americans, but the perceived threat to the country was more salient so system justification processes predominated. In contrast, in the economic recession of 2008–2009 it was evident that the country would survive, but many Americans were not at all sure that their economic welfare would endure, so uncertainty management became the most common response. There is much to be learned from research that looks for changes around this 'tipping point' of system justification versus uncertainty management. In addition, the psychology of social and political change might benefit from empirical examination of how patterns of personal uncertainty and perceived system threat are distributed across the population of a given nation at different points in time. As some members of a nation or culture come to re-evaluate their situation in terms of fairness, while others 'explain away' injustice in the interest of system justification, one would expect to see substantial social conflict. Let us consider briefly, then, what sort of events might trigger alarm activation on a cultural level, if the logic of Fairness Heuristic Theory and Uncertainty Management Theory is indeed applicable to temporal patterns that play out on a broad scale. Tost and Lind (2010) list three categories of events that can activate fairness-related alarm and thus prompt a switch from the assimilation of fairness experiences to initial fairness positions (and justification of the system) that is posited to be a feature of use-phase fairness cognitions to the re-evaluation and enhanced sensitivity that is supposed to exist in the judgment phase. These three categories of events are 1) those events that stimulate the human alarm system either directly or by calling up thoughts about personal uncertainty, 2) very stark violations of expectations with respect to personal treatment or outcomes, and 3) events or actions that clash undeniably with very basic moral or philosophical beliefs.

A cultural version of the first category of fairness-related alarm would require that feelings of personal uncertainty be provoked at about the same time in a substantial proportion of the population. One of the examples used above was the onset of an economic downturn of sufficient magnitude and breadth of effect as to make large numbers of people uncertain about their future, such as that occurring in the last years of the last decade. As noted earlier, an interesting finding from the experimental studies on fairness and uncertainty management (see generally Van den Bos and Lind, 2009) is that the uncertainty does not need to be in the same context as the fairness effects it provokes. Thus, early studies on fairness and uncertainty management (e.g., Van den Bos, 2001) used uncertainty manipulations that simply asked experimental participants to recall uncertain situations—*any* uncertain situations—and then observed heightened sensitivity to fairness experiences in a supposedly separate experimental task. In another study (Van den Bos et al., 2008), a flashing warning light positioned in the general vicinity of data collection for a field study on fairness was enough to enhance fairness effects. On the individual level, then, it appears that personal uncertainty in one area can 'bleed over' to switch on enhanced fairness evaluations in an entirely different part of life. The example introduced earlier of uncertainty from the 2008–2009 recession perhaps fostering especially intense resentment of executive and trader bonuses has the uncertainty and the fairness re-evaluation in the same part of American culture. It is perhaps not surprising, though, that at the same time a substantial minority of Americans showed a rapid change of attitude with respect to universal health care. Instituting such a reform to American health care had been a popular issue in the 2008 presidential campaign, but by the late summer of 2009 there was a surprisingly negative reaction to a law mandating such reform. The political opponents of health care reform had found fertile ground for their arguments castigating the procedural fairness of the legislative process that produced the reform and criticizing the individual rights implications of the new law. Might it have been the case that widespread uncertainty about jobs and financial security opened people up to fairness-based political arguments, even though those arguments concerned a topic that really had little to do with the financial crisis? Of course, there are many other arguments that might be applied post-hoc to explain these political events, but the possibility of a change in the perceived fairness of the system is intriguing.

A second category of situations prompting Alarm Activation involves stark violations of strong expectations with respect to treatment or outcomes. Examples of such a stark violation of expectations in American history might be the hugely negative economic outcomes experienced in the Great Depression, which called into question the whole structure of governmental social support. This example falls into the category of violations of expectations, and not simply an alarm from personal uncertainty, because there was little doubt—the negative outcomes in the Depression were known, not probabilistic—and they stood in stark contrast to the 'boom' years of the early and mid-1920s. Whereas most Americans were only alarmed for the future in the recession of 2008–2009, in the 1930s most Americans experienced radical and unexpected reduced quality of life. Again, of course, this is only speculation concerning what was happening in the psychology of fairness at a given point in the history of American culture.

The final category of alarm that might prompt a change from Use Phase assimilation and justification processes to Judgment Phase re-evaluation is the occurrence of events or important actions that constitute a violation of rules or principles that are seen as basic to the culture. Skitka's (2002) work on moral mandates provides examples of such re-evaluations in individual fairness reactions. The application of this idea to temporal trends in culture and fairness involves some action or event that touches on widespread concerns and that violates a fundamental principle of the culture. An example might be the widespread distaste and subsequent political reforms in American political processes after the Watergate Scandal of the 1970s. The scandal involved actions in a presidential campaign that simply were 'beyond the pale' for most Americans, and the resulting changes in public opinion about restrictions on political campaign activities and acceptance of public financing of presidential campaigns may well have been driven by a post-Watergate re-assessment of whether American politics was fair.

Judgment Phase fairness processes

Once a fairness Alarm Activation has occurred, the impact of information about the fairness of all social relationships will be enhanced. As new information and experiences relevant to the assessment of fairness of any given relationship is encountered it will be used to revise fairness impressions. Memories of instances of past fair or unfair treatment will be retrieved and factored into this re-evaluation process. As revised fairness assessments are formed, they will in turn alter pre-existing inclinations to bond with the social entities in question and to guide cooperative or pro-social behavior, along the lines suggested by Fairness Heuristic Theory.

In the evaluation of whether one is being treated fairly or unfairly, circumstances and cultural factors may well enter into consideration, with greatest attention being given to treatment dimensions and outcomes that are linked to the core values and societal ideals within which the fairness judgment is being made. Thus, on an intra-societal basis Ohbuchi's (2008c, this volume) writings help us understand differences in what is considered fair and proper in, for example, an investment bank versus a religious monastery (or between individuals of different class or political persuasions; see Ohbuchi, this volume). On a cross-cultural level, as Ohbuchi notes (2008c), this analysis of societal ideals may well be key to understanding what constitutes fairness in devout cultures or in traditionally hierarchical societies. When combined with the core heuristic process posted by Fairness Heuristic Theory, this would mean that in a very religious society following Alarm Activation causing transition into the Judgment Phase there would be a quick assessment of whether, for example, societal authorities are behaving in a religiously appropriate manner and this assessment would serve as the basis for deciding whether the perceiver's relation to the society was fair and proper. Once a fairness impression was thus established as a heuristic, later religiously-linked actions would be assimilated to this impression, so that later impious acts by authorities might be 'explained away' to make them fit the initial judgment. In addition, a positive initial fairness judgment, in this case based on evidence of piety or religious devotion by authorities, would lead to greater engagement and identification with the society and later in a new Use Phase, via system justification processes, to rationalizing away negative social outcomes or failures of the society on other justice principles.

Of course, the revised fairness judgment might be negative. The person in question might decide that their treatment or the actions of the social entity in question was unfair. If this were to happen, the Judgment Phase would result in disengagement from the social entity or, at the extreme, enmity toward it. Indeed, when an event or a change in circumstance prompts Alarm Activation and subsequent experiences push an individual toward the belief that their relationship with an organization or social structure is fundamentally unfair, remarkably strong reactions—what Lind et al. (2000) term a 'vendetta effect'—can be the result. In this instance the psychological dynamics of the subsequent Use Phase would be predicted to exhibit 'anti-System Justification' processes, in which experiences and subsequent impressions of the social entity would be assimilated to a negative, rather than a positive, judgment, and actions would be destructive, not supportive, of the welfare of the social entity in question.[2] It is from such fairness judgment processes, one might hypothesize, that revolutions are born.

Time, culture, and fairness

This approach to understanding how fairness works in different cultures suggests some differences and similarities in fairness phenomena that would not be expected from traditional cross-cultural psychology. First, the current line of thought predicts that in the Fairness Judgement Phase one would see conceptually similar primacy and assimilation effects on fairness judgments in, for example, a devoutly religious society and an avidly secular, economically oriented society, but that the key elements in arriving at the initial fairness judgment would differ depending on the societal ideal in each. That is, the pattern of reaction to a pious authority in the former and an equitable authority in the latter would be the same except for the criterion used to judge fairness.

But of course 'the criterion used to judge fairness' is a very important issue. In the discussion above, I have followed the lead of Ohbuchi (2007b, 2008c) and Deutsch (1975) in suggesting that all groups and societies choose fairness rules and criteria that turn on a balance of entitlement and treatment, but that the critical dimension of entitlement is based on social ideals in the society in question. In the context of Fairness Heuristic Theory logic, the key criterion question concerns what information or experience will be taken as an indication of individual security with respect to group actions. There is always an interpretive process involved in the judgment of balance and security, however, and the interpretation of fairness-linked experiences can be affected by cultural differences. Thus, in the Van den Bos et al. (2010) studies on voice and performance in the US and the Netherlands, referred to earlier, the two cultures studied differed in when voice was seen as appropriate and desirable. When cultural values dictated that voice was appropriate, then provision of voice was seen as relevant to judgments about those who controlled the process. Voice was thus a fairness criterion in both countries, but whether it was seen as relevant to evaluations of the person's relationship to the authority differed depending on cultural-moderated interpretations.

The connections between various fairness principles and the societal ideals they support appear to be invariant across cultures. Thus there is probably little or no cross-cultural variation in whether the fairness principle of equitable distribution of benefits (i.e., distribution of outcomes proportionate with performance in tasks benefiting the group or society) is associated with individual rights and individualized performance. The key question is how much emphasis the society places on individualized performance versus some other ideal, and in what social context each ideal predominates.

If we look at much of the existing social psychological literature on cultural differences in fairness judgments and related phenomena, one striking feature of many studies is that all members of a given culture are viewed as perfect representatives of that culture. That is, we tend to discuss the fairness judgment processes within various cultures as though every member of the culture carried an identical set of values and interpretations that drive potential differences from another culture, all members of which carry a different identical set of values and interpretations. Of course, this is not the case—that is evident from the fierce political debates that occur in many nations over what is fair national policy on one issue or another. Unfortunately we seldom look at intra-cultural differences in attitudes about the sort of societal values that drive preferences for some fairness criteria over others. Ohbuchi's chapter on demographic differences in societal values in this volume (Chapter 3) is a noteworthy exception. Some of the findings about education and values reported there raise the question, for example, of whether studies comparing the fairness judgments or actions of students in Japanese universities to, for example, those of students in American universities really represent how fairness is judged in the general national cultures in each location. It may well be the case that the comparison of highly educated respondents in each location leads us to underestimate how different the two fairness cultures are.

In summary, then, the present theoretical approach to cross-cultural fairness focuses attention on similarities of fundamental process and on differences in societal values and interpretations of fairness-relevant events. Similarities across cultures are likely to reflect the fundamental balancing of interests (in the terminology of Fairness Heuristic Theory and its successors; or the balancing of treatment and entitlement in Ohbuchi's fairness formula, 2007). Differences across cultures can result from differences in the societal values that are deemed most important in the context in question, from differences in how fairness-relevant experiences and events are interpreted or from events that put the cultures at different points in the Use-Phase–Alarm Activation–Judgment-Phase process.

Of the issues raised here, it is the possibility of temporal cultural trends in fairness judgments that may well be the most intriguing topic for future research and theory. As noted at the outset, the psychology of fairness has benefited from cross-cultural comparisons, sometimes by seeing that fairness phenomena are widespread, indeed probably ubiquitous, features of human social psychology (e.g., Lind et al., 1978), sometimes by revealing interesting differences in fairness processes play out that are relevant to our fundamental understanding of relevant fairness phenomena (e.g., Van den Bos et al., 2010). What we have seldom looked at (with the exception of work like that of Ohbuchi, 2008) is the way changes in the social environment reflect and are reflected in the psychology of justice.

The connections suggested here between the psychology of fairness and various historical trends are, of course, pure speculation with no data at all to support the fairness processes that are suggested. The examples are advanced to argue for two points. First, that there may well be interesting changes in any given culture's social and political life that are driven by widespread impact of fairness processes. These fairness-based changes, if they occur and if they are due to psychological processes like those suggested here, can be quite radical. Thus, the first argument made from these examples is that they might account for some interesting and radical changes in social and political behavior.

The second reason for raising the historical examples goes to the very fact that these examples are only speculative. It was necessary to rely on assertion and probably naïve historical analysis *exactly because there are no studies on this topic*. If the social psychology of justice begins to look at fairness differences that occur at different times within a single culture, rather than looking only at fairness differences that occur at the same time in different cultures, we might be able to form a more dynamic understanding of how fairness works. The conceptual origin for this chapter lies in Ohbuchi's (2008c) argument that there have been changes over time in Japanese concerns for different types of justice. If more social justice researchers begin to look at such trends and changes, it seems likely that our understanding of the social psychology of fairness and its implications will benefit greatly.

2 Social Inequality and Sense of Fairness in Japan: Multi-Level Sense of Fairness, Social Ideals and Rationalization Mechanisms

Nobuyoshi Kawashima

Japan has been experiencing widening social inequality in recent years. Social inequality is defined as a state of imbalance in both the quantity of social resources in possession such as wealth, power, prestige and information and the distribution of opportunities to acquire them (Hara, 2008). Japan's inequality problem has been the subject of vigorous debate since the late 1990s. It is argued that social inequality has increased on the back of the collapse of the economic bubble and the ensuing recession and has been spurred further by the structural reform policy of the Koizumi administration (i.e., the promotion of regulatory reform and competition) (Tachibanaki, 2006). The widening of social disparity is mentioned in the Government's annual report on the Japanese economy and public finances for FY2009 (Cabinet Office, 2009). In short, social inequality can be regarded as one of the more serious social problems facing contemporary Japan.

The causes of inequality include individual socio-economic status such as income, gender, educational background and occupation. Income is the result of resource distribution in the present moment and the most direct indicator of an individual's social status. In contrast, gender and educational background relate to inequality of opportunity in the sense that they determine one's future occupation and income. With regard to gender in particular, inequality has been alleviated by the push for gender-equal participation in recent years but gender gaps still exist in wages and the proportion of senior managers (Suzuki, 2008). The employment status—whether one is a permanent employee or not—has also attracted much recent attention as an important factor of disparity (Tachibanaki, 2006).

The widening social inequality is weakening people's perception of fairness in Japanese society. Mabuchi (2000) found that a sense of fairness has declined among the Japanese since the late 1990s. Among more recent data, a joint opinion survey conducted by Japan's Yomiuri Shimbun and Britain's BBC in 2009 has found that 72 per cent of the Japanese respondents chose 'Not fair' to the question 'Do you think that the economic wealth is being distributed fairly?' (Yomiuri Shimbun, 2009). A sense of fairness is a subjective judgment on whether an individual is being given appropriate treatment based on his or her deservedness (Ohbuchi, 2008). A sense of unfairness increases antisocial behavior (Tanaka, 2008; Tyler, Boeckmann, Smith and Hue, 1997; Tyler and Smith, 1998) and adversely affects health (Kawachi and Kennedy, 2004; Kawashima and Ohbuchi, 2011). Since it is a determinant of both social behavior and individual wellbeing, identifying the mechanisms behind this increasing sense of social unfairness in Japan is an important subject of study for social psychology.

Multi-level sense of fairness

Researchers have argued that one's experience of inequality and one's judgment about its fairness vary depending on the perspective of the person who is making the judgment (Brickman, Folger, Goode and Schul, 1981; Deutsch, 1985; Lerner, 1980; Walster, Walster and Berscheid, 1978, for example). Brickman et al. (1981) differentiate between what they call microjustice, which concerns the treatment of a particular individual (or a particular group), and macrojustice, which concerns society as a whole. While a sense of micro fairness (justice)[1] is a judgment about the treatment of an individual and an evaluation based on benefits the individual is presently receiving or expects to receive in society, a sense of macro fairness is a judgment made by an individual from the perspective of a member of society about whether society is operating fairly for the entire nation (Ohbuchi and Fukuno, 2003).

A multi-level sense of fairness is known to produce varied social and individual outcomes (Dalbert, 1999; Kawashima, Ohbuchi, Kumagai and Asai, 2010; Kawashima and Ohbuchi, 2011; Ohbuchi and Fukuno, 2003). Kawashima et al. (2010) studied the effects of the senses of micro fairness and macro fairness on remonstrative acts deviating from normative behavior such as 'no inclination to follow social rules such as traffic rules' and 'not voting in elections'. The study found that a sense of micro unfairness increases deviant remonstrative behavior whereas a sense of macro unfairness has no such effect. It also found that while a sense of unfairness on both levels increases norm-compliant remonstrative acts such as 'participating in or supporting activities opposing government policies' and 'participating in citizens' movements to raise local and social issues', this effect is stronger with a sense of micro unfairness than a sense of macro unfairness.

In her study of the multiple aspects of Beliefs in a Just World (BJW), Dalbert (1999) examined the effects of Personal BJW (e.g., 'I am usually treated fairly') and General BJW (e.g., 'I think basically the world is a just place') on subjective well-being and self-esteem. She found that Personal BJW shows a stronger positive correlation with subjective well-being and self-esteem than the General BJW. The more personal an experience of injustice is, the more threatening it is for the self and therefore the more strongly it will be denied (Dalbert, 2002). Thus, it is considered that if one is compelled to admit that an injustice has been done to oneself, the threat to the self increases, which influences various aspects of one's social behavior and personal well-being.

While the importance of taking the multiple levels of the sense of fairness into account has been demonstrated by many studies, the causes of the multi-level sense of fairness have not been investigated fully. Since judgments about micro fairness and macro fairness are made independently of one another, they are likely to be influenced by different factors. We shall discuss the factors determining the multi-level sense of fairness in relation to social inequality in the next section.

Factors of a sense of micro fairness

Tyler et al. (1997) emphasizes relative differences in the degree of self-involvement in relation to a multi-level sense of fairness. Judgments about micro fairness in many cases have a high level of self-involvement. The persons making judgments are concerned about their self-interests and make judgments about fairness on the grounds of the quality of treatment given to them in society (fair or unfair). In contrast, judgments about macro fairness have a low level of self-involvement. Those who are making judgments are detached from self-interests and evaluate the level of fairness from a perspective of the appropriateness of profit sharing in society as a whole (fair or unfair). It is surmised that the senses of fairness and unfairness in this case are formed based on the perception of whether society is being operated according to appropriate social ideals (Ohbuchi, 2001; Kawashima and Ohbuchi, 2010).

The supposition that self-interest determines a sense of fairness has often been considered within the framework of the stratification model. The stratification model is based on the hypothesis that social inequality is judged to be unfair because it diminishes the self-interests of the disadvantaged (Mahbuchi, 1996). The disadvantaged are often dissatisfied as their self-interests are restricted. Many of them would compare themselves with the privileged and find the inequality unfair. It goes without saying that low-income earners are more economically disadvantaged than high-income earners. And one's socio-economic status such as educational background and employment status have a strong connection with one's social disadvantage in a sense that they create income inequality. Consequently, the stratification model of social fairness assumes that a sense of fairness is closely related to an individual's socio-economic status (Marshall, Rose, Newby and Vogler, 1988; Miyano, 1998).

This argument leads to the conclusion that an individual's socio-economic status is an important factor of a sense of micro fairness. One's socioeconomic status is closely linked to the condition of one's self-interest in society. An individual's socio-economic status is therefore an important determinant in making a judgment about micro fairness that emphasizes self-interest but this is not the case with macro fairness, which focuses on distribution throughout the entire society rather than the treatment of individuals. Let us consider the following example. The high-income executives of large corporations can feel that they are fairly treated in society comparing their advantaged status with disadvantaged ones and have a strong sense of micro fairness. At the same time, however, they may get a strong sense of unfairness in society as a whole when they come across news reports about social inequalities on TV. Thus, the effect of one's socio-economic status on macro fairness is weak whereas the effect on micro fairness is strong.

Kawashima, Ohbuchi, Kumagai, and Asai (2009) conducted a social survey in eleven cities throughout Japan in February and March 2009 in order to verify this hypothesis. In this survey, a sense of micro fairness was measured by two items—'I am not fairly treated in this society (inverted)' and 'I am unfairly treated in this society (inverted)'—and a sense of macro fairness was measured by three items—'The current state of Japanese society cannot be considered fair (inverted)', 'The present-day Japan cannot be called a fair society (inverted)' and 'The present-day Japan is operated fairly'. Using the average values of the items corresponding to the senses of micro fairness and macro fairness as the respective composite scores, they carried out multiple linear regression analysis with these scores being dependent variables and demographic variables being independent variables. It was found that higher-income earners had stronger senses of both micro fairness and macro fairness but the effect on a sense of micro fairness was greater than on a sense of macro fairness. Furthermore, additional mediation analysis found that the effect of income on a sense of macro fairness was an indirect one mediated by a sense of micro fairness.

Kawashima et al.'s (2009) findings indicate that socio-economic status is an important factor of a sense of micro fairness. One's socioeconomic status is strongly linked to the condition of one's self-interest in society and the condition of one's self-interest appears to be reflected directly on the judgment of one's treatment in society. At the same time, the condition of one's self-interest does not appear to have a strong influence over one's judgment about macro fairness in society as a whole.

In fact, many studies on the relationship between macro fairness and socio-economic status have not found a stronger sense of fairness among people with higher socio-economic statuses. The Social Stratification and Mobility Survey (SSM Survey)[2] which has been conducted every ten years since 1955 in Japan, measured a sense of fairness by asking 'Generally speaking, do you think that the society is fair nowadays?' in 1985 and 1995. In the analyses of the results, no positive correlation was found between socio-economic statuses such as income and educational background and a sense of fairness in either data set (Oda and Abe, 2000; Umino and Saitō, 1990).

According to Kawashima et al. (2009), one of the reasons for the failure of these studies to find any relationship between a sense of fairness and socioeconomic status was that they overlooked the multiplicity of the sense of fairness. The sense of fairness measured by the 1985 and 1995 SSM Surveys was similar to a sense of macro fairness (Oda and Abe, 2000; Umino and Saitō, 1990). However, the condition of one's self-interest in society is reflected more strongly in one's judgment about the fairness of the way one is treated than one's judgment with respect to society as a whole. It is therefore not surprising that these studies focusing on a sense of macro fairness did not find any clear relationship between socio-economic status and a sense of fairness.

Factors of a sense of macro fairness

The effect of socio-economic status

Some recent social surveys have begun to demonstrate the presence of relationships between some socio-economic variables and a sense of macro fairness. A question about macro fairness, which was the same as the one in the SSM Survey, was used in the Japan Survey on Information Society 2002 (JIS2002)[3] which found a stronger sense of macro fairness among older people and higher-income earners than younger people and lower-income earners (Nagamatsu, 2004). A similar tendency has been found in more than one survey conducted in the latter half of the 2000s. A sense of macro fairness has been found to have a positive correlation with age and income in Kawashima et al. (2009) and with age and educational background in Kawashima and Ohbuchi (2009). In short, the effects of age and socio-economic status on macro fairness judgments, which were not found in surveys through to the end of the 1990s, have been observed in surveys since 2000.

The following explanation is possible with respect to age. Japanese society has been grappling with a slowing economy since the latter half of the 1990s and experienced a social situation in which many people are faced with income stagnation despite their hard work. It is likely that the older people whose hard work was rewarded in the rapidly growing economy and the subsequent favorable economic climate of the past still consider society as a fair place based on their past experiences even in today's grave social conditions. To younger people with no such past experiences, however, the worsening social conditions in recent years directly lead to a declining sense of fairness. Hence, the younger they are, the weaker their sense of macro fairness in the surveys after the second half of the 1990s.

The change in the relationship between socio-economic status and a sense of macro fairness can be explained by the weakening of a sense of micro fairness. As mentioned earlier, it has been pointed out that there is growing inequality in Japan (Cabinet Office, 2009). This means that the relative proportion of people of low socio-economic status is increasing and the number of people who have a sense of micro unfairness is likely to be on the increase. As shown by Kawashima et al. (2009), a decreasing sense of micro fairness leads to a decrease in a sense of macro fairness. Thus, the positive correlation between a sense of macro fairness and income found in the post-2000 surveys can be explained at least partially by growing inequality and the resultant decline in a sense of micro fairness: but the possibility of socioeconomic status directly curtailing a sense of macro fairness cannot be ruled out entirely. This is an important issue to consider in future surveys.

With respect to educational background, however, some studies have found that a sense of macro fairness is higher among people with higher education (Kawashima and Ohbuchi, 2009) and others show completely opposite findings (Oda and Abe, 2000; Kawashima and Ohbuchi, 2010). Stratification models suggest that people with higher educational background tend to have more socially advantageous status and hence a strong sense of fairness. In contrast, the information quantity hypothesis (Mabuchi, 1996) proposes that more highly educated people, having more accurate information about society, have a stronger sense of unfairness because society is naturally an unfair place. Moreover, the enlightenment effect hypothesis (Kimura, 1998) predicts that more highly educated people tend to sympathize with unfortunate others and aspire for equality, and hence view society as unfair. While it is difficult to determine from the currently available data which hypothesis is correct, it is important to remember that educational background, unlike income, appears to have more than one implication in its relationship with a sense of fairness.

The effect of social ideals
Besides socio-economic status, the SSM Surveys and the JIS2002 also suggest relationships between social awareness or assessment and a sense of macro fairness. Umino and Saitō (1990) raised a possibility that a sense of macro fairness is determined by attitudes towards social systems (e.g., likes and dislikes for political parties, a sense of political efficacy, authoritarianism etc.) and the recognition or assessment of one's own status mainly in relation to one's occupation (status identification, income satisfaction level etc.) based on the analysis of the 1985 SSM Survey. Nagamatsu (2004) found a strong tendency towards a sense of macro unfairness among those who estimate that there is a higher number of 'people who make the same level of effort as you do and who are better off or worse off than you are'. Oda and Abe (2000) analyzed the effect of unfair experiences and social mobility experiences using the 1995 SSM Survey data but found that these variables had very little effect on a sense of macro fairness.

The hypothesis that one's sense of fairness is determined by one's assessment of society has been discussed within the framework of the group-value model. The group-value model proposes that people consider social inequality to be unfair because it runs counter to their social ideal. According to Lind and Tyler (1988; Tyler et al., 1997), fairness is one of the important group-values and individuals can enhance their personal and group self-esteem when they perceive that the group they belong to is operated in a fair manner. Consequently, if the treatment given to oneself or others does not comply with the group's ideals or norms, the individuals must feel a sense of unfairness (Ohbuchi, 2007a).

For this reason, the perception that society is realizing its ideals (the perception of social ideal realization) is considered to be an important determinant of macro fairness judgments. The proper operation of Japanese society means that many of its members are receiving fair treatment. The perception of social ideal realization therefore increases a sense of macro fairness. Ohbuchi (2001) measured people's perception that society is operated based on three criteria of distributive fairness (equity, equality and need) and analyzed the relationships between them and a sense of macro fairness. The study found that all three types of perception showed a strong correlation with a sense of macro fairness and at the same time that the equality criterion exerted the greatest effect on a sense of macro fairness.

Some important issues remain with regard to the relationship between social ideals and a sense of macro fairness. The first issue is a change in the social ideals of the Japanese people. Ohbuchi (2001) suggested the possibility of the equality criterion being the most important social ideal for people based on a social survey conducted in 2000. However, Japanese society has yet to come out of the prolonged economic slump and social inequality is now gaining wider recognition among people as a social problem. It is conceivable that these changes in social conditions are causing some changes in people's social ideals.

The second issue concerns the complex nature of social ideal realization. The three criteria of distributive fairness are not mutually exclusive and they are often applied in a complex manner (Ohbuchi, 2008b; Tyler et al., 1997). It is therefore possible that economic inequality based on efforts and contributions exist while at the same time a certain level of equality is established or a safety net is provided for the poor. Assuming this complex realization of the fairness criteria, simple questions such as 'Do you think economic equality has been realized?' or 'Do you think effort- or performance-based distribution is being carried out?' do not reflect actual situations. We need to find out which ideal is applied to which part of the social structure in order to measure people's perception based on real situations. For this purpose, it is necessary to analyze the inequality structure of Japanese society and examine in detail how the three criteria are being realized.

In the next section, we shall examine social ideals in contemporary Japanese society—what kind of society do the Japanese think is desirable?—based on a recent social survey. This is followed by a discussion about the content of the perception of social ideal realization—how the criteria of distributive fairness are realized in present society. Finally, we shall consider to what extent people feel that an ideal society is being realized and how this feeling relates to a sense of macro fairness (and micro fairness).

Social ideal in contemporary Japan

According to Deutsch (1985), each social group adopts a set of fairness criteria according to the group's goal. In a society with a goal of increasing productivity, equitable distribution based on performance and contributions to the group is considered fair treatment. In contrast, a society with an emphasis on social harmony considers that equal distribution of resources to all members is regarded as fair treatment. Finally, a society with a goal of protecting the socially weak gives priority to distribution on the basis of need.

In Japan, the concept of equitable treatment based on performance and results is spreading as a social ideal in recent years. According to the World Value Survey of twenty five countries in 2005–2006, 65.9 per cent of the Japanese respondents supported the statement that 'We need larger income differences as incentives for individual effort' rather than 'Income should be made more equal' (Dentsu Communication Institute/Nippon Research Center, 2008). As only 47.9 per cent of the Japanese chose 'We need larger income differences' in the same question in 1995 (Dentsu Communication Institute, Inc., 2005), the importance of the equity criterion appears to be increasing among the Japanese. However, it is important to remember that this question implies an ideal society compared with the present Japanese society. It means that the respondents are stating their view of the relative importance of fairness criteria, not the absolute importance, and the finding does not warrant a conclusion that the Japanese strongly support the equity principle alone and disregard the equality criterion.

In fact, the findings of more recent social surveys demonstrate that an inclination towards social harmony and protection of the weak is still strong among the Japanese. As Ohbuchi (Chapter 3 in this volume) reported, our survey in 2010 found strong support for the equality and need principles as well as the equity principle among people. In actual social or group situations, a complex distribution system combining these three criteria are often used (Ohbuchi, 2008b). For example, many corporations and firms adopt a dual remuneration system with a basic salary based on the equality criterion and an additional performance-based pay for equity distribution. Allowances for dependents and sick leave are also measures based on the need principle.

In summary, it appears that the people of contemporary Japan wish to expand the equity principle while they continue to support the equality and need principles as important. After pointing out the strong orientation towards equality among the Japanese by international standards, Miyano (2000) predicted that the recent expansion of their equity orientation would help clarify differences between their equality and equity orientations in making judgments about fairness. This would be the case also with the need principle and it is likely that the spread of the new equity principle throughout Japanese society has been prompting reevaluation of the two traditionally important fairness criteria. Based on the above, we believe that people's perception of whether Japanese society has realized each of these three criteria influences a sense of fairness independently.

In that case, how are these three criteria of distributive fairness actually realized (or not realized) and how do they influence the people's sense of fairness in contemporary Japanese society? The recent widening of inequality in Japan appears to contradict the principles of equality and need while it is in accord with the equity principle. If the distributive criteria are applied in combination (Ohbuchi, 2008b; Tyler et al., 1997), however, the equality criterion is satisfied and a sense of fairness is maintained when people perceive that a certain level of distributive equality is achieved even though some inequality exists. Similarly, the perception that social security for the poor is in place is likely to play a role in maintaining a sense of fairness in an unequal society. We shall consider how assessment is made with respect to whether each fairness criterion has been realized based on Japan's social structure in the next section.

Inequality and the perception of social ideal realization in contemporary Japan

Inequality in contemporary Japan
The existence of social inequality in contemporary Japan has been identified by many surveys and studies. For example, relative poverty rate in Japan, which is the proportion of people whose income is below half of the population median, is one of the highest among the OECD countries (OECD, 2006). While the percentage of students who enroll in senior high schools exceeds 90 per cent, the percentage of students enrolling in universities in 2009 was only 56.2 per cent (Ministry of Education, Culture, Sports, Science and Technology, 2009), suggesting the existence of inequality in education.

Yet, the inequality in Japan expressed in the form of these numbers does not necessarily relate to urgent problems such as starvation or destitution. Hara and Seiyama (2005) argue that Japanese society has become an 'affluent' society through the rapid economic growth of the 1960s to mid-1970s and achieved basic equalization in the process. They divide social resources into two types—the standard of living that is desired and considered within reach by a majority of people is 'basic goods' and anything above and beyond is 'upper goods'—and argue that the existing inequality in Japan is about upper goods as a majority of people have already attained basic goods. Hara (2008) cites the following examples of basic goods:
1. enough income to keep one from poverty or hunger
2. enough food, clothing, shelter and consumer durables to maintain human dignity
3. upper secondary education (senior high school education).

By comparison, upper goods include income high enough to enable living beyond a certain standard, an opportunity to enroll in universities, and so on.

Looking at the imbalance in upper goods, one's perception about the proper operation of the equity principle plays an important role in one's judgment about fairness. If one feels that high income and university education are products of luck or chance, one's sense of fairness decreases. If one perceives that they are based on individual contributions to society or group, one's sense of fairness increases.

In Japan, effort is regarded as an important criterion for assessment of one's contribution to society or group (Saitō and Yamagishi, 2000). Thus, the perception of reciprocity that resources are distributed according to effort and hard work in Japanese society is likely to increase a sense of fairness from an equity perspective.

It has been a common view of researchers that while imbalance exists in upper goods, there is no severe imbalance in the distribution of the three social resources comprising basic goods in Japan. According to Hara (2008), basic goods satisfy human needs for not only material affluence in food, clothing and shelter but also psychological aspects such as pride and self-esteem. Although new inequality phenomena such as NEET (Not in Employment, Education or Training) and net cafe refugees (or cyber homeless) cast some doubt on this argument, the affluence perception that basic goods are widely distributed to many people in Japanese society is expected to increase a sense of fairness from an equality perspective.

While basic wealth is spread widely, the number of people who have difficulty acquiring the minimum level of social resources has been increasing in recent years as demonstrated by growing numbers of non-permanent workers and unemployed. Article 25 of the Constitution of Japan guarantees that 'All people shall have the right to maintain the minimum standards of wholesome and cultured living' and provides the basis for the existing social security system consisting of various social insurances and welfare benefits. While many problems have been raised with respect to Japan's social security system (Tachibanaki, 2006), the social security system realizes the need principle as long as it aims to assist those who are unable to maintain the minimum standards of living in an unequal society. Therefore the kindness perception that these safety nets for the needy exist is likely to help increase a sense of fairness even if inequality in society widens.

The perception of social ideal realization and a multi-level sense of fairness
Our social survey in 2010 asked respondents to evaluate Japanese society in terms of their perception about the realization of social ideals that corresponded to the three distributive fairness criteria. Three questions were asked in each of the three areas: the reciprocity perception (e.g., 'Japanese society has given due recognition to effort and hard work and will continue to do so'), the affluence perception (e.g., 'No matter how bad social conditions will become, we will be able to maintain a certain standard of living as long as we live in Japan'),

and the kindness perception (e.g., 'Japanese society extends a helping hand to the poor'). Using the average scores of the question items as the composite scores, the percentages of affirmative responses above the midpoint were calculated. They were 36.6 per cent for reciprocity, 34.5 per cent for affluence and 24.5 per cent for kindness. The percentages of affirmative respondents were well below half in all three areas of perception and this tendency was particularly marked with the kindness perception.

These results show the existence of a great gap between the ideal society and the perceived society. Although the importance of the three distributive fairness criteria are strongly recognized in contemporary Japan (Ohbuchi, Chapter 3 in this volume), many people today perceive that equitable distribution based on effort and hard work, equal distribution of the requisite minimum resources, and need-based distribution to the needy are inadequate. The particularly low level of the kindness perception is likely to be linked to a critical scrutiny of Japan's social security policy.

Further, we conducted multiple linear regression analyses using the three types of realization perception as independent variables and a multi-level sense of fairness as a dependent variable and gender, age, educational background, household income and occupation as control variables (Kawashima and Ohbuchi, 2010). As a result, on the one hand, the reciprocity perception exhibited the strongest effect in increasing both a sense of macro fairness and a sense of micro fairness. A sense of macro fairness was shown to intensify as the affluence perception and the kindness perception increased. On the other hand, the kindness perception enhanced a sense of micro fairness but the affluence perception did not. And the effect of the kindness perception on a sense of micro fairness was weaker than that on a sense of macro fairness.

The fact that the effects of the three types of perception on a sense of macro fairness remained after controlling for the effects of the demographic variables supports our hypothesis that perceptions about the realization of social ideals is a factor of a sense of macro fairness. Furthermore, the finding that the reciprocity perception had the strongest effect contradicted Ohbuchi's study (2001), which found that the equality criterion had the strongest effect on a sense of macro fairness. Although it is not possible to make a simple comparison as different indicators were used in these studies, the fact that the equity principle based on effort and hard work was found to be the strongest determinant of a sense of macro fairness serves as evidence for the increasing prevalence of the equity principle in Japan in recent years. Although we hypothesized that the perception of social ideal realization was a factor of a sense of macro fairness, we did not expect to find that the reciprocity perception and the kindness perception would increase a sense of micro fairness as well. While the perception of social ideal realization was a measure of one's perception that society as a whole is satisfying the criteria, each respondent was of course a member of society. For this reason, some of the respondents may have made a connection between the perception of social ideal realization and their own circumstances when answering the questions. The reciprocity perception exhibited a particularly strong effect on a sense of micro fairness perhaps because in explaining the imbalance of self-interest which was considered important in making judgments on a micro fairness, attributing the cause of the imbalance to effort and hard work was most easily associated to a sense of micro fairness.

We have so far examined the relationships between the condition of one's self-interest, the perception of the realization of social ideals and a multi-level sense of fairness. The theory is built on the assumption that people are able to objectively understand both their own circumstances and the condition of society as a whole and can assess the degree of fairness in society dispassionately based on their understanding. However, admitting one's own disadvantage is a threat to one's self-esteem or sense of control (Lerner, 1980; Mikula, 1993; Tyler et al., 1997). And the perception that the society in which one lives is an unfair society produces negative emotions such as anxiety and fear (Jost and Banaji, 1994; Jost and Hunyady, 2002). These motivational tendencies point to a possibility that people in objectively unequal circumstances may strengthen their perception of fairness by rationalizing their circumstances. We shall reexamine the relationship between social stratification and a sense of fairness from a rationalization perspective in the next section.

Mechanisms to rationalize inequality

System justification theory

The theory of system justification proposed by Jost et al. (Jost and Banaji, 1994; Jost and Hunyady, 2002) is a social psychological theory to explain the tendency of rationalizing inequality observed among people of low socio-economic status. According to Jost et al., people have a general tendency to try to reduce fear and anxiety. However, the perception that they are living in an unfair, irrational and undesirable society evokes these unpleasant emotions (Kay, Gaucher, Napier, Callan and Laurin, 2008). If people of low socio-economic status suffer social disadvantages but are unable to change the situation easily, they tend to modify their perception and view the status quo as fair, reasonable and desirable in order to avoid unpleasant emotions such as anxiety and fear.

Rationalization of status quo is likely to have a particularly significant meaning among the people of low socio-economic status. According to the theory of cognitive dissonance (Festinger, 1957), people who are going through painful experiences may strengthen their commitment to the painful situations in order to rationalize their pain rather than trying to remove or end such situations (Wicklund and Brehm, 1976). Jost, Pelham, Sheldon and Sullivan (2003) considered that this mechanism would apply to people of low socio-economic status. People of low socio-economic status firstly have the cognitions that 'the system is putting me (and my group) at a disadvantage'. At the same time, however, they have the cognitions that 'through our acquiescence, my group and I are contributing to the stability of the system'. In order to resolve this dissonance between these conflicting cognitions, people of low socio-economic status sometimes defend the fairness or legitimacy of their society more strenuously than do people of high socio-economic status (Hunt, 2000; Kay, Jost, Mandisodza, Sherman, Petrocelli, and Johnson, 2007).

Jost and Hunyady (2005) suggest the existence of various ideologies that relate to rationalizing the status quo. One of them is BJW, a belief that the individual gets what he or she deserves and what he or she gets corresponds to his or her worth (Lerner, 1980). Those who have a strong BJW among people of low socio-economic status consider that they are in their current circumstances because they deserve them and not because the society in which they live is unfair. This belief is likely to reduce unpleasant emotions.

Stratification model and rationalization
In contrast to the system justification theory, the stratification model argues that people of low socio-economic status have a sense of unfairness based on their disadvantaged circumstances (Mabuchi, 1996; Marshall, Rose, Newby and Vogler, 1988; Miyano, 1998). However, to discuss the relationship between socio-economic

Figure 2.1: The effect of interaction between a belief in a just world and educational background on macro fairness

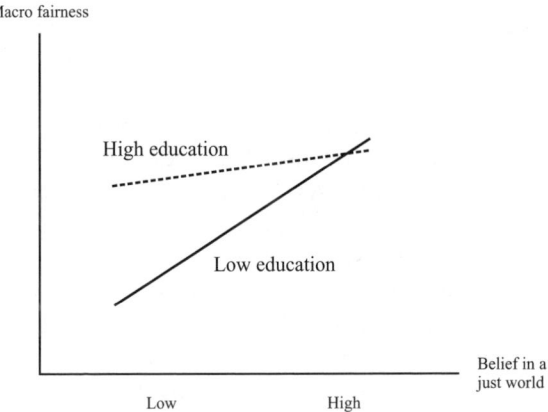

Source: Kawashima and Ohbuchi, 2009.

status and a sense of fairness, individual differences in justification tendencies must be taken into account. On the one hand, strong believers in a just world who are placed in disadvantaged positions may think that they deserve such treatment and maintain their sense of social fairness whereas those with weak just world beliefs may consider them unfair and have a strong sense of unfairness. On the other hand, since people of high socio-economic status have a sense of fairness based on their privileged status, they are less motivated to rationalize and therefore the level of BJW has no effect on the sense of social fairness among people of high socio-economic status.

When Kawashima and Ohbuchi (2009) measured a sense of macro fairness and BJW in their 2008 survey, they found that people of low socio-economic status rated the fairness of society lower than did people of high socio-economic status contrary to Jost et al.'s (2003) theory. However, the effect of interaction between socio-economic status and a BJW was significant and the low-status (low-education) people with a strong BJW had a stronger sense of macro fairness than those with a weak BJW whereas a BJW had no main effect on the sense of macro fairness of the high-status (high-education) people (Figure 2.1).

American studies on system justification observed among low-status people have assumed that they are in a state of inner conflict between self-interest recovery and uncertainty avoidance and suggested that the latter often takes precedence over the former in the real world (Jost and Hunyady, 2002; Jost et al., 2003). The finding that low-status people with a strong BJW regarded society as being fair just as did high-status people in Kawashima and Ohbuchi (2009) demonstrated that a tendency to rationalize inequality in order to avoid anxiety and fear did exist among some Japanese. At the same time, however, Kawashima and Ohbuchi also found that the low-status people did not always shut their eyes to their disadvantages stemming from inequalities. As shown in Figure 2.1, there are people of low socio-economic status who are more inclined to look at the reality of their self-interest rather than anxiety and fear arising from the perception of social unfairness and assess society as unfair.

We were able to demonstrate the effects of rationalization in focusing upon the relationship between socioeconomic status and macro fairness. However, we have not yet investigated if a similar mechanism operates at the level of micro fairness. The rationalization of status quo, which the system justification theory emphasizes, differs from the rationalization of self-interest and self-esteem, and therefore, for people of low socioeconomic status, the two types of rationalization contradict with each other (Jost, Liviantan, Van der Toorn, Ledgerwood and Mandiosodza, 2010). If the individuals' sense of micro fairness reflects their self-interest rather than their sense of macro fairness, their inner conflict would be more conspicuous at the micro level. It is a significant future research agenda to examine if the rationalization of status quo is observed with respect to the sense of micro fairness among the people of low socioeconomic status.

Another issue relates to the substance of the rationalization mechanism. Jost and Hunyady (2005) argue that people adopt a number of substantially different ideologies, their descriptive contents, and illustrative references to rationalize social systems: BJW, the protestant work ethic, meritocratic belief, economic system justification, fair market ideology, power distance, social dominance orientation, opposition to equality, right-wing authoritarianism, and political conservatism. Many of them are value systems or belief systems that have European or American cultural foundations. One expression of this is the 'equity principle' which rationalizes resource allocation based on one's ability or performance. The Japanese take into account not only the equity principle but also the equality principle and the necessity principle in making judgments about fairness (Ohbuchi, Chapter 3). Future studies on the rationalization mechanism of the Japanese therefore will need to measure beliefs that match their values.

Conclusion and issues

We have examined in this chapter the factors of a sense of fairness and why widening inequality leads to a decrease in the sense of fairness. Assuming the multiple levels of sense of fairness, we have demonstrated that a sense of micro fairness with respect to one's own circumstances is strongly related to socio-economic status but a sense of macro fairness with respect to the condition of society as a whole is not. This suggests that an increase in the proportion of the underprivileged due to widening inequality results in an increase in the proportion of people who feel they are not receiving fair treatment. At the same time, it has been shown that a sense of macro fairness is closely linked with the perception of whether Japanese society is operated according to desirable ideals, i.e., the perception of social ideal realization. However, the perception of realization in each of three social ideals based on the distributive fairness criteria was generally low, suggesting a possibility that widening inequality is lowering a sense of macro fairness with respect to society as a whole.

Further, we turned our attention to the existence of a rationalizing mechanism which would increase a subjective sense of fairness in the face of objectively unequal society or circumstances. While a sense of macro fairness was lower among low-status people than high-status people in Japan, the low-status people with a strong BJW, who considered that they would get what they deserved and receive the treatment they deserved, had a higher sense of macro fairness than those with a weaker BJW. These findings demonstrate that while people make objective and rational judgments about fairness when faced with inequalities, the judgment process is interfered with by a motivational mechanism in some cases.

There are some unanswered question about the mechanism behind the relationship between social inequality and a sense of fairness. We hypothesized that the condition of self-interest has a stronger effect on micro fairness judgment than macro fairness judgment and found a strong link between socioeconomic status (income) and a sense of micro fairness. However, some low-status people may rate the condition of their self-interests higher through comparison with people in an even lower status and some high-status people may feel disadvantaged compared with more privileged people (relative deprivation). Consequently, we need to prove our hypothesis about the link between the condition of self-interest and a multi-level sense of fairness by measuring the perception of the condition of self-interest as a mediator of the relationship between socio-economic status and a sense of micro fairness. Another important question concerns what reference group individuals use in their judgments of fairness. In this chapter, we attempted to measure the multidimensional sense of fairness by using questionnaire items such as 'I feel I am not treated fairly in this society' or 'the current state of Japanese society cannot be considered to be fair.' These questions assume that Japanese society at large is the most important reference group in the respondents' sense of fairness. However, people belong to a variety of groups—such as occupational, regional and age groups—and their judgments differ depending upon which reference groups they have in mind. It is important for future research to investigate how individuals form their sense of fairness in their own groups and how this sense affects their health and social behavior.

3 Social Class and Values in Japan[1]

Ken-ichi Ohbuchi

In the 2009 general elections the Japanese people chose to entrust government to the Democratic Party instead of the Liberal Democratic Party, which had been responsible for government for over 50 years. This change in government was probably due to the people's expectations of Democratic policies on such matters as the economy, education, social security and environmental issues, but at the same time, was probably also the result of a sense of dissatisfaction by many Japanese with the edifice of vested interests constructed over many years under the LDP administration, beneficial to only a portion of people involved.

To understand collective behavior, such as election behavior and public opinion, it is necessary to apprehend changes in people's social values. Social values are people's beliefs and preferences about such things as what sort of society is preferable, how human beings should live, and how social and interpersonal problems should be resolved. Social values have at their core moral values (what is right) and life values (what is the sensible way to address problems), but also include beliefs relating to world view (what are fundamental world principles), social view (what are the principles that move society) and the human view (what is the nature of humanity).

In this chapter I will investigate three issues pertaining to Japanese values that have in recent years become a source of debate: social fairness, collectivism, and religion and traditional values. I will introduce relevant theories and empirical studies while at the same time considering them in light of data from social research that I have recently conducted.

Social fairness

Fairness is a criterion for assessing social action and decisions. 'Social' refers to actions or decisions that affect the treatment of people. A definitive example of where people have a strong interest in fairness is in relation to their pay and promotion within a company.

The most hotly debated definitive example of justness and injustice in Japan is jury verdicts. These determine how a subject person will be treated and can literally be matters of life and death. No matter the social situation, however, people expect to be treated as appropriate to their qualifications and rights, and are dissatisfied if such is not the case. This is the notion of fairness.

Fairness criteria and Japanese preferences

The sense of fairness discussed above can be expressed as a formula: Treatment/Deservedness (Ohbuchi, 2007a). Deservedness refers to qualifications and rights (Olson, Roese, Meen and Robertson, 1994). Therefore, fairness is defined as a certain social decision treating the people involved in a manner befitting their qualifications and rights. Where a social decision is associated with distribution of resources it is called distributive fairness, and where it is distribution of rights to speak in (ability to influence) a decision-making process, it is known as procedural fairness. We will now consider the relationship between Japanese values and social class as they pertain to distributive fairness.

There are three criteria for fairness that are widely accepted in modern society when determining distributive fairness: equity, equality and need. They arise from differing deservedness in the fairness formula. Deservedness in equal distribution is a function of group membership. Rights to receive education, medical care, welfare services and other state-provided services are afforded equally to all citizens, but distribution is restricted to Japanese nationals, and rightful criteria of eligibility to receive is group membership of Japanese nationality. Groups in which equal distribution of this nature takes place, according to Deutsch (1975), are groups that maintain relationships that are as close as family and that mutually cooperate. Groups in which equal distribution is adopted are run with the objective of social harmony, and deservedness in distribution is group membership.

Conversely, another deservedness condition constitutes a ground in equitable distribution. In a company, staff who work hard are given preferential treatment in the form of high pay and promotion. In equitable distribution of this nature, individual performance is the deservedness condition which determines treatment. Many economic and social resources awarded in modern society, such as assets, honor and status, are based on individual performance. Equitable distribu-

Figure 3.1: Difference in preference for distributive fairness criteria in Japan and the USA

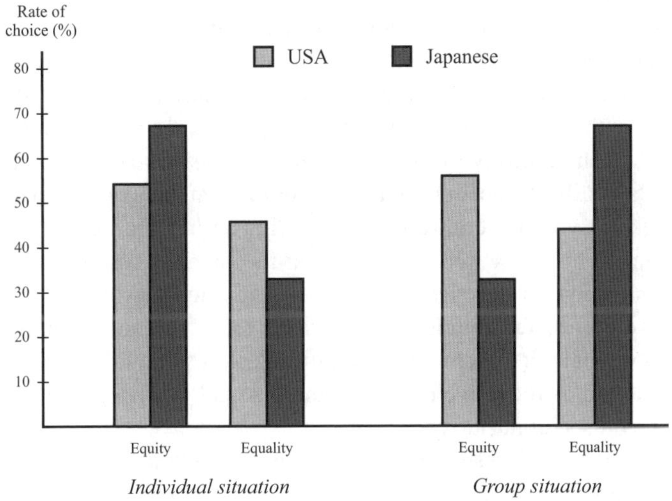

[Bar chart showing Rate of choice (%) comparing USA and Japanese preferences for Equity vs Equality in Individual situation and Group situation]

Source: Kano, 1980.

tion guarantees individual freedom and encourages maximization of individuality. Therefore, the doctrine of such groups is individual freedom and rights.

Deservedness for distribution according to need is degree of hardship, in other words, how great is the need for resources. In a society where the public norm is to receive a certain level of education, to be healthy and to live a cultured life, children, the elderly and people with disabilities who are unable to attain that norm through their own ability are given aid, and the special provision of social and material resources is probably deemed fair distribution. In that situation, deservedness to receive these special distributions is a person's level of desperation, or degree of hardship. A society that emphasizes distribution according to need is a society that has welfare and protection of the weak as its social doctrine.

Research into fairness undertaken prior to 2000 indicates that Japanese have a liking for equal distribution. Cross cultural research undertaken in 1991 found that only 20 per cent of US respondents replied positively to the statement 'the fairest method of allocating assets and income is to divide them equally among everyone', while almost twice as many Japanese (39 per cent) agreed (Miyano, 2000).

Kano (1980) conducted an experiment with three-person groups of people who work, and compared the case where each individual chose a method of distribution and the case where the choice was made by the three in collaboration. He found that as individuals, Japanese chose equitable distribution, but as groups they were more likely to choose equal distribution. Kano compared the results of this study with those from a similarly designed experiment conducted by Deutsch and Mey in the USA. The comparison reveals (Figure 3.1) that in both individual and group circumstances, Americans consistently chose equitable distribution rather than equal distribution. Kano's research indicates that the Japanese do not have an unconditional preference for equality, but when a group is formed the preference for equality almost doubles, in seeking to maintain harmony between members. This orientation to equality has been interpreted as reflective of the Japanese social attitude, with its emphasis on social harmony.

Recent values research, however, provides a different view of the Japanese. From 2005 to 2006 a global values survey was implemented in countries around the world. The survey included the question 'In an ideal social system, should income be more equal, or should there be greater disparity in income in order to stimulate individual human effort?' Comparing the responses from 25 countries, only 34.1 per cent of Japanese responded 'it should be equal', placing Japan a low 22nd (Dentsu Communication Institute/Nippon Research Center, 2008). Two-thirds of Japanese respondents said 'there should be greater disparity', a proportion that was higher than Germany, France, China and the USA. This research, in contrast to the conventional view, indicates that Japanese view equal distribution of resources negatively.

Results of our recent social research point to even more complicated aspects to the Japanese sense of fairness. In March 2010 I randomly selected 2400 Japanese adults and conducted a survey of values, obtaining responses from 986. Respondents were asked 'What sort of society should Japanese society be?' and were asked to rate their degree of support for equitable distribution (example: 'Preferential treatment is given to people who are very able and get results'), equal distribution (example: 'An equal society in which there are no differences'), and distribution according to need ('The weak (children, the elderly, people with disabilities) are adequately protected'). Respondents whose ratings were at the median or higher were deemed supporters, and calculation of that proportion gave high results for each, with equitable at 79.1 per cent, equal at 78.2 per cent and according to need at 94.8 per cent. This shows that these criteria are broadly accepted by modern Japanese, but support for the criterion of need was highest and equality was not particularly preferred. This indicates that Japanese have a strong interest in protecting the weak, and that most Japanese judge distribution of resources from that perspective to be fair.

The results of this research suggest that in modern Japan the sense of fairness is complicated. Earlier values research indicated that until about 20 years ago the equality orientation was strong in Japan, but after the economic bubble burst in the 1990s and due to the inclination of society overall to competitive principles, it seems that of necessity social values have changed. While there is a feeling of inevitability about the introduction of performance-based reward, it also seems that many Japanese do not desire an increase in disparity. A survey of managers conducted after the bubble economy burst found that, while they acknowledge that a performance-based human resources management practice is necessary, they deemed a difference in wages of around 20 per cent to be adequate (National Institute of Labor Administration, 1998). It seems, therefore, that among the Japanese there is a belief that even with equitable distribution, less disparity is better.

Conversely, in the long economic recession after the bubble burst, more people in Japan have become unemployed and more must content themselves with atypical jobs. Confronted by these circumstances most Japanese experience social insecurity and want a safety net established for those in distress (Ohbuchi, 2008). The strong need orientation apparent among the Japanese in our research results appears to reflect the strength of this insecurity.

Differences in sense of fairness according to social class

All three criteria of fairness are generally supported by the Japanese, but our social research data shows differences according to social class. Analysis of variance using average ratings revealed differences in degree of support for equality and equity according to annual income ($F(3,915) = 11.690$, $p < 0.001$; $F(3,915) = 2.357$, $p = 0.070$). As Figure 3.2 shows, the trends were for support for equal distribution to be greater the lower the annual income and, in contrast, support

Figure 3.2: Difference in preference for fairness criteria according to annual income

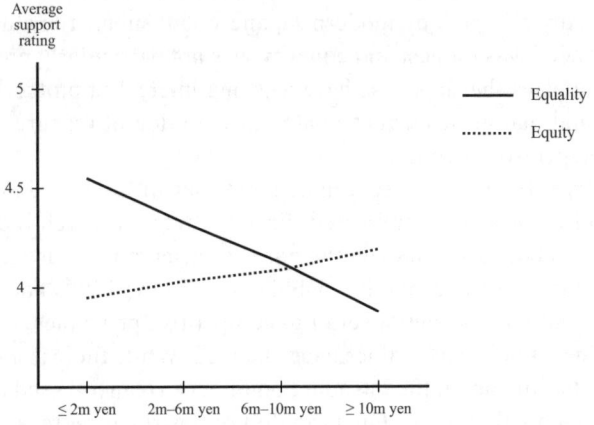

for equitable distribution to be greater the higher the annual income. In relation to yet another index of social class, level of education, the same difference was seen in support for equality and equity (F(3,940) = 12.382, p < 0.001; F(3,939) = 5.271, p < 0.001). Figure 3.3 shows the tendency for the lower the level of education, the greater support for equality, and in contrast, a tendency for people with higher levels of education to support equity. These results show clearly that those in the lower classes desire equal distribution and those in the higher classes assert equitable distribution.

Annual income and level of education are linked, but there is a need to consider the different reasons for preference for fairness criteria. As annual income is a manifestation of the circumstances of remuneration distribution, people with low incomes feel dissatisfaction with their unfortunate circumstances and probably hope for equal distribution as a means of improving their lot. Conversely, because people who have obtained high annual incomes will want to justify that as the just fruits of their own effort and talent, they can be expected to assert equitable distribution.

While annual income is a manifestation of current circumstances, in a society like Japan's where schooling is considered paramount, level of education is seen as qualification for remuneration distribution, according to the fairness criterion of equity. A person with a high level of education expects high remuneration appropriate to that level, and from that point of view their support for the equity criterion

Figure 3.3: Difference in preference for fairness criteria according to education

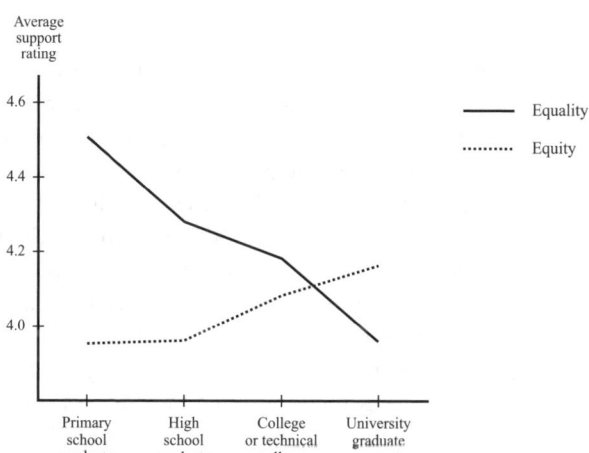

is understandable. Conversely, if a person with a low level of education were to abide by the equity criterion, low remuneration would be deemed appropriate for them and they therefore appear to reject this and conversely assert equality, which supports equal distribution irrespective of schooling. The results of our research demonstrate that preference for fairness criteria is strongly linked to social class and there is a tendency for people from both lower and higher social classes to support distribution criteria (equity vs. equality) that are advantageous to their own position.

In an analysis of age difference the main effect of age was significant in analysis of variance of equity ($F(5,928) = 2.480$, $p < 0.05$). In multiple comparisons using the Bonferroni test, however, there was no significant difference between any age groups, and there was no marked difference due to age in relation to preference for fairness criteria.

Finally, no differences according to social class or age were seen in relation to the need criterion. As we saw earlier, degree of support for need was high, and results of analysis here indicate that there is wide support among Japanese, irrespective of class or age. This probably reflects people's social insecurity arising from unstable employment after the bubble economy burst and the subsequent growing disparities.

Collectivism

The debate about Japanese collectivism

A point of debate in recent years in relation to Japanese values has been the cultural dimension of individualism versus collectivism. One important investigation has been the large-scale occupational value survey conducted by Hofstede on IBM staff in 50 countries around the world (Hofstede, 1980). Hofstede identified four factors, one dimension of which was individualism versus collectivism. Individualism emphasizes individual preference and achievement and expresses the tendency to give higher priority to individual objectives than group objectives, while conversely, collectivism emphasizes harmony within a group and the tendency to give higher priority to group objectives than individual objectives (Muramoto, 2009). At the extreme of individualism were positioned the USA and the nations of Europe, while at the extreme of collectivism were the countries of Central America. In this dimension Japan was located in the middle, and was more individualistic than Korea, Taiwan and the other nations of East Asia.

According to Hofstede's research results, Japan certainly exhibited more collectivism than western nations, but it was not a society in which collectivism was extremely strong. Well-known *Nihonjinron* pre-dating Hofstede, such as Benedict's *The chrysanthemum and the sword* (1946), Chie Nakane's *Japanese society* (1970) and Hamaguchi's inter-individualism theory (1982) had all stressed the collectivism of Japanese society, and Hofstede's research precipitated an increasingly vigorous debate, triggering various empirical research projects seeking to establish that Japan is collectivist.

The tendency to view Japan as collectivist was strongly backed by Kitayama's theory of cultural self (Markus and Kitayama, 1991). He claimed that compared to Americans and other westerners, who see themselves as individuals independent of other people, Japanese and other Asians see their existence as interdependent; linked to other people. The self-concept prescribes people's social cognitions, feelings, and behavior toward others. For example, research has shown that an American's sense of happiness is linked to their level of self-esteem, but an important factor in happiness for the Japanese is close companionship with others (Uchida, Kitayama, Mesquita, Reyes and Morling, 2008).

Of course, the view that Japan is collectivist has also been criticized. A significant criticism has been directed at the claim exemplified in the words of Shōtoku Taishi, 'Harmony is to be valued', an argument that the aim of Japanese collectivism is to maintain social harmony. Self-control and the avoidance of social conflict have long been held to be precepts of social behavior in Japan. However, Takano (2008) challenges this assumption, quoting Sugimoto and Mouer (1995) and Befu (1980) to point out that throughout history there has certainly been no shortage of conflict within and between Japan's social groups. Sugimoto and Mouer have shown that in the period immediately after the Second World War labor disputes occurred more frequently in Japan than in the West. Befu points to the number of peasant uprisings in the Edo period and the number of tenant farmer disputes from the Meiji era on to demonstrate that actions that disrupted harmony within groups were not uncommon in Japan.

After reviewing comparative cultural studies and investigating sociological and economics data, Takano (2008) declared the theory of Japanese collectivism to be 'an illusion'. He reasons that the root of the widely accepted present-day theory that Japan is highly collectivist can be traced to Benedict. Cultured Americans highly value individualism as founded in the modern Enlightenment; in contrast, there was a tendency to deem other, unmodernized regions to be collectivist. This contrast was an implicit premise of Benedict's Japanese cultural research. She emphasized the Japanese collectivist behavior of the militaristic era—apparent in peoples of all nations under external threat—in developing her theories on Japanese culture, and in the process gave concrete form to the cultural stereotyping to which Americans are wont. Takano claims that that gave rise to a plethora of *Nihonjinron*, and the theory of Japanese collectivism became a strong, commonly accepted theory.

Kitayama (1999) criticized Takano et al. for having arbitrarily selected their data, a claim which Takano (2008) has disputed. Unlike Takano, I have not exhaustively investigated the relevant data, but the cross cultural research between Japan and America that I have conducted has produced results which indicate that the Japanese are collectivist. The research investigated cultural styles in resolving disputes (Ohbuchi, Sato and Tedeschi, 1999), based on 501 American students and 407 Japanese students responding to an Oyserman (1993) scale, and found that the Japanese are significantly more collective than Americans (standard score M = 0.35 vs -0.30, t(844)

= 11.52, p < 0.01). Therefore, for the moment at least, I ascribe to the theory of Japanese collectivism, but as I discuss below, there are major variations among individual Japanese in relation to this value and I am therefore also skeptical about assertions that the Japanese are uniformly collectivist.

Group pre-eminence and orientation to personal relations

Collectivism is a complex value. The characteristics cited as collectivism may be classified in two general orientations: group pre-eminence (group norms, group achievement, and maintaining group order) and orientation to interpersonal relations (closeness, social support, and harmonious relations). Proponents of the former value set hold that for the nation and society, group members will unite in cooperation, see the group's success as synonymous with their own success, and must strive for the prosperity of the group even at the expense of the individual. Frequently cited examples of the group-preeminence characteristics include the pre-war militaristic state system with the Emperor at its pinnacle, and the management style and company-centered sensibilities of employees in Japanese companies which were an important pillar of the decades of rapid economic growth. The theories of Benedict and Nakane emphasized group pre-eminence.

Others have argued the Japanese collectivism thesis by focusing on the characteristics of the latter, the orientation to interpersonal relations. The theory of Hamaguchi (1982) emphasizes the value that Japanese place in a non-instrumental way on establishing intimate and trusting interpersonal relations with others, arguing that Japanese regard being in interdependent relationships in which each is considerate of and helps the other as the natural way for humans to be. Hamaguchi says 'Japanese collectivism is not immersion and subordination of the individual to an organization ... it is a concept in which the organization and its members seek to share benefits and live together' (1982: 7). He further explains that what is important for Japanese is being in relationships with others in a group, rather than the group itself.

Triandis and Gelfand (1998) propose a concept of the underlying dimensions of collectivism that is close to this one on the basis of empirical research. They identified underlying sub-dimensions for individualism and collectivism that are respectively, horizontal and vertical. The horizontal dimension expresses whether maintaining personal relations and solidarity is emphasized or not. Horizontal Individualism (HI) expresses the tendency for the self to desire independence from others, while Horizontal Collectivism (HC) conversely expresses the tendency to perceive similarities in others and to seek strong solidarity with peers. The Vertical dimension is interest in status. Vertical Individualism (VI) is the tendency to seek status and achievement as an individual through competition with others, while Vertical Collectivism is the tendency to emphasize group status and prestige and to adopt a competitive attitude toward other groups. The group pre-eminence collectivist category corresponds to Vertical Collectivism, while an orientation to interpersonal relations corresponds to Horizontal Collectivism.

Differences in collectivism according to social class (variations)

Whatever the values, there are individual differences among the Japanese. That is also probably the case for collectivism. Based on data from my own recently completed social research I have attempted to compare collectivism between social classes to see how collectivist values are distributed among the Japanese. I calculated a Horizontal Collectivism score (HC-HI) and a Vertical Collectivism score (VC-VI) from responses to a Triandis and Gelfand scale, and analyzed the relationships to age, annual income (family income) and schooling. The average for all respondents was +0.17 for Horizontal Collectivism, and +0.83 for Vertical Collectivism, with the data suggesting that overall, Japanese have a tendency to collectivism.

I used household income and education as indices for social class. It was not the case that both were completely congruent in our data; for example, the correlation, $r = 0.401$, $p < 0.001$, was not high. However, in contrast to the 60.8 per cent of people with incomes of 10 million yen or more who were graduates of university or post graduate programs, 82.7 per cent of people with incomes of 2 million yen or less had graduated from high school or lower, indicating a certain relatedness between schooling and income; that is, Japan is a society in which schooling is considered paramount and living standard (social class) is dependent on schooling.

I first divided the respondents into four groups according to income and compared the two types of collectivism. There was no apparent difference in income in Horizontal Collectivism, but there was in Vertical Collectivism ($F(3,930) = 3.23$, $p < 0.05$). As Figure 3.4 shows, Vertical Collectivism is stronger among people with low

Figure 3.4: Difference in collectivism according to annual income

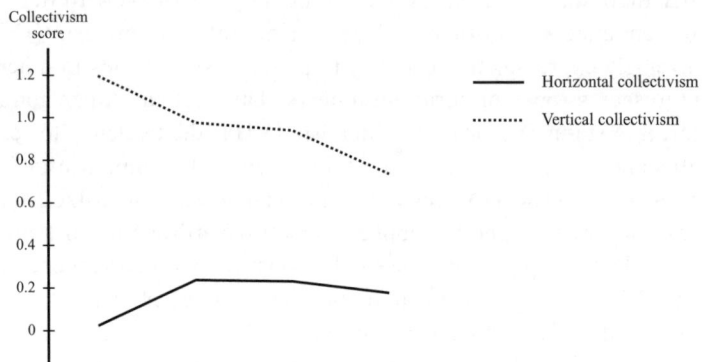

incomes, and gets weaker the higher the income. In the analysis that looked at relationship to schooling, the same trend was apparent, with Vertical Collectivism being strongest among those with the lowest level of schooling (Figure 3.5). These results indicate that Vertical Collectivism is a value of people in lower social classes.

As there are expected to be differences in values according to age, I also investigated this point. The results of comparison according to age are given in Figure 3.6, and the age difference between the two types of collectivism is extremely clear. Horizontal Collectivism is strong among younger people and weak in those who are older ($F(5,942) = 4.92$, $p < 0.001$). Vertical Collectivism is exactly the opposite, being strong among older people and weak in those who are younger ($F(5,940) = 2.53$, $p < 0.05$). This indicates that for the Japanese the type of collectivism is completely different between young and old.

The results of this research indicate that among the Japanese, Vertical Collectivism is strong in lower social classes and among older people and weak in upper social classes and among younger people, while Horizontal Collectivism is strong among younger people. This suggests that occupational experience may have a major effect on the formation of collectivist values. It may be surmised that the fact that Vertical Collectivism is strong among people aged 30 or more is because they have belonged to a company or other organization, had the experience through that of acquiring important

Figure 3.5: Difference in collectivism according to education

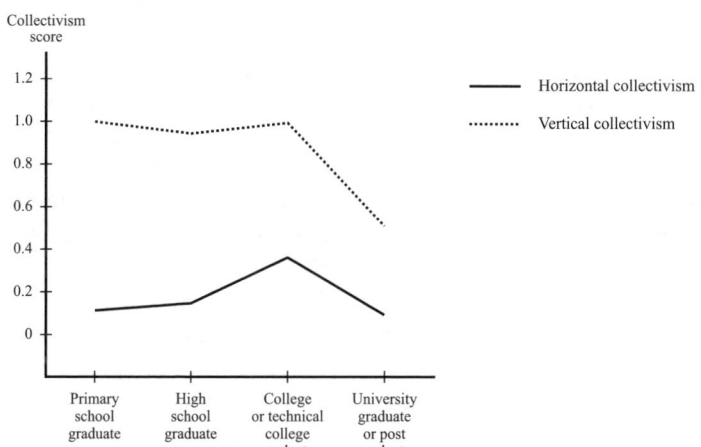

Figure 3.6: Age difference in collectivism

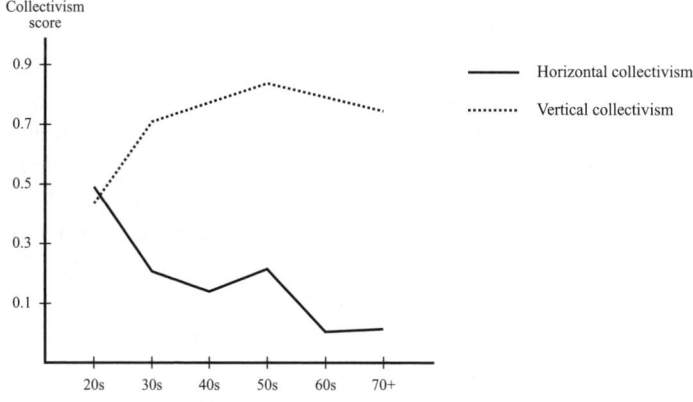

life resources, and have come to recognize the importance of the group in an individual's life. This result also suggests, however, that type of occupational experience will have differing effects on people's values. People with higher levels of education typically enter professional occupations and believe that they acquire status and income through their own professional skills, so that compared to the average company employee their reliance on an organization is low. This is probably why Vertical Collectivism is relatively weak among those with high levels of schooling. It can probably be further deduced that because they also have high levels of income, the relatively low level of Vertical Collectivism among persons with high income is due to the same factors.

In contrast, younger people (particularly in their 20s) have not yet entered an occupation, or if they have, have not been employed for long, and therefore have a weak sense of self as defined by organization. It can be deduced that they have not yet come to form group pre-eminence values. Rather, it is probably because they value their friends and other close relationships that they evidenced strong characteristics of Horizontal Collectivism.

I am unable to be definitive as my research is not comparative between different cultures, but in so far as the raw Triandis and Gelfand scores are concerned, Japanese incline to collectivism in both vertical and horizontal dimensions. Our analysis, however, indicates that the nature of this collectivism differs according to social attributes, and in that sense our research provides another perspective on the debate surrounding Japanese collectivism.

Religion and traditional values

Generally speaking Japanese are said to have no religion. Certainly in social surveys, most Japanese respond that they do not have a religion. In a Japan Broadcasting Corporation opinion poll only 33 per cent of Japanese responded to the question 'Do you have a religion?' with the answer 'I do', which is significantly different from 93 per cent of Americans (NHK Broadcasting Culture Research Institute, 1984). The World Values Survey conducted in 2005 gave very similar results (36.5 per cent) (Dentsu Communication Institute/Nippon Research Center, 2008). In fact, probably only a very small portion of Japanese would have completed the special rituals to become members of the faithful, such as baptism or Buddhist confirmation, and there would not be many Japanese who are in the habit of regularly attending a church or temple. Another survey by the Japan Broadcasting Corporation (the 'Consciousness Structure Attitudes and Awareness of Japanese Today' survey, conducted every five years since 1973) shows that the proportion of people who have engaged in continuous religious activity, such as the practice of prayer or worship, has been in the order of 10 per cent since its inception, and has declined in recent years (NHK Broadcasting Culture Research Institute, 2010).

Japanese religious attitude

Among experts, however, there is a view that the apparently irreligious Japanese life style is not in the strictest sense of the words, no religion. While at a glance it appears to contradict the above survey results, in the World Values Survey only 12 per cent of Japanese responded 'I am an atheist'. Further, only 26.7 per cent responded 'I hardly ever or never go to a shrine or temple' (Dentsu Communication Institute/Nippon Research Center, 2008), meaning that most Japanese, while perhaps not regularly, are on occasion visiting such religious facilities. Conversely, in a recent 'Consciousness Structure Attitudes and Awareness of Japanese Today' survey, 42 per cent responded they 'believe in the existence of Buddha', and 33 per cent responded they 'believe in God', while on the other hand only 24 per cent responded 'I do not believe at all in matters associated with religion or faith' (NHK Broadcasting Culture Research Institute, 2010). These survey results suggest that Japanese in fact are involved in a variety of religious activities, and further, conduct their lives while accepting religious concepts.

Why then, do Japanese respond in the negative to the question 'Do you have a religion?' It is probably because they understand the question to be asking whether or not they belong to a particular religious body like Christianity or Islam. Certainly the majority of Japanese do not undertake religious activity associated with a particular religious body, but religious activity itself is broadly observable in the lives of Japanese. Buddhist shrines, Shinto altars and religious charms are found in Japanese homes, and nearly all Japanese visit a shrine to mark the New Year and go to temples for funerals. At important milestones in a person's life, such as building a new home, launching a business, or sitting exams, they pray at a shrine. Old customs that have their origins in religious events, such as the *obon* festival of the dead, the *ohigan* Buddhist celebrations of the equinox and the *shichigosan* celebrations of children reaching the ages of three, five and seven, continue to this day. Taken together, the only conclusion is that Japanese lives have strong religious overtones.

These actions are ritualistic and customary, and it is the opinion of some that they do not constitute religion, but in as much as there is a sense that if those things are not done, one feels bad, then something is inherent therein that can be called religious sentiment. Many

Japanese stepping onto the grounds of a shrine or temple feel a sense of solemnity, and if they recall that they have not visited the family gravesite for many years, feel guilt, so that it may be surmised that underneath such feelings lies a sense of belief in the existence of the gods and Buddha, or of the soul. That sense is not always based on rational or logical thought. For example, even if objectively there is no such existence, conceptually, acting in a manner that is respectful of it provides respite for the heart. In so far as such attitudes and mental preparedness have an actual effect on the hearts and actions of the Japanese people, then they are something that in the broad sense may be termed 'religion'.

Japanese religion is in this way different from monotheistic religions such as Christianity or Islam, in that it is polytheistic, with the subject of worship being different types of gods, and at the same time it is syncretistic, in that their application is separated as appropriate to events. The NHK Broadcasting Culture Research Institute survey (1984) called Japanese religious awareness 'folk religion'; underlying that is the notion of animism, which manifests in events and rituals that are closely linked to the communal life of an agrarian society, and at the same time it has the nature of syncretism, being accepting of and merging imported religions (Buddhism and Confucianism). Japanese religion is not severe in that life is lived in accordance with faith, or actions judged in accordance with doctrine, but instead there is apparent in it the magnanimity to accept gods with many different origins without the exclusiveness of monotheism.

Japanese social values and religion

Given contact with a diversity of religious facilities and taking part in everyday life events and customs that have religious meaning, it is likely that a religious world view and rules of virtue may also have affected Japanese values. We turned our focus to the traditional Japanese philosophies of Buddhism, Confucianism and Shinto, and through social research investigated how much these traditional values are shared by modern-day Japanese (Ohbuchi, Sato and Miura, 2008; Ohbuchi and Kawashima, 2009a; Ohbuchi and Kawashima, 2009b). The Japanese traditional values scales we developed comprise four scales for Buddhism, four for Confucianism, and six for Shinto. From the average in Figure 3.7, as half or more scales are at the midpoint or higher, it is apparent that traditional philosophies have at least some effect on modern-day Japanese values. We will

Figure 3.7: Degree of support for traditional Japanese values

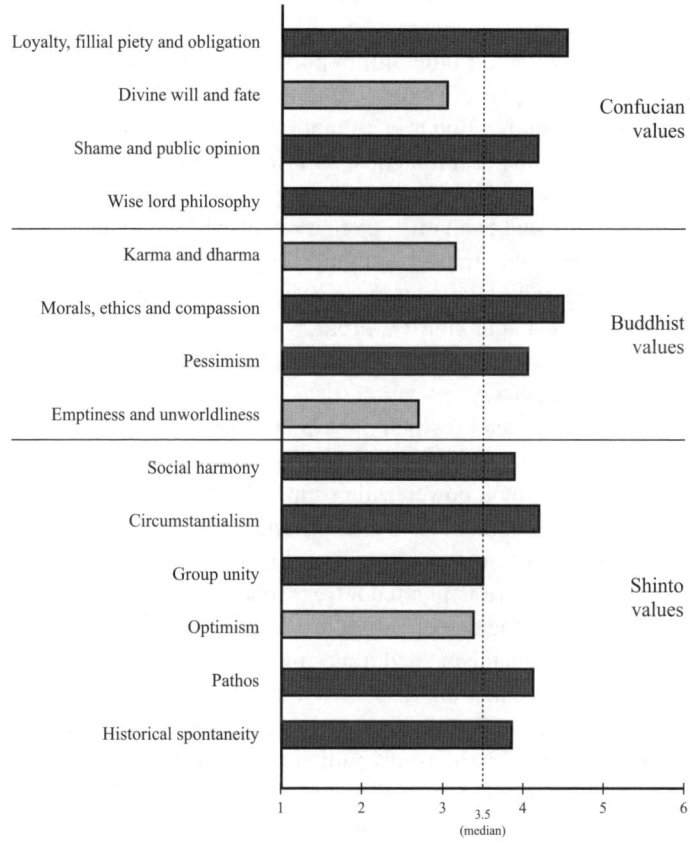

Source: Ohbuchi and Kawashima, 2009.
Note: The darker bars are higher scores than the median of the scale (3.5).

consider the traditional values of modern-day Japanese based on 2009 survey data (Ohbuchi and Kawashima, 2009b).

One of the value areas in which the effect of traditional philosophies can be seen is life values, which describe the principles an individual should abide by in life. In relation to this point, Figure 3.7 suggests three different types of life values. The first is indicated by loyalty, filial piety and obligation (Confucianism) and group utilitarianism (Shinto), in which it is expected that class (the vertical society) will be respected and the individual will contribute to the group and fulfill the role they have been given in that context. It is a life value that corresponds to Vertical Collectivism. The second is a value expressed through shame and public opinion (Confucianism), the morals, ethics and compassion of Buddhist philosophy, and the social harmony found in the Shinto philosophy. It is a life value that addresses meeting people's expectations by controlling self-interest, orientation to cooperation and collaboration, and giving priority to maintaining human relationships. In broad terms it corresponds to Horizontal Collectivism. The third is a life value that addresses relativism (Shinto), and is an attitude that rejects absolute and universal principles and holds that one should respond to circumstances as they arise and undertake matters as is right. It could be described as accommodative and flexible thinking, but it is also a way of thinking that gives rise to a lack of consistency and systems that are irresponsible (Ohtsuka, 2008).

Another value area in which the effect of traditional philosophies can be seen is social view. It is a passive social view which holds that society is moved by a power which supersedes the human, and it is beyond the power of humans to cause change in historical spontaneity (Shinto). Level of support was low, but in divine will and fate (Confucianism) there is posited a transcendent power, or 'divinity', which determines the fate of individuals and society. It is for that very reason that Confucianism encourages individuals to comprehend the transcendence of knowing divine will, or obeying divine will, and to engage proactively in the resolution of problems. In the Shinto philosophy, however, the transcendent power that moves society is held to be beyond the power of humans to affect, and the emphasis is on powerlessness, wherein the individual should simply allow themselves to go with the flow. The Shinto philosophy, however, also contains within it optimism in the form of the precept 'the best approach is to go with the flow', which indicates a sense of trust in the goodness of the transcendent power. Human proactivity is instead looked down upon as trivial wisdom, and Shinto embraces blind trust in the transcendent power that the Japanese call 'nature'. The fact that there was a higher degree of support for those scales expressing Shinto nature than Confucianist divinity illustrates that Japanese assume the effect on society's movement of a power (nature) that transcends human ken, but tend to see it as something friendly and protective of humans (Japanese), and it is apparent that this gives rise to a lack of proactivity in favor of a passivity in the face of problems to be resolved (Kamijima, 1968; Kono, 2004: Ohbuchi, 1998).

A number of influences from traditional philosophies are also apparent in the human view, but all have in common that humans are seen as fleeting. Pessimism (Buddhism) is a human view that emphasizes the emptiness and arduousness of life, through precepts such as 'life is suffering' and 'this world is transient'. Conversely, pathos (Shinto) recognizes this fleeting nature of human life and evaluates it positively as having given rise to the delicate sensitivity of the Japanese people, their empathy with others and their gentleness.

As outlined above, the results of our social research show that the traditional philosophies of Confucianism, Buddhism and Shinto have a wide range of effects on contemporary Japanese values (Ohbuchi, Sato and Miura, 2008; Ohbuchi and Kawashima, 2009a; Ohbuchi and Kawashima, 2009b).

Differences in traditional values according to social class

Based on the data from the social research that I undertook in 2010 I looked at how traditional values differ between social classes and found differences according to annual income in karma and dharma, pessimism, emptiness and unworldliness, divine will and fate, and optimism ($F(3, 928) = 4.891$, $p < 0.01$; $F(3,925) = 9.809$, $p < 0.001$; $F(3,929) = 5.499$, $p < 0.001$; $F(3,925) = 6.174$, $p < 0.001$). As is apparent from Figure 3.8, the trend was the same in all value dimensions, with traditional values held more strongly, the lower the income.

Educational differences were apparent in even more value dimensions: karma and dharma, $F(3,953) = 9.919$, $p < 0.001$; morals, ethics and compassion, $F(3,952) = 3.573$, $p < 0.05$; emptiness and unworldliness, $F(3,950) = 14.440$, $p < 0.001$; loyalty, filial piety and obligation, $F(3,954) = 6.462$, $p < 0.001$; divine will and fate, $F(3,954) = 14.586$, $p < 0.001$; shame and public opinion, $F(3,951) = 19.364$, $p < 0.001$; social harmony, $F(3,952) = 10.203$, $p < 0.001$; group utilitarianism, $F(3,949) = 9.859$, $p < 0.001$; and optimism, $F(3,950) = 9.413$, $p < 0.001$. As can be seen in Figure 3.9, all Buddhist, Confucianist, and Shinto dimensions are included, and there is no bias to any particular religion. In that sense also, the results indicate that these religions have a wide range of effects on Japanese values.

Figure 3.9 shows that the trend is the same as for income, being higher the lower the level of education for all value dimensions. Among these are included dimensions that correspond to Vertical Collectivism (group utilitarianism, loyalty, filial piety and obligation)

Figure 3.8: Difference in traditional values according to income

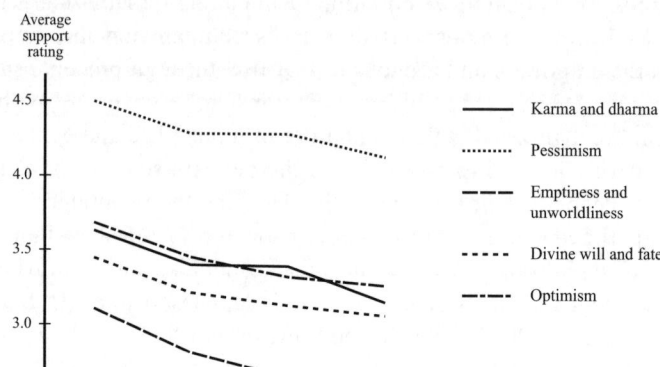

Figure 3.9: Difference in traditional values according to education

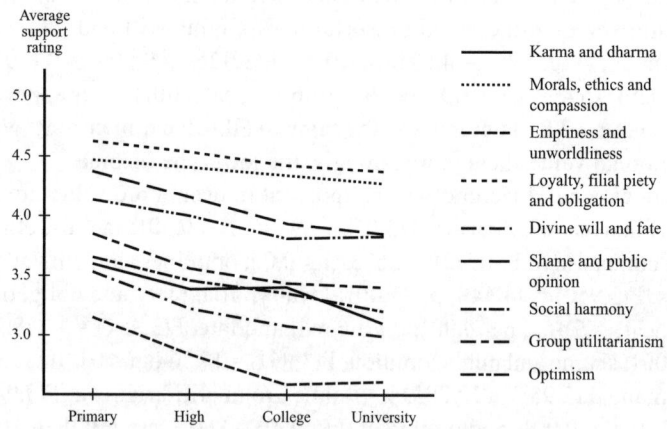

and to Horizontal Collectivism (social harmony, shame and public opinion), but unlike the section on Japanese collectivism, all are strongly supported by the lower social classes. In other words, no matter the index looked at, the relationship between social class and traditional values is clear: these values are stronger, the lower the class.

Why is it that people of lower class have strong traditional values? There are several possible interpretations of this result. The first may be that in a society like Japan in which schooling is considered paramount, people with a lower level of education are not only placed in a position of disadvantage occupationally, but also have many occasions in which they feel inferior to others, and there is therefore a tendency for them to have lower self-esteem. This low self-esteem probably works against the formation of individualistic values with their emphasis on the power and supremacy of the individual. At the same time it may be that because such people feel themselves to be a weak and powerless existence, they come to rely more strongly on interpersonal relations and the groups to which they belong, and it is possible this also manifests the mental conditions for acceptance of an existence that transcends the individual.

Second, because people with lower levels of education do not have professional techniques or qualifications they are typically engaged in jobs that do not require special skill or knowledge, such as the service or manufacturing industries. Because such people are not given major responsibility or authority, they are probably unable to take particular pride in their job, and conversely, they may typically accumulate interdependent experiences in which they are cooperating with others and helping each other. These communal experiences are limiting of the self and encourage the formation of 'other' oriented attitudes, and may well enhance affinity for traditional values.

Third, it is necessary to discuss the possibility that dissatisfaction with an unfortunate environment and the resulting desire for restoration will encourage a return to traditional values. There are several psychological mechanisms that are conceivably in play here. First, if respondents with low levels of schooling and low income are as a result dissatisfied with themselves and their lives, it should be reflected in their values. The fact that pessimism, from among the Buddhist values, is strongest among those with low levels of schooling, income, class and satisfaction, would indicate that. Further, among this group may be those who will not lay the blame for their lot with their own shortcomings, but seek to lighten their sense of responsibility by attributing their lot to fate. The interpretation could be that such people will support Confucianist divine will and fate. Further, there may be people who focus on the values of the groups to which they belong to compensate for their dissatisfaction and use that as a basis in seeking to restore their self-esteem. Such people may develop stronger group oriented values (loyalty, filial piety and obligation, group utilitarianism) from among Confucianism, Shinto and the Japanese classics. Finally, there are conceivably people who will place their current unsatisfactory lot in the relative context of a larger spatial-temporal world that includes the next world, and seek to find other significance for their current circumstances. This is the interpretation for believers in Buddhist karma and dharma.

Assuming that an unfortunate environment encourages acceptance of traditional values, we considered the reasons, but for the fourth interpretation, it is necessary to posit the reverse causal relationship. That is the view that a person originally familiar with traditional values, who is other oriented and weakly individualistic, will be likely to have a low level of schooling. Such a person is not ambitious, is self-restraining, and will tend to live in a way that is in harmony with their surrounds and gives priority to group interests. Among such people it may be that there are those who do not go out of their way to aim for a high level of schooling or high income, who are satisfied with the basics and who seek a life of self-sufficiency. However, just because they are that way it is not necessarily the case that such people are satisfied with their lives. A sense of satisfaction with life is positively correlated with schooling and income ($r = 0.181$, 0.329, with both ps < 0.01) and it is not the case that people who are in an unfortunate position enjoy their 'honorable' poverty.

Whether or not they enjoy their poverty, the fourth and final interpretation suggests that traditional values in a modern society like Japan could inherently work against individual achievement and success. Our research results reveal a tendency for traditional values to be supported by older people (in their 60s). This suggests that the young Japanese today grew up with their parents in an environment in which traditional values were strong. It was probably the case that the culture emphasized devotion to one's parents, appearances, consideration, and pre-eminence of the group.

Many children when they enter their teens shed these traditional values in favor of a tendency to emphasize individualistic values, but among them may be young people who strongly internalize the traditional values they inherited from their parents' generation as their own, and who do not turn to individualism. They will first consider the feelings and circumstances of others, control their own assertiveness, and become adults who act in accordance with the virtues of humility and self-sacrifice. People such as this who are weakly individualistic have low motivation to seek to maximize their own abilities, or to achieve or be superior in achieving things ahead of others and are not driven to participate actively in exam hell to achieve a high level of schooling by winning through no matter what.

As a result, they are unable to use the best route for upward movement between classes—schooling—and remain in the same class as their parents, or shoulder the risk of moving downwards to a lower class. The foregoing is no more than a speculative interpretation, but in so far as our traditional values are present in the competitive modern Japanese society, the author wishes to point out the possibility that those values could fulfill a role that works against individual success and achievement.

Social class and values in Japan: Conclusions

The Japanese sense of fairness has been extensively debated among Japanese social scientists. In research prior to 2000 it had been stressed that Japanese favor equal distribution, but subsequent empirical data has not always been in accord with that finding. Our survey results demonstrated that Japanese most want distribution according to need, but at the same time there are major differences between classes in relation to equality and equity. People of the lower classes favor equality more than equity, and people of the higher classes conversely favor equity more than equality.

In recent years the theory of Japanese collectivism has also become a hotly debated topic among Japanese researchers. I, on the one hand, support the theory, but have focused on individual differences among the Japanese, and in particular, differences between social classes. Collectivism has two aspects, vertical (group pre-eminence) and horizontal (relationship orientation), but my social research (2010a) on Japanese values demonstrated that Vertical Collectivism is strongest among people of the lower social classes, and is relatively low among members of the upper classes.

Japanese religion has also attracted the interest of social scientists. While the Japanese have described themselves as being without religion, there is no shortage of religiosity in their behavior and feelings. Those feelings are traditional and cannot be fully expressed in terms only of polytheism and syncretism. I posited that the traditional religions of Buddhism, Confucianism and Shinto have had an effect on the formation of Japanese values, and measured the traditional values of modern-day Japanese. I was thus able to identify many value dimensions associated with those religions, most of which were strongly supported by people from lower classes.

The fact that the lower classes favor equal distribution more than equitable distribution is a function of self-interest. However, looking at class differences in collectivism and traditional values, their preference for equality seems not to reflect interest in benefits in a personal material sense, but their own unique view and way of life in relation to people and society. Those values may have been formed as the result of their being in unfortunate circumstances, but conversely, collectivist values restrain individual achievement and may prevent social movement. The research identified the broad influence of social class on values, and attempted their interpretation from several perspectives, including the views just expressed. Nevertheless, the psycho-social mechanisms of the effect social class has on values is as yet inadequately explained.

4 Invisible Inequality: Occupational Prestige

Yoshiya Shiotani

Considerable attention has been focused in Japan recently on issues of social inequality, and primarily on economic disparity. Social inequality is not limited to economic aspects. As well as economic disparity, there are disparities in social evaluations. Needless to say, people need money to secure the material bases to support their lives. People also need to be acknowledged and respected by others. However, evaluations of a person by others or the society vary depending on the person's social attributes, including education level, occupation, and employment status. Of these, this study focuses on the social evaluation of occupations. While differences in social evaluations of different occupations are not as visible as economic disparities, they are nevertheless present in contemporary Japanese society. The purpose of this chapter is to review previous studies on the social evaluation of occupations, called occupational prestige studies, and to critically review their main findings.

This report consists of three parts. First, in order to show the academic positioning of occupational prestige studies, part 1 describes social stratification research, which deals with social inequality in general, and the role played by occupational prestige studies in this area. This is followed by an explanation of the current mainstream method of measuring occupational prestige and a demonstration of specific examples of occupational prestige scores (OPSs) assigned to different occupations. This section concludes with an overview of the history of social surveys on measuring occupational prestige. Part 2 organizes six points at issue regarding the reliability and validity of the OPS as a scale of occupational status, and analyzes arguments as to whether the theoretical prerequisites for using the OPS are met or not. Part 3 provides a discussion and presents a conclusion.

Social stratification research and the occupational prestige score (OPS)

The role played by occupational prestige studies in social stratification research

Occupations are the most important indicator of social status in social stratification research (Hara and Seiyama, 2005; Naoi and Suzuki, 1978). This is due to the 'fact that social resources, including income, prestige and power, are distributed exclusively through occupations' (Naoi, 1978: 284). Occupations bring various forms of inequality to people and function as a de facto or rudimentary order that stratifies people (Naoi, 1979). Occupations not only satisfy economic needs in individuals' lives but also provide social relationships for establishing individuals' roles in the society (Nakao, 2000). Occupation has therefore been understood to better explain differences in social resources between individuals than any other social status variable.

Traditionally, social stratification research has conducted analyses of concepts such as social mobility and status attainment by using two approaches to occupational status: the 'big-class schema' and 'gradational schema' (Jonsson, Grusky, Carlo, Pollak and Brinton, 2009). The big-class schema approach classifies occupations into categories, each of which is of reasonable size, such as professional, managerial, clerical or sales, instead of regarding them as specific, individual occupations, such as turners, pharmacists or cooks. One example of this approach is the research conducted by Featherman and Hauser (1978) in the US, which analyzed the association between parents' and children's occupational classes by conducting a log-linear analysis of the intergenerational mobility table. In contrast, the gradational schema is an approach that regards occupational status as a continuous variable by assigning social status level scores to individual occupations. Examples of such scores include the 'occupational prestige score' (National Opinion Research Center [NORC], 1947) and the 'socioeconomic index' (Duncan, 1961), both of which are discussed in this article. An example of research based on the gradational schema is Blau and Duncan (1967), which conducted a path analysis of the status attainment process on the US data. Scales of occupational status, such as the OPS, have been created based on the social evaluation of occupations.

These tasks have substantially been conducted by occupational prestige studies, which deal with the social evaluation of occupations.

As an area of social stratification research, a number of empirical occupational prestige studies have been conducted (Hodge, Siegel and Rossi, 1966; Nakao, 2000). While topics dealt with by occupational prestige studies range widely, these studies have mainly focused on constructing scales of the social status of occupations and analyzing the reliability of the scales (Wegener, 1992). By aggregating individuals' subjective ratings of the social status of occupations, occupational prestige studies have developed a scale of the social status of occupations called the 'occupational prestige score' and have demonstrated the reliability of this score as a scale of social status by comparing OPSs between groups with different social attributes, between societies with different cultures, and between different points in time. Occupational prestige studies have not only provided the OPS as an analytical tool to researchers who adopt the gradational schema, but also served to strengthen their theoretical belief that a continuous, one-dimensional structure of the social status of occupations exist in society (Stehr, 1974).

The greatest contribution of occupational prestige studies to social stratification research is the creation of continuous scales of occupational status, such as the OPS and socioeconomic index (SEI), which have enabled path analyses of the status attainment process. After Blau and Duncan (1967), these analyses have played a leading role in innovative empirical studies in social stratification and mobility research (Kanomata, 1984: 35). The analytical method used in earlier studies, conducted separate analyses for 'intergenerational mobility' and 'intragenerational mobility'. The innovation of path analysis introduced a new methodology in which the entire process is dealt with as one continuous flow, from infancy and childhood, when social status and lifestyle is directly inherited from one's parents, to adolescence when one begins to establish one's own social status through education (Tominaga, 1979: 18). Since the path analysis corresponds to a multiple regression equation in a sequential-simultaneous form, a prerequisite for its application is that all status variables have been quantified (Tominaga, 1979: 18). The OPS and SEI satisfies this prerequisite, enabling a path analysis of the status attainment process.

Method of measuring occupational prestige and the OPS

Occupational prestige is the relative social status of an occupation in a society (Nakao, 2000), representing the socially-shared attractiveness associated with the occupation (Tsuzuki, 2000). The procedure that has been adopted for measuring occupational prestige consists of collecting individuals' ratings of various occupations by social surveys and assuming that the mean value for each occupation represents the social status of the occupation. For instance, the following wording was used in the 1995 National Survey of Social Stratification and Social Mobility (SSM Survey) conducted in Japan:

> Here is a form listing various occupations. People in general might distinguish these occupations, saying that some are higher or lower than others. If you are asked to classify these occupations into five levels, how would you classify them? For each occupation, please choose one of the following: 'Highest', 'relatively high', 'average', 'relatively low', and 'lowest' (Tsuzuki, 2000: 39).

Each respondent is asked to evaluate the social status of 56 different occupations, from 'president of a large company' to 'musician', by classifying them into the five categories described above. The researchers assign 100, 75, 50, 25 and 0 points to the 'highest', 'relatively high', 'average', 'relatively low', and 'lowest' categories, respectively. The OPS for an occupation is the mean value of all ratings for the occupation given by all respondents to the survey. The OPS is regarded as reflecting the relative social status of the occupation in society. This method of measuring social prestige, called category rating, has become the mainstream method for measuring occupational prestige.

Table 4.1 presents OPSs calculated by the procedure described above. The highest level of prestige is enjoyed by some managerial jobs, such as president of a large company and Member of Parliament, as well as highly professional occupations such as physician, judge, university/college professor and pilot. The occupations associated with lowest prestige include unskilled physical labor jobs, such as cannery worker, security guard, road worker and miner, as well as some service occupations, such as shop clerk and waitress.[1] Positioned between these occupational categories are occupations associated with mid-level prestige, including: semi-professional occupations, such as primary school teacher and child minders; clerical jobs, such as sales representative at a large company and bank employees; and skilled physical labor jobs, such as carpenter, restaurant cook, and barber.

History of social surveys on occupational prestige

The first attempt to measure occupational prestige using social survey was by Counts (1925). Counts measured the social status of occupations in the US by asking a total of 450 respondents, including high school and college/university students and teachers, to rate 45 different occupations. The results of this research indicated a high level of consensus on occupational status ratings between the different groups of respondents, with the correlation coefficient for each occupation between groups with different social backgrounds always being 0.9 or higher. However, Counts' intention in this research was not to develop a scale of occupational status, such as the OPS. As a pedagogue, Counts' investigations were aimed at providing better vocational guidance to children.

The idea behind the current OPS, i.e., the idea of developing a scale of occupational status based on people's subjective evaluations of occupations in order to serve social mobility research, was first presented by Smith (1935). Smith conducted a social survey in the US and asked his respondents to rate different occupations by assigning a score ranging between 0 and 100 to each occupation, and calculated the mean value for each occupation as a measure of its occupational prestige. Smith says, 'The scale will make possible the measurement of direction, amount, and speed of vertical mobility of an individual' (Smith, 1935: 47).

Before the 1950s, occupational prestige studies were typically small-scale social surveys of residents of specific communities, until the NORC (1947) conducted measurement of occupational prestige based on a nationwide social survey in the US. Using a five-level category rating system, the NORC assigned OPSs to ninety different occupations. The NORC's survey was the vanguard of modern occupational prestige measurement and provided a model for subsequent occupational prestige studies (Nakao, 2000). The socioeconomic index (Duncan, 1961) discussed later in this chapter was created based on the research data provided by the NORC.

Subsequently, occupational prestige was measured in the US in the mid-1960s and the late 1980s. In the 1960s, Siegel (1971) developed a scale of occupational prestige that applies to all of the occupations covered by the national census, by combining the results of surveys conducted in 1963, 1964 and 1965 (Nakao, 2000). Over the next two decades, this scale provided the foundation for the SEI and served as

Table 4.1: Occupational prestige scores (from 1995 SSM Survey)

Occupation	OPS	SE
Physician	90.1	14.8
President of a large company	87.3	16.7
Judge	86.9	16.9
College/university professor	84.3	17.1
Pilot	82.5	17.9
High-level bureaucrat	77.5	21.2
Member of Parliament	74.9	22.7
Licensed architect	72.0	16.2
Certified public accountant	70.8	16.1
Stewardess*	70.0	17.2
Professional athlete	69.0	19.8
Owner of a small or medium business	68.9	15.8
Musician	66.6	16.0
Automobile design engineer	66.3	15.7
Pharmacist	65.7	15.1
Dress designer	64.6	15.3
Primary school teacher	63.6	15.6
Section chief of a large company	63.2	14.6
Head priest of a temple	60.3	18.2
Nurse*	59.7	17.0
Policeman	57.9	15.3
Sales representative of a large company	57.4	14.2
Section chief of a city office	56.9	13.3
Construction or public works foreman	56.7	13.7
Bank clerk	56.4	12.9
Section chief of a small or medium business	56.1	12.9
Carpenter	53.1	15.4
Childminder*	52.9	13.0
Wholesale shop owner	52.9	11.1
Furniture maker	52.1	13.5
Restaurant cook	51.6	13.3
Owner of a retail business	51.3	11.2
Train driver	51.3	10.7
Machine assember of a large company	51.1	14.3
Electrician	50.4	13.1
Barber	49.7	11.5
Bank teller	49.4	10.0
Bus driver	48.9	11.5
Train station employee	47.8	11.0
Car salesperson	47.2	11.9
Office clerk of a small or medium business	47.0	10.6

Table 4.1: continued

Car mechanic	46.8	11.9
Machine assembler of a small or medium business	46.7	14.5
Fisherman	46.5	16.2
Postman	46.2	12.0
Farmer	45.6	17.6
Baker	44.6	13.2
Insurance salesperson	44.3	13.8
Pressman	44.0	13.7
Shop clerk	42.4	14.0
Cannery worker	42.2	13.7
Spinner	42.0	15.1
Security guard	39.9	16.1
Roadworker	39.0	17.6
Waitress*	38.1	15.5
Miner*	36.7	19.0

Source: Tsuzuki, 2000.
Notes:
OPS = occupational prestige score; SE = standard error.
*: As the term was used in the survey.

a basis for Treiman's (1977) international occupational prestige scale (Nakao, 2000). A resurvey of occupational prestige was conducted in 1989, in response to the 1980 modification to the occupational classification system made by the US Bureau of Labor Statistics (Nakao and Treas, 1994). In this resurvey, a nine-level category rating system was used and OPSs were assigned to a total of 740 different occupations.

In Japan, the first attempt to measure occupational prestige was the SSM Survey of six major cities conducted in 1952 (Naoi, 1978). This was followed by Nishihira's (1964) survey conducted in the 23 wards of Tokyo, which measured occupational prestige of 98 occupations. Measurement of occupational prestige based on a national survey was conducted in 1955, 1975 and 1995. All three measurements were conducted as part of the SSM Survey. The SSM Surveys have been conducted every ten years since 1955 and have measured occupational prestige once every 20 years. Occupational prestige was measured for 32, 82, and 56 different occupations in 1955, 1975 and 1995, respectively. All of these surveys used the five-level category rating system. In 2004, occupational prestige was measured in Korea. Sixty-six different occupations were measured using a five-level category rating system (2003 Nen Kaisō Chōsa Kenkyūkai 2007 [2003 Stratification Survey Research Group]).

Reliability and validity of the OPS

Comparison of OPSs between different time points

Hodge, Siegel and Rossi (1966) investigated changes in occupational prestige structure in the US three times: in 1925, 1947 and 1963. The correlation coefficients between OPSs at different time points were very high, with the lowest value being 0.934. Hodge et al. concluded that there were no substantial changes in the structure of occupational prestige (ranking of occupational prestige) in the US between 1925 and 1963. A similar trend has been observed in Japan. Hara (1999) analyzed data from 1955, 1975 and 1995. The correlation coefficients between OPSs between 1955 and 1995 were very high, at 0.932. As an indicator of people's perceptions of occupational status, the ranking of OPS showed no changes corresponding to the significant developments in the industrial, employment and occupational structures that resulted from the rapid industrialization of postwar Japan. One possible reason for this is that the economic compensation obtained through occupations, the educational credentials necessary to be employed in an occupation (Hara, 1999; Hodge et al., 1966) and the functional importance of occupations (Hodge et al., 1966) are not affected by rapid changes in industrial society.

Of course, we cannot argue that there was no change in occupational prestige during this period. Hodge et al. (1966) reported that disparities in prestige between different occupations narrowed slightly between 1947 and 1963 in the US, as a result of the increasing prestige of blue-collar jobs and a corresponding decline in the prestige of many managerial, clerical and sales jobs. Hara (1999) also pointed out that the overall mean value of all OPSs increased between 1955 and 1995 in Japan and that occupations with relatively lower prestige tended to have received the greater increases in scores. These changes were observed to result from an increasingly frequent avoidance of the lower rating categories (i.e., the 'lowest' and 'relatively low' categories in the category rating system) and their substitution with the 'average' category (Hara, 1999). Possible reasons put forward for this include: (1) the general improvement in income levels and educational achievements produced by the rapid economic growth of the postwar period, which resulted in weaker associations between occupation and socioeconomic conditions, as well as the disappearance of many of the occupations that are obviously associated with poverty (low prestige); and (2) the diffusion of a type of an egalitarian ideology represented by the idea that 'all legitimate trades are equally honorable' (Hara, 1999).

Goyder (2005) also reports a reduction in disparities in prestige between occupations. Goyder investigated changes in occupational prestige between 1975 and 2005 using data from surveys conducted in Belgium and Canada. This study reported greater 'equalization' in the OPSs, with 25 out of the 80 (31%) individual occupations investigated showing greater than ten points of change in OPS. However, the correlation coefficient between OPSs at different times was 0.930, because of no changes in the ranking of occupational categories, such as professional, managerial and clerical jobs (not individual occupation).

Nietz (1935) was one of the first studies that investigated the influence of social changes on occupational prestige. To investigate the influence of the Great Depression, a significant social change in the US, on occupational prestige, Nietz compared the occupational ranking in 1928 (i.e., before the Great Depression) and 1934 (i.e., in the midst of the Great Depression). Of the 40 occupations investigated, 10 showed a change in ranking by four or more places. Scores rose for occupations such as policeman, soldier, insurance salesperson, etc., while they dropped for occupations such as bus driver and grocery shop owner. However, there were virtually no changes in score for the occupations ranked first (banker) to eleventh (primary school teacher) or the bottom ones ranked thirty-fifth (miner) to fortieth (ditch digger). Another characteristic common to both 1929 and 1934 was the overall structure: professional and managerial jobs occupied top-ranking positions, followed by clerical, skilled and sales jobs, and finally by unskilled, physical labor jobs in both surveys. 'In general, the depression and the recovery had less influence on the ratings than might have been expected' (Nietz, 1935: 459).

Comparison of OPSs between culturally different societies

The earliest international comparisons of OPSs include the research by Inkeles and Rossi (1956), who compared OPSs between six industrialized societies (i.e., the US, Britain, New Zealand, Japan, Soviet Union and Germany). The mean correlation coefficient was 0.91, indicating considerable consensus on social evaluations of occupations between the six societies despite their different cultural background. Inkeles' and Rossi's interest in this issue was to analyze whether 'structure advocates' or 'culture advocates', whose conceptual positions are diametrically opposed, present a more sound argument. Structure advocates argue that, since the modern occupational system brought by industrialization is highly consistent across nations, there is little room for traditional cultural patterns to influence the system. Culture advocates, in contrast, argue that each culture has its own value system, which assigns different scores to different occupations in the standardized modern occupational system. Based on the high correlation coefficients between OPSs observed in different countries, Inkeles and Rossi concluded that the structure advocates' argument appeared to be more reasonable than the cultural advocates'.

The most comprehensive international comparative study on occupational prestige was conducted from the structure advocates' perspective. Treiman (1977) argued that industrialization, regardless of where it occurs, brings about similar occupational organizations and differences in rewards, and compared occupational prestige scores between 60 different societies using the results of 85 surveys. A comparison of OPSs between the US and other societies revealed a mean correlation coefficient of 0.837, with the minimum and maximum values being 0.54 (Zaire) and 0.98 (Canada), respectively. The structure of occupational prestige is quite similar in all countries, although not identical. Differences in the structures of occupational prestige derive primarily from levels of economic development and the high scores of blue-collar jobs in socialist countries (Trieman, 1977). Based on this analysis, Treiman proposed the Standard International Occupational Prestige Score corresponding to the 1968 standard international occupation classification. This enabled international comparisons of occupational prestige using a one-dimensional scale.

Comparison of OPSs between groups with different attributes

Studies comparing the occupational prestige structures at different points in time or in different societies principally analyzed the reliability of the OPS. This section will discuss comparisons of OPSs between groups with different attributes. In addition to analyzing the reliability of the OPS, this comparison intends to check whether the theoretical prerequisites for using the OPS are met or not. The theoretical prerequisites here include: (1) all occupations can be ranked along a one-dimensional scale; and (2) people have common perceptions about the social status of occupations. As long as the OPS is a quantitative scale, it is obvious that prerequisite (1) must be met. Furthermore, prerequisite (2) is necessary to justify the process of constructing a scale of occupational status by aggregating people's subjective ratings of occupations.

For instance, let us consider a society consisting of two groups with an equal number of members. Let us suppose that the members of group X rated the social status of occupations A, B and C as 100, 0 and 50, respectively, while group Y rated the same as 0, 100 and 50, respectively. Thus the mean scores for occupations A, B and C across the two groups are all 50. We cannot, however, regard these scores as an index of occupational status in that society and conclude that the three occupations have the same social status. The three occupations simply happen to have the same score as a result of calculation and these scores do not represent the views of the members of either group X or Y. While this example is based on two groups, the situation is the same if the views of two individuals are used. This example section is related to prerequisite (2). Prerequisite (1) will be discussed later.

Do people with different social attributes share common perceptions about the social status of occupations? Here again, the correlation coefficient has been used as an index of the degree of consensus on occupational evaluations between different groups. The results are similar to those derived when comparing different points in time or different societies. Specifically, while significant differences are observed in some specific occupations, a very high degree of consensus is found in the overall occupational scores between groups with different attributes. Naoi and Suzuki (1978) compared OPSs between groups that differed in area of residence, age, education level, employment status, occupation, firm, or individual income in Japan. They found that the correlation coefficient between OPSs of the different groups ranged from 0.938 to 0.995. A similar tendency has been repeatedly reported by other studies conducted in western countries, including Counts (1925), the NORC (1947), Goldthorpe and Hope (1972), and Tarohmaru (1998a), suggesting a consensus on this tendency.

However, with respect to the scores of individual occupations, there have been frequent reports of systematic differences, called 'egocentrism', as well as random differences in scores. Egocentrism refers to the tendency of people to rate their own and similar occupations higher than others. In the US, Coutu (1936) surveyed college/university students to measure the prestige of 20 professional occupations using paired comparison. Students at medical, law and engineering schools assigned the highest scores to physicians, lawyers and engineers, respectively. Medical students also assigned higher ratings to dentists, nurses, osteopaths and other medical professions than did law or engineering students. Blau (1957) analyzed data on male subjects from the 1947 NORC survey which used a five-level category rating system. There was a quite small, but consistent, overall bias for higher scores assigned to the rater's occupation, with white-collar workers tending to assign white-collar jobs higher scores and blue-collar workers tending assign blue-collar jobs higher scores. However, the rater's position had virtually no influence on the ranking order of occupations.

Other studies have reported differences among people with different social status in the range of occupational rating, as a different phenomenon from egocentrism. Wegener (1990) conducted a nationwide social survey in Germany and measured occupational prestige using a technique called magnitude estimation. This is a psychophysical method of constructing a ratio scale, developed by Stevens (1975). In this method, the social status of a certain occupation A is used as the standard with a rating of 100, and the social statuses of other occupations are rated by respondents using numbers. Wegener calculated the range of scores assigned to each occupation (i.e., the maximum and minimum numbers) and found a tendency that the evaluation differences in occupational status between different occupations was greater in respondents with higher social status. However, other studies have not reported as clear a tendency as Wegener (1990). Shiotani (2010) measured individuals' perception of occupational status in Japan using a unique technique called the 'free measurement system'. In this system, respondents are asked to classify different occupations into any number of categories based on the level of social status and to rate the categories of occupations using numbers between 1 and 100. No statistically significant association was found between respondents' social attributes and the range of scores assigned to occupational categories (i.e., the maximum and minimum numbers).

As exceptional cases seen in occupational prestige studies, British people referred to as 'deviants' by Young and Willmott (1956) assigned very unique ratings to occupations (the term 'deviant' does not mean a criminal but someone who assigns very different ratings to occupations from the average ratings). The scores assigned to occupations by deviants are exactly the opposite of the commonly seen ratings, assigning the lowest scores to the most prestigious white-collar jobs, such as company executives and certified public accountants, and the highest scores to the least prestigious jobs, such as farmhands, truck drivers and street cleaners.

In terms of the OPS, there is considerable consensus on occupational evaluations across groups with different attributes. However, the above discussion has not completely confirmed theoretical prerequisite (2) for the OPS. In addition to the discussion presented in this section on the degree of consensus on occupational evaluations between groups, we must analyze the degree of consensus on occupational evaluations between individuals. The next section will present arguments on this issue.

Comparison of occupational evaluations between individuals

The purpose of analyzing the degree of consensus on occupational evaluations between individuals is to more directly confirm whether or not theoretical prerequisite (2) for the OPS (i.e., 'people share common perceptions about the social status of occupations') is met. A series of debates on this issue were published in the journal *Social Forces* in the 1980s. Balkwell, Bates and Garbin (1980) surveyed 259 American college/university students and argued that prerequisite (2) is met by demonstrating that the mean inter-individual correlation coefficient of occupational scores was 0.745. By contrast, Guppy (1982) argued that the high inter-individual correlation of 0.745 was due to the limitation of the sample population to college/university students and, therefore, the results did not support prerequisite (2). Guppy hypothesized that a group from a higher stratum is associated with a greater degree of intra-group consensus on occupational scores. As supporting evidence, Guppy referred to five studies of different samples and demonstrated that while studies whose sample was limited to college/university students or professionals were associated with higher inter-individual correlation coefficients of occupational scores (0.70 and 0.75, respectively), research using random sampling and including respondents from a variety of strata were associated with low correlation coefficients (between 0.42 and 0.48). Guppy also attempted to confirm the validity of his hypothesis by analyzing data from the 1964 NORC survey. When the sample population was divided into three groups based on education level and the mean inter-individual correlation coefficient within each group was calculated, higher values were associated with higher education levels.

This tendency has been confirmed by Hodge, Kraus and Schild (1982), who were opponents of Guppy (1982) in that debate. Hodge et al. (1982) retested Guppy (1982) and found that lower degrees of consensus on occupational evaluations were associated with groups with lower education levels, lower prestige occupations or lower income levels. These results support Guppy's (1982) argument. Furthermore, Guppy and Goyder (1984) analyzed data from the NORC surveys conducted in 1947, 1963 and 1964, and demonstrated that in each survey, lower degrees of consensus were associated with groups with lower education levels or lower occupational status. The tendency that lower degrees of consensus on occupational ratings are associated with lower strata has not been confirmed in data from Japan (Tarohmaru, 1998b), however, a consensus has developed on this tendency in occupational prestige research.

Once a consensus was reached on this issue, the next issue to be addressed was: 'What causes the disparities in the degree of consensus between strata?' Balkwell et al. (1982) and Hodge et al. (1982) argued that people in the lower strata tended to experience random errors in the process of understanding the structure of occupational prestige due to their lower cognitive ability, resulting in lower degrees of inter-individual consensus (the cognitive error hypothesis). Guppy (1982), however, thought that while people have stable perception (image) of occupational status regardless of their social position, higher diversity of perception in members of the lower strata results in lower degrees of consensus among them (the reality diversity hypothesis).

Which hypothesis is valid is a very important question in occupational prestige studies. If the cognitive error hypothesis is valid, theoretical prerequisite (2) for the OPS is considered to be met, whereas if the reality diversity hypothesis is adopted, prerequisite (2) is rejected. The cognitive error hypothesis considers that, while random errors arising from lower cognitive ability result in lower degrees of consensus, people across all strata of the society intrinsically have common perceptions of occupational status. This hypothesis assumes that there is an external reality that precedes individuals' perceptions of occupational status or, in other words, a scale of occupational prestige in the form of social facts (Stewart and Blackburn, 1975). Therefore, the hypothesis considers that random errors are canceled out by averaging individuals' occupational ratings and we can extract a scale of occupational prestige as a social structure. If the cognitive error hypothesis is valid, creating and using the OPS can be justified as described above. By contrast, if the reality diversity hypothesis is supported, for example, under the circumstances where, apart from people with standard perceptions of occupational status, there are some people with unique perceptions, such as the deviants referred to by Young and Willmott (1956) in the lower strata, theoretical prerequisite (2) for using the OPS (i.e., 'people have common perception about the social status of occupations') no longer holds.

In order to test the two hypotheses, Balkwell et al. (1982) calculated inter-individual correlation coefficients after controlling for cognitive ability. The sample of American college/university students was divided into two groups, depending on whether students' fathers had graduated from college/university. Being college/university students, members of both groups are assumed to have the same level of cognitive ability (Balkwell et al., 1982). If Guppy's (1982) reality diversity hypothesis is correct, then the group whose fathers had graduated from college/university should show a higher degree of consensus than the other group whose members' fathers did not graduate from college/university. However, the mean inter-individual correlation coefficient was 0.74 and 0.75 in the former and latter groups, respectively, showing virtually no difference. Based on this result, Balkwell et al. (1982) argued that Guppy's hypothesis cannot be supported. In addition, Hodge et al. (1982) demonstrated that there is a correlation at a level of 0.497 between the number of years of education and the level of knowledge about occupations, and argued that the cognitive error hypothesis is more likely to be valid. In response, Guppy and Goyder (1984) analyzed 1947, 1963, 1964 NORC data and a 1965 Canadian replication of the 1964 NORC study. They conducted a multiple regression analysis, in which the units of analysis were pairs of respondents, the dependent variable was the inter-individual correlation coefficient of occupational scores, and the independent variables were dummy variables, such as whether both halves of the pair had graduated from college/university or not. As a surrogate parameter of cognitive ability, a variable named 'general knowledge' was added to this multiple regression model, in order to analyze the effects of combinations of attributes after controlling for cognitive ability. The results showed that 16 per cent and 15 per cent of the variance of the degree of consensus between inter-individual correlation coefficients was explained by 'general knowledge' and the stratification variables, respectively. The effects of combinations of stratification attributes did not disappear after controlling for cognitive ability. It was thus concluded that cognitive errors explain some, but not all, of the disparities between social strata in the degree of inter-individual consensus on occupational ratings (Guppy and Goyder, 1984). Thus, the debate between the cognitive error hypothesis and the reality diversity hypothesis was settled as a compromise between the two hypotheses, with the conclusion being that both factors seem to be influential.

One-dimensional nature of occupational prestige

This section discusses arguments surrounding the one-dimensional nature of occupational prestige. With a few exceptions, almost all stratification theories have tacitly assumed that there is a weak-order relationship between the rank orders of occupations or, more specifically, when comparing the social status of occupation A with occupation B, the relationship between the two occupations can be determined as A>B, B>A or A=B (Tarohmaru, 1998b). However, Tarohmaru (1998b) objected to this assumption that 'all occupations are comparable', arguing that the comparability of occupations should be determined based on consensus of members of the society.

Tarohmaru created a 'discrepancy ratio' index and used it as a basis for determining the comparability of occupations. The discrepancy ratio is expressed as d_{xy}/N_{xy}, where d_{xy} is the number of all respondents who rated occupation Y higher than occupation X, despite occupation X's higher occupational prestige score than occupation Y, and N_{xy} is the number of all respondents who rated both occupations X and Y. Using data from the 1995 SSM Survey, Tarohmaru made pairs of occupations from the 56 different occupations surveyed, and calculated the discrepancy ratio in each of the 1540 sets ($_{56}C_2$=1540). Assuming that occupations can be ranked in order according to their OPS only if the discrepancy ratio is 0.19 or lower, Tarohmaru described the ranking order of occupations as a partial order system (i.e., an order system allowing inclusion of incomparable factors).

There was an overall tendency that occupations with higher OPSs are associated with higher dissensus on ratings. Occupations associated with particularly high dissensus are those ranked between high-level bureaucrat (OPS=77.5 points, ranked sixth) and section chief at city office (OPS=56.9 points, ranked 23rd). Professional athlete was associated with particularly high dissensus and was incomparable with seven other occupations. As for the relatively less prestigious occupations ranked below section chief at city office, almost all of them could be determined as ranked higher or lower than their partner, with carpenter and child-minder being the only exceptions.

However, there were 26 incomparable pairs of occupations, which represented only 1.7 per cent of all pairs of occupations. This should not be a critical flaw for the validity of the OPS. This suggests that the OPS is a satisfactorily valid stratification index if used and interpreted carefully. However, 'it would be better to abandon the illusion that all occupations can be ranked in a weak-order system based on occupational prestige. Rather, the intersubjectively shared stratification structure should more appropriately be described as a 'partial order system' (Tarohmaru, 1998b: 25).

Kraus, Schild and Hodge (1978) hypothesized that the OPS, being a one-dimensional, continuous scale, is a sociological creation of researchers that may not reflect reality. When measuring occupational prestige, researchers define *a priori* the dimension(s) of occupational rating, as seen in ranking and category rating techniques, and in many cases the dimension is single. The OPS has high correlation even between groups with different attributes and is stable over time. However, this may be an artifact arising from methodological problems rather than because the structure of occupational prestige shared by people is truly reflected in the OPS.

Based on this hypothesis, Kraus et al. surveyed 463 urban residents in Israel and asked them to classify at their discretion various occupations according to 'similarity'. The standards for judging similarities and the number of occupational categories were left to each respondent's discretion. A similarity matrix was created from the data so obtained, and the dimension based on which similarities were judged was extracted using smallest space analysis. The analysis was conducted after dividing the sample population into three subgroups. In all subgroups, two dimensions (dimensions one and two) were extracted. While the correlation coefficients for dimension two between different subgroups were low, those for dimension one were 0.96 or higher. In addition, the correlation coefficient between dimension one and the OPS was as high as 0.92. Based on these results, Kraus et al. concluded that occupational prestige measured by previous studies is not a sociological creation but is rooted in people's collective consciousness. Occupational prestige provides the most important standard for people to distinguish differences between occupations.

What does the OPS measure?

Finally, let me discuss arguments about the validity of the OPS. The OPS is calculated by averaging individuals' ratings of occupations. What, then, does the OPS so calculated actually measure? According to Tarohmaru (1998c), when we say 'occupational prestige', the term 'prestige' is interpreted in three different ways: (1) 'prestige in the narrow sense', i.e., a person with high prestige is respected by others and can exercise social power based on his/her prestige; (2) 'prestige in the broad sense', i.e., prestige does not always carry with it honor or social power but refers to the general goodness or desirability of an occupation (Goldthorpe and Hope, 1972); and (3) 'prestige as a reflection of socioeconomic status', i.e., occupational prestige is an estimate of 'objective status' that combines the economic status and social status (i.e., education level) of an occupation. The OPS is merely an estimate, including errors, of socioeconomic attributes of an occupation (Featherman and Hauser, 1976).

Empirical studies on the validity of the OPS have shown that the second interpretation above is more appropriate than the first. The 1964 NORC survey measured, in addition to occupational prestige, ratings occupations along other dimensions, including 'autonomy and independence of the job', 'income from the job', and 'pleasure in the job' (Nakao, 2000). In eight of the nine dimensions, there was high correlation with the OPS, with correlation coefficients of 0.90 or higher (Nakao, 2000). In the Japanese SSM Surveys, occupational ratings by category are followed by questions about how much emphasis is placed on 'skill level', 'degree of responsibility' and other dimensions in assigning ratings to occupations. The 1995 SSM Survey investigated 11 different dimensions. There were seven criteria on which 'great emphasis' or 'some emphasis' was placed by 70 per cent or more of all respondents (Tarohmaru, 1998a). These seven dimensions are: 'skill level', 'degree of responsibility', 'education level', 'level of respect from others', 'level of contribution to the society', 'income level', and 'amount of power over the society'. Various criteria were thus emphasized, in addition to 'amount of respect from others' which seems to correspond to 'prestige in the narrow sense'.

While the aforementioned studies have analyzed the nature of measurement of the OPS based on respondents' subjectivity, studies about interpretation (3) have considered what is measured by the OPS, by analyzing the relationship between occupational prestige and two objective indices: education and income. These studies have assessed the plausibility and validity of the OPS through comparison with indices of socioeconomic status. The socioeconomic index (SEI) is a scale of occupational status developed by Duncan (1961) in order to assign scores representing occupational status to occupations that were not covered by the 1947 NORC survey. Duncan (1961) created the SEI using individual occupations as the units of analysis. A multiple regression analysis was conducted by using: the proportion of respondents who assigned the highest ratings to the occupation (i.e., respondents who assigned the rating of 'excellent' or 'good' in the five-level rating system) as the dependent variable; and the proportion of persons with high levels of education (i.e., persons who had completed high school or above) and the proportion of persons with high income (i.e., persons whose income was $3500 or more in 1949) as independent variables. As a result, the following regression equation was obtained:

> (Proportion of respondents who assigned the highest ratings to the occupation) = 0.55 (proportion of persons with high levels of education) + 0.59 (proportion of persons with high income) − 6.0

By substituting the values of the proportion of persons with high levels of education and that of persons with high income into the above regression equation, scores representing occupational status were assigned to occupations whose OPS was not measured. The determination coefficient in this regression equation was 0.83. This means that 83 per cent of the variance of occupational prestige can be explained by education and income. This provides a basis for researchers to support the third interpretation above.

Furthermore, efforts to compare the OPS and SEI include substituting the respective scale values into the status attainment process model and deciding which scale is better based on the level of explanatory power of the model. Such efforts have generally concluded that the SEI is better than the OPS as an index of occupational status. For instance, if education, first occupation and father's occupation are used as independent variables, the model's explanatory power (i.e., determination coefficient) for American men's current occupations was 0.439, 0.361 and 0.294 in the case of Duncan's SEI (1961), Siegel's OPS (1971) and Treiman's OPS (1977), respectively (Featherman and Hauser, 1976). In addition, Treas and Tyree (1979) inserted the three measures of occupational status above into a structural equation model and found that the error variance was smaller when the SEI was used.

However, some studies have raised objections to these findings. Kerckhoff, Campbell, Trott and Kraus (1989) compared the status attainment process model between the US and UK. When the SEI is used, the analytical results were very similar between the two countries. By contrast, when the OPS is used, differences were observed between the two countries, with data from Britain showing a stronger influence of father's occupation on respondents' current occupation. As a result, Kerckhoff et al. (1989) concluded that social evaluations of occupations' desirability may be more important in intergenerational mobility in Britain than in other societies, and observed that the OPS and SEI are likely to be measuring different dimensions of the social mobility process.

Discussion and Conclusion

This study has thus reviewed studies of occupational prestige and organized points at issue presented by previous studies. The discussion and conclusion is given below.

While the OPS is a simple scale of occupational status calculated by averaging individuals' ratings of occupations, it has very high robustness. If comparisons are made between different points in time, between culturally different societies, or between groups with different attributes, the correlation coefficient between OPSs is 0.90 or higher. However, in order to use the OPS as a scale of occupational status, two theoretical prerequisites must be met: (1) All occupations can be ranked along a one-dimensional scale; and (2) people share common perceptions about the social status of occupations. It has been confirmed that prerequisite (1) is practically met. However, it remains a matter of debate whether prerequisite (2) is sufficiently met. When the OPS is compared between groups, the correlation coefficient is 0.90 or higher. By contrast, the correlation coefficient between individuals' ratings of occupations is around 0.50, representing some, but by no means complete, consensus (Tarohmaru, 1998b).

How should we understand this issue? It does not seem to have been discussed sufficiently in occupational prestige studies. These studies have paid more attention to consensus than dissensus on occupational ratings. The reason for this can be understood in terms of the theoretical load in observation, which Iseda (2003) describes as, 'our perceptions cannot be completely independent from our background theories'. Functionalism was one of the more enduring social theories of the 20th century. It is fair to say that the history of occupational prestige studies has been one of cyclical reinforcement of functionalist theories and analytical methods involving calculation of correlation coefficients between OPSs (Stehr, 1974). Functionalism is good at explaining consensus on values between persons. As such, it is not appropriate for explaining dissensus (Stehr, 1974). Analytical methods showing high correlation went very well with the functionalist theories which argued for consensus on values. Functionalist theories have promoted use of the analytical methods involving the calculation of correlation coefficients between OPSs and, at the same time, the analytical methods showing high correlations have lent support to the validity of functionalist theories (Stehr, 1974). There is a possibility that, of the various phenomena relating to occupational ratings, information indicating consensus on ratings may have received more favorable attention, due to theoretical biases in observation.

We could point out that behind this 'more favorable attention' was, in addition to the issue of the theoretical bias in observation, a strong desire to produce a tool to express the social status of occupations as a continuous quantity. Before the OPS was developed, researchers had no option but to express occupational status in the form of categories. The development of the OPS made it possible to express occupational status as a one-dimensional continuous quantity. Since this allows statistical analysis based on correlation coefficients, strong demand arose for the development of occupational status scales. For researchers hoping for the development of occupational status scales, information indicating consensus on occupational ratings was more attractive than that indicating dissensus on occupational ratings. It is possible that, for this reason, more favorable attention was given to consensus on occupational ratings.

There was vigorous debate over inter-individual consensus and dissensus on occupational ratings in the 1980s. By then, however, landmark social mobility studies using occupational status scales had already been completed by Blau and Duncan (1967), Sewell, Haller and Ohlendorf (1970) and others. Social mobility studies were experiencing a return of the 'big-class schema', as seen in the intergenerational mobility study using log-linear analysis conducted by Featherman and Hauser (1978). Under the circumstances, arguments over the degree of consensus on occupational evaluations may not have been of much interest to the many researchers of social stratification who were not specialists in occupational prestige. By the 1970s, an academic consensus had been reached that the OPS has very high temporal and spatial stability and is robust across different social attributes. It is likely that this was regarded as a basis for using the OPS and resulted in the spread and establishment of the OPS as a convenient scale of occupational status before the issue of the degree of inter-individual consensus was sufficiently discussed.

Even if the above points are taken into account, however, occupational prestige studies should be considered to have made a great contribution to social stratification research. The development of occupational status scales, such as the OPS and SEI, enabled path analysis of the status attainment process. Occupational prestige studies methodologically supported the 'gradational schema', a paradigm in social mobility research, and thus brought prestige to social mobility research. While the current mainstream paradigm in social mobility research is the big-class schema rather than the gradation schema, the return of the big-class schema arose from criticisms of the gradational schema. In this sense, it would be fair to say that occupational prestige studies have great historical significance in social stratification research.

5 Distributive Justice in Economic Theory, and the Capability Approach

Jun Matsuyama

Introduction

Distributive justice and contemporary Japan

The scarcity of resources relative to wants raises what are the fundamental questions of economics: how much of what should be produced; how should it be produced; and for whom should it be produced? When considering such fundamental economic questions, a definition of what is economically *desirable* is needed. Desirability has been investigated in economics from two perspectives: efficiency and fairness. Efficiency here means using scarce resources without wastage to increase the general welfare of society. Fairness is related to how to fairly (equitably) divide up products. This type of issue is regularly termed distributive justice, and is described in Aristotle's *Nicomachean Ethics*. His discussion, of course, reflects the political shape of Athens in the 4th century BCE, and addresses distributive justice as a question of the distribution of honor and wealth among the polis citizenry (Urmson, 1998: 127).

Cake making is a frequently used example to explain the relationship between these two perspectives. Using ingredients without wastage to make a larger cake is a matter of efficiency. By contrast, how to fairly divide the baked cake between several people is a question of distributive justice. Whereas in the former case it is clear that a larger cake is desirable, the latter case is not as simple. For example, some may consider it good to divide the cake *equally*, but others may consider it good that it be divided according to degree of *contribution*. In fact, the Japanese Social Stratification and Social Mobility (SSM) Surveys conducted in 1995 and 2005 reported that between 70 and 80 per cent of respondents supported the contribution principle of distribution, known as the principle of performance-based distribution (Ishida, 2008: 57–58).

Yet, in Japan today, distributive justice is a real problem (Hirano, Kamemoto and Hattori, 2002: 157).[1] Social security, for example, is an approach to economic disparity that is presumed to have a close connection with distributive justice. In particular, a government apportioning the taxation burden among the populace to fund the implementation of its policies is an issue of distributive justice. In fact, there are survey results that show that as a method of obtaining fiscal resources, 62.5 per cent of Japanese approve the system of progressive allocation of burden in proportion to income (Ishida, 2008). As Ishida (2008: 58) points out, it can be presumed that the Japanese 'are inclined to accept the principle of performance-based distribution at an ideological level, but also are supportive of policies to rectify excessive disparity, while at the same time being wary of excessive egalitarianism'.

Welfarism vs. its alternatives

It is commonly held that economics has traditionally focused primarily on the issue of efficiency and paid scant attention to that of fairness.[2] Furthermore, almost all matters regarding distributive justice have been exclusively based on *welfarism*.[3] Welfarism, as used here, is a criterion for deciding superiority and inferiority in a variety of situations, where the determination is based solely on each person's utility. For example, if the utility of a situation consequent on telling a lie is greater than the situation where a lie is not told, then irrespective of the rightness or wrongness of lying, the former situation will be determined to be better than the latter.

In respect of welfarism, however, the question that has continued to be asked is whether it is an appropriate criterion for distributive justice. Welfarism is criticized as subjectivist because it focuses only on the subjective measure of utility and cannot appropriately reflect cognitive distortion in the evaluation of a situation. According to Sen (1992: 77-78), welfarism is an inappropriate approach for analyzing entrenched inequality and poverty. He reasons that humans who are continuously living an extremely and severely distressed life will become accustomed to that life.[4] Rather than being eternally grief stricken, people will seek to derive happiness from tiny improvements. As a result, despite what is objectively a wretched situation, the possibility emerges that the effect on subjective health and welfare is not so severe. This means that it is possible that welfarism fails

Table 5.1:   Utilities in different situations

Situations	x	y	z
Utility of A	49	50	99
Utility of B	49	50	1
Total	98	100	100

Source: This table was created by the author with reference to Sen (1979b, p. 547).

to appropriately reflect distortions in health and welfare arising from entrenched inequality and poverty. Further, welfarism does not focus on inequity and disparity between individuals; rather social welfare can be defined as the sum of individuals' utilities. Let us consider a specific example of distribution of goods. In an initial situation **x**, for example, there are two individuals, **A** and **B**, the utility of each of whom is given in Table 5.1.[5] In situation **y**, through a re-allocation of goods, a situation results that in terms of total utility is preferable to situation **x**. Conversely, an unequal situation **z** arises as a result of, say, competition. From the welfarist perspective situation **z** is deemed preferable to situation **x** since total utility of situation **z** is greater than that of **x**, i.e.100>98, while situations **y** and **z** are judged indifferent due to their having the same total utilities. This consequence is nevertheless intuitively rather difficult to accept. In this case, the example reveals that welfarism does not take into account distribution aspects between individuals.

This type of criticism of welfarism, and of utilitarianism more generally, allows critics to begin to advocate alternatives to distributive justice. According to Sen, the central issue is not 'why equality?', since critics are all egalitarian with respect to some *focal variable*. 'Equality of what?' is the important question. The focal variables specifically refer to alternative measures to utility, such as Rawls' primary goods, Dworkin's resources or Sen's functionings and capability. Above all, the core interest of egalitarians is to overcome the problems of welfarism, such as subjectivism and ignorance of the distributional issue. They therefore are positioned as non-welfarists.

In this chapter, we will discuss the advantages and disadvantages in each theory through simple examples that can appeal to our intuitions. In order to look at what approaches are actually being proffered for the problems of present day Japan, the theories will be linked to

Japanese research into debates on distributive justice. This chapter is thus structured as follows. First, we develop Rawls' theory of justice by contrast with welfarist. Second, we elaborate on the capability approach, which is posited as an alternative theory to the welfaristic approach and to Rawls' approach. Third, we present an overview of what is known as Dworkin's equality of resources, which is based on the concept of individual responsibility, and briefly summarize the views of both the advocates and critics of this approach. Fourth, we summarize Sen's views of responsibility and investigate the relationship between responsibility and the capability approach. Fifth, we review inherent problems in the capability approach which still remain unsolved. Finally, we sum-up our discussions.

Rawls' theory of justice and primary goods

In *A Theory of Justice* (1971), Rawls advocated the concept of *primary goods*. The primary goods to which he refers are goods that every rational human being could be expected to want, such as rights, freedom and opportunity, income and wealth and a social basis of self-respect (Rawls, 2010: 86). Focusing on primary goods as a measure of individual well-being, rather than utility, Rawls avoids the problem of subjectivism. Prior to advocating primary goods, Rawls proposes the rules of justice, which are known as the two principles of justice. In his principles, the most important fundamental are freedoms. As long as these are compatible with similar freedoms of other people, then Rawls' first principle of justice is the principle that every person should have equal right to the broadest possible fundamental freedoms. The second principle is twofold, comprised of the principle of fair equality of opportunity and the difference principle. The former is the principle that each person is provided equally with opportunities. The latter is the principle that distribution is equitable where the primary goods of the most unfortunate are maximized; it works to ameliorate inequality by redistribution of goods. Rawls' order of priority of these principles is: the first principle of justice (the broadest possible freedoms), the principle of fair equality of opportunity, and finally the difference principle. Rawls argues that using the two principles of justice encourages equality on the one hand, while giving maximum consideration to the most unfortunate on the other.

Many have argued, particularly in economics, that the difference principle accounts not only for efficiency, but also for equality. Let us apply Rawls' difference principle to the situations **x, y** and **z** in Table 5.1.

In this table the various situations were measured by utility, but here we will reassign to the values in Table 5.1 an index of primary goods. This means that in situation **z** the goods held by individual **B** will be a lesser amount than in situations **x** or **y**. Thus, situation **z** would not be judged preferable to situations **x** or **y**. This judgment is in contrast to the judgment from welfarism. For situations **x** and **y** the amount of goods held by the most disadvantaged individual in situation **y** is greater than that held in situation **x** and therefore situation **y** would be deemed preferable to situation **x**. Consequently, it invites a judgment that is more in accord with our intuition than does welfarism. The difference principle is not only a theoretically persuasive rule; research indicates it is also persuasive in reality. Using a questionnaire, Tachibanaki and Urakawa (2006) conducted an empirical study of which of the variety of principles relating to income distribution was preferred by the Japanese people and concluded that the difference principle enjoys the most support.

Sen acknowledges that Rawls' approach makes it possible to incorporate various values other than utility, such as freedom, into the theory of distributive justice. At the same time, however, Sen identifies two problems with this approach. The first is the problem of evaluation. According to Rawls' approach each person's well-being is evaluated by the amount of primary goods, which are *'means'* to freedom. This, however, is because what is important is not what means are available to a person, but 'the freedoms they actually enjoy to choose the lives that they have reason to value' (Sen, 1992: 125). Sen, therefore, asserts that capability, an expression of the actual freedom being enjoyed, is the appropriate focal variable. The second point he makes is that Rawls' approach does not take *human diversity* into account. The diversity referred to here is the vast differences in people's concepts of the good, and the fact that the ability to convert goods into a satisfactory form is different for everyone. Rawls takes diversity into account in the former sense but not in the latter sense. As an example, let us consider the issue of distribution of goods to a person with a disability (individual **A**) and to a person with no disability (individual **B**). In distribution justified by the difference principle the person with the disability would only receive, at most, the same amount of goods as the other. If individual **A** needs more goods to do the same thing as individual **B**, even if both receive an equal portion of primary goods, there still remains a profound inequality between them in terms of the freedoms of individuals **A** and **B**, which means what each can realize from using their own goods. This example says that Rawls' approach does not appropriately take physical diversity into account.

The capability approach

Welfarism and individual diversity

How are the two criticisms of Rawls' approach raised in the previous section overcome by Sen? Before entering into the main argument, in this sub-section we discuss what distribution of goods welfarism justifies in case of individual diversity being taken into account. One type of welfaristic egalitarianism is *equality of marginal utility*. This principle requires equal distribution of each person's marginal utility. Here we will follow on from the example in the earlier section and consider the problem of distribution of goods given to two individuals where individual **A** is a person with a disability and individual **B** is a person with no disability. Let utility functions of individuals **A** and **B** be $U_A(x) = \sqrt{x}$ and $U_B(x) = 2\sqrt{x}$, respectively. The fact that $U_A(x) < U_B(x)$ for all $x > 0$ represents individual differences in the ability to convert those goods to utility. The marginal utility functions for individuals **A** and **B** are respectively, $MU_A(x) = 1/(2\sqrt{x})$ and $MU_B(x) = 1/\sqrt{x}$. Figure 5.1 depicts the marginal utility functions MU_A and MU_B.[6]

The amount of individual **A**'s goods are measured from left to right (x_A axis) while the amount of individual **B**'s goods are measured from right to left (x_B axis). The marginal utility of individuals **A** and **B** is measured on the MU_A and MU_B axes, respectively. The distribution of goods that would make each person's marginal utility equal is given by **x***. For any total amount of goods distributed, the ratio of distribution of goods between individuals **A** and **B** that would make each person's marginal utility equal is $x^*_A : x^*_B = 1:4$. In other words, according to equality of marginal utility, individual **A** always receives only one quarter of the goods of individual **B**. Equality of marginal utility is 'harsher' to individual **A** than Rawls' primary goods approach.

Functioning and capability

We have seen that it is not possible to appropriately address people's diversity in both the equality of marginal utility and the Rawlsian approach. How then does the capability approach address this point? The focus in the capability approach is neither utility, nor primary goods, but a *functioning*. A functioning is a concept that expresses 'what he or she manages to do or to be' (Sen 1985a: 7). 'It has to be distinguished from the commodities which are used to achieve those

Figure 5.1: Marginal utility functions of individuals A and B

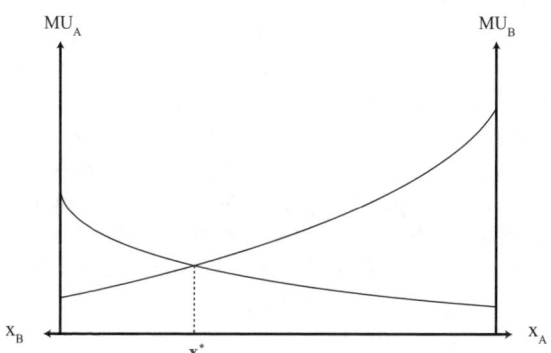

functionings' (Sen 1985a: 7). Consider that just having goods, say, a bicycle, is different from enjoying bicycle riding, which means that he or she can realize the *characteristics* of a bicycle, that is, the property of being capable of *movement*.[7] The characteristics referred to here are 'the various desirable properties of the commodities in question' (Sen 1985a: 6). To account for the diversity of people, it is not sufficient only to focus on the characteristics of a good. That is because even given the same bicycle, that is, even if individuals **A** and **B** have the same characteristics of bicycle, individual **B** *can* freely ride the bicycle, but individual **A** *cannot realize* the bicycle's characteristics due to his or her disability. Therefore, in order to account for individual diversity, there is a need to consider what each person *can actually do* with a good. Note that individual diversity, of course, depends not only on individual features (e.g. disability, illness and pregnancy), but also on social and natural constraints (e.g. laws, ethnicity and disaster). Formally speaking, the set of *utilization functions* f_i of individual i is denoted as F_i. The set of utilization functions F_i may be interpreted as expressing the individual features of individual i. The achieved functioning is given by the vector $b_i = f_i(c(x_i))$ achieved from a vector of characteristic $c(x_i)$ by using utilization function f_i in F_i which he or she chooses, where c is a characteristic function that maps a vector of goods into its characteristics. The capability of individual i is defined as the set of feasible functionings as follows:

$$Q_i(X_i) := \{b_i : b_i = f_i(c(x_i)) \text{ for some } f_i \in F_i \text{ and for some } x_i \in X_i\},$$

where X_i describes the set of a vector of goods that an individual i is able to use. Given budget constraints X_i and individual features F_i, the set $Q_i(X_i)$ expresses 'the freedom that a person has in terms of the choice of functionings' (Sen, 1985a: 9).

Equality of capability requires that differences among person's capabilities are equalized as much as possible (See Yoshihara, 2004). Let us again consider the earlier distribution question.[8] As the difference between individual **A**, who has a disability, and individual **B**, who has no disability, is attributable to the differences in individual features, F_i, let us suppose F_A F_B. Therefore, for any distribution of goods x, the capability of individual **B** includes the capability of individual **A**, i.e. $Q_A(x)$ $Q_B(x)$. Further, we suppose that the capability of each person will enlarge monotonically with respect to the amount of goods. In other words, for i = **A**,**B**, if $x \leq x^*$, then $Q_i(x)$ $Q_i(x^*)$. Under equal distribution, no disparity with respect to goods will arise between individuals **A** and **B**. However, a disparity in capability will have arisen due to the differences in individual features. Therefore, if equal capabilities are required, by re-distributing $e > 0$ from individual **B** to individual **A** differences between $Q_A(x+e)$ and $Q_B(x-e)$ are alleviated compared to differences between $Q_A(x)$ and $Q_B(x)$, which means that, it becomes possible to justify a greater distribution of goods to individual **A**.

Luck egalitarianism

In this section we will focus on one of the major approaches in current theories of distributive justice, Dworkin's (1981) theory of *luck egalitarianism*. Luck egalitarianism asserts that in relation to those parts of a person's circumstances not within the scope of personal responsibility, equalization is justified, but if inequality has arisen as a result of personal responsibility, it may be tolerated. Dworkin emphasized the issue of personal responsibility, which was not adequately developed by either Rawls or Sen. Dworkin criticized welfarism for its inability to properly distinguish people with disabilities and those with *expensive taste*.

Following on again from the previous example, individual **A** is a person with a disability, individual **B** is able, and we will now consider individual **C**, who is able and has expensive taste. Expensive taste refers to having tastes that—to achieve the same degree of satisfaction—cost more. For example, individual **B** may be satisfied by beer, but individual **C** must drink premium champagne to be satisfied. The objective circumstances of individuals **A** and **C** are clearly different, but to achieve the same utility, they require more goods than individual **B**. Now let us again consider the issue of distribution of goods. Suppose individuals **A** and **C** have identical utility functions. If we consider equality of marginal utility for individuals **A** and **C**, as we saw in Figure 5.1, the same amount of goods will be distributed to individuals **A** and **C**. However, doubt arises concerning the same treatment of individuals **A** and **C**. This demonstrates that welfarism is absolutely neutral towards individual **A** with a disability, and individual **C** with expensive taste.

Dworkin advocates *equality of resources* as an alternative to welfarism.[9] The resources referred to here are divided into two: external resources and internal resources. The former refer to transferable resources, such as goods and income, while the latter refer to resources intrinsic to an individual, such as individual production skills, disabilities, or talents. Equality of resources accounts not only for external resources, but also for internal resources. From this perspective, if a shortfall in external or internal resources arises as a result of factors that are other than the responsibility of the individual, they are the subject of compensation. From the side, where inequalities have arisen through factors attributable to personal responsibility, there will be no remediation.[10]

Let us reconsider the earlier example of the question of distribution of goods. Suppose that individual **C**'s expensive taste is due to personal responsibility.[11] If goods are to be distributed equally among individuals **A**, **B** and **C**, then individuals **A** and **C** will obtain the same degree of satisfaction because of the same utility function. According to luck egalitarianism, individual **A** as the subject of compensation is justified. The responsibility concept distinguishes between individual **A** with a disability and individual **C** with expensive taste. By introducing the concept of personal responsibility, Dworkin's theory of equality of resources has succeeded in shifting the focus to the question of people with disabilities.

Criticism of luck egalitarianism

As we saw above, luck egalitarianism has certain merits. However, there are objections to luck egalitarianism. Seiyama (2004) claims that basing moral decisions on the responsibility concept is fraught with a major theoretical challenge: the line between responsibility and irresponsibility may often be arbitrary. For example, a certain person attempts suicide, does not manage to die, and is left with major physical and emotional disabilities. The person's action—attempted suicide—could ultimately be considered a personal decision, but what is rather more important, or most important, are the socio-economic factors that caused that action. Consequently, if it is clearly asserted that the individual is responsible for an act of attempting suicide, then conceivably there are certain elements of arbitrariness in drawing such a line.

Anderson points out that luck egalitarianism does not satisfy the most fundamental condition of egalitarian theory: "its principles express equal respect and concern for all citizens" (1999: 289). Luck egalitarianism could lead to precipitating a dishonorable stigma to the disabled and the stupid and untalented etc., which is one of Anderson's examples. According to Anderson, under a system of luck egalitarianism an institution called something like the State Equality Board could be established that will send out letters like this one:

> To the disabled: Your defective native endowments or current disabilities, alas, make your life less worth living than the lives of normal people. To compensate for this misfortune, we, the able ones, will give you extra resources, enough to make the worth of living your life good enough that at least *one* person out there thinks it is comparable to someone else's life.
>
> To the stupid and untalented: Unfortunately, other people don't value what little you have to offer in the system of production. Your talents are too meager to command much market value. Because of the misfortune that you were born so poorly endowed with talents, we productive ones will make it up to you: we'll let you share in the bounty of what we have produced with our vastly superior and highly valued abilities. (Anderson 1999: 305)[12]

The criticisms through a thought experiment that we have outlined above do not intend to reject luck egalitarianism. Rather, they may be considered to be important for clarifying problems that could arise. Luck egalitarianism constitutes one of the dominant theoretical positions in modern theory of distributive justice. It is expected these criticisms will be a basis on which further debate may take place.

Responsibility and the capability approach

So, what does Sen think of the concept of responsibility?[13] He clearly recognizes a degree of importance in personal responsibility when he says: 'Any affirmation of social responsibility that *replaces* individual responsibility cannot but be, to varying extent, counterproductive. There is no substitute for individual responsibility' (Sen 1999: 283, emphasis original). However, while acknowledging the importance of personal responsibility, he appears to distance himself somewhat from treating it as a core issue, arguing that 'The arbitrarily narrow view of individual responsibility has to be broadened' (Sen, 1999: 284–285). Sen also maintains that 'the substantive freedoms that we respectively enjoy to exercise our responsibilities are extremely contingent on personal, social, and environmental circumstances' (Sen, 1999: 284). For example, children who are unable to receive primary education, or people who live in a repressive society, are not only disadvantaged from a well-being perspective, but are also disadvantaged in their ability to live a responsible life. Forcing personal responsibility on such people must be considered to be impossible.

Sen makes the following claims in relation to the mutual interdependence of responsibility and freedom:

> The argument for social support in expanding people's freedom can, therefore, be seen as an argument *for* individual responsibility, not against it. The linkage between freedom and responsibility works both ways. Without the substantive freedom and capability to do something, a person cannot be responsible for doing it. But actually having the freedom and capability to do something does impose on the person the duty to consider whether to do or not, and this does involve individual responsibility. In this sense, freedom is both necessary and sufficient for responsibility. (Sen 1999: 284, emphasis original)

As Suzumura and Gotoh (2001: 282–283) point out, Sen's emphasis is not the perspective of personal responsibility, rather the broad perspective of responsibility, which they call *our responsibility*. Our responsibility means here the responsibility of each person to rationally and publicly deliberate and act when building desirable social systems.

Hence, Sen's concept of responsibility divides into two levels. One is the responsibility of an individual to achieve personal objectives, and the other is the responsibility of a citizen to formulate public rules and systems. His concept of responsibility may be described as stratified, compared to the concept of responsibility as a criterion for justifying compensation in responsibility egalitarianism. Within its purview also is the nature of individuals and society. What precedes personal responsibility is securing capability for every person: what builds just society is done by us with our responsibility through public deliberation.

Unsettled problems of the capability approach

We will now review inherent problems of the capability approach which still remain unresolved: ranking capability sets and listing capabilities.

Ranking capability sets

As we have seen, according to the definition of capability, an individual's capability is defined as a *set* of functioning vectors. Consequently, to determine the superiority or inferiority of the capabilities of individual **A** and individual **B**, there is a need to establish and by some means order the capability set of each person. However, as a capability set is not a number like income, the method is not simple. Here we will look at an overview of approaches for ranking capability sets. First, as the simplest scenario, let us consider the situation where the capability set of **B** includes that of **A**. This situation should correspond to the intuitive sense that the capability set of individual **B** is better than that of individual **A**. This method is called ranking based on inclusive relationship. Generally, there is not necessarily an inclusive relationship between two arbitrary sets, however. A common method of ranking sets is by comparing the maximum value in the set, which is called elementary evaluation (Sen, 1985: 39).[14] For example, let us take the case where the capability set Q_A of individual **A** has been given as a finite set $\{1,5,8\}$ and the capability set Q_B of individual **B** is $\{2,3,5,6,7\}$. Here, the elements of the set are evaluations of functionings. As the maximum value in the former set exceeds that in the latter (max $Q_A = 8 > 7$ max Q_B), the capability set of individual **A** is deemed better than that of individual **B**. There is another conceivable method. Compared to individual **A**, the maximum value in the capability set of individual **B** may be inferior, but there are more choices ($\#Q_B = 5 > 3 = \#Q_A$). Consequently, seen from the perspective of freedom of choice, the capability set of individual **B** could be said to be better than that of individual **A**. The method of ranking sets by greater or lesser numbers of elements in the set is sometimes called the cardinality criterion. In the element evaluation method only the ultimate choice is considered, the method implicitly reflects consequentialism. In comparison, what is considered in the cardinality criterion is not consequences: the focus is freedom of choice, or process aspects. As demonstrated above, the difference in ranking between capability sets is attributable to the implicit assumptions in each criterion (consequentialism vs. freedom of choice). It is not possible to address this in detail here, but the axiomatic characterization of ranking sets has been studied by a lot of researchers and forms a current research field in social choice theory.[15]

Listing capabilities

In the capability approach, a functioning has an important meaning. In other words, it incorporates the Aristotelian question: what is a good life? This question is often called the issue of listing capabilities, and features in a variety of debates.[16] The issue on the list is associated with the question of whether it is possible to determine what a good life is for a human being, or if it has been determined, how it can really be justified. Aiming to demonstrate the significance of the capability approach, Sen (1985: 46–47) cited the following *tentative* list of capabilities: (1) GDP per head; (2) Life expectancy; (3) Infant mortality; (4) Child death rate; (5) Adult literacy rate; and (6) Higher education ratio. According to Sen, a list of capabilities like the foregoing has the shortcoming that it is unfairly concentrated only on matters relating to life, death and education, and ignores many other latent capabilities, such as: (7) Prevalence of undernourishment; (8) Extent of morbidity; (9) Adequacy of basic clothing; and (10) Ability to be housed and sheltered. It has frequently been observed, however, that he has not as yet proposed a *convincing* list of capabilities (see Nussbaum, 2005). Sen (2004: 333, n.1) gives two reasons for not specifying a *plausible* list. One is the difficulty of deciding on a list alone without specifying the purpose of analysis, and the other is that specifying such a list would effectively shrink the domain of public reasoning. The latter reason is particularly important for Sen, reflecting his view of public discussion, which should involve dialogue with as many others as possible, and emphasize reasoned and introspective judgments. Consequently, he considers that a list of capabilities should be formed through rational judgment in public deliberation, and thus it is not up to him to decide on such a list.

The question of a list of capabilities is related to the debate about a means of measuring quality of life using Townsend's (1993) concept of relative deprivation (Abe, 2008: 180–188). Townsend does not rely on one-dimensional indices such as income for a person's quality of life. He measures quality of life multi-dimensionally, not only from the perspective of basic nutrition, such as being able to eat meat or fish once a week, but accounting for the social aspects of a person, such as inviting a friend to the house. An entirely predictable criticism is that the importance of being able to eat meat or fish once a week, or of inviting a friend to the home, differs between individuals and between countries and eras, so a case can be made that they may not necessarily be appropriate criteria. What has been developed to address these problems is the 'agreed standard' approach. This approach is a means of having society at large choose the necessities that enable a person to live a basic life, rather than it being the choice of individual researchers. Abe (2008), in *Kodomo no hinkon* (The poverty of children), lists the social necessities for children using the agreed standard approach. For example, the citation of 'breakfast' and 'picture or children's books' suggests that what is important for a child's quality of life is not limited to basic nutrition and knowledge, but also family engagement.

Conclusion

This chapter has discussed welfarism and the contemporary theories of distributive justice developed by Rawls, Dworkin and Sen. While it has not been an exhaustive discussion of all of the points of debate in the various theories, the following two points have emerged above all as requirements that should be satisfied by modern theories of distributive justice: to take account of the diversity of individuals and the concept of responsibility. The author is of the view that as a theory that satisfies these two requirements, the capability approach is superior to the other three theories in question. As we have seen, irrespective of theoretical and empirical studies into the capability approach, research continues to be generated and is in every sense current and ongoing.[17] It goes without saying that how to apply the capability approach to questions of disparity and poverty, and especially those questions in Japan, is a crucial issue. For example, as one policy for alleviating child poverty, Abe (2008: 228) cites all children being able to receive equal support. What this chapter asserts for that is a policy, the target of which is securing equal capabilities for all children.

Part 2:
Conflict and Cooperation in Social Relations

6 Intergroup Unfairness and Group Identification

Tomohiro Kumagai

Intragroup fairness has been the central issue for both theoretical and empirical studies on social justice, whether from the perspective of equity theory (Adams, 1965), relative deprivation theory (Stouffer, Suchman, DeVinney, Star and Williams, 1949), distributive justice (Deutsch, 1975) or procedural justice (Thibaut and Walker, 1975; Folger, 1977). These studies have examined the effects of the ways people are treated within a group—for example, when people perceive the group to be fair, they increase their commitment to it or their cooperation within it. However, people are interested in the question of fairness not only within a group but also between groups. Evaluation of the way one's own group is treated by other groups and the way one's own group treats other groups must have some impact on one's intergroup behavior. Intergroup fairness has been of central interest from the early period of intergroup relations studies. For instance, the well-known minimal group experiments by Tajfel, Billig, Bundy and Flament (1971) reported unfair distribution between the ingroup and the outgroup.

In this chapter I discuss the issue of intergroup social unfairness from the perspective of social identity, especially group identification. In doing so, I address two aspects of intergroup fairness, that is, unfair treatment of the ingroup by the outgroup and unfair treatment of the outgroup by the ingroup, based on the findings of empirical studies, including my own, of the Japanese people.

Intergroup conflict and social unfairness

How does social unfairness relate to intergroup conflicts? One of the principal causes of wars, ethnic conflicts and collective actions such as demonstrations and riots is the perception that one's own group has been harmed. Such harm can include not only physical damage inflicted by an outgroup but also symbolic and psychological harm. The degree of retaliation depends on how the victim perceives the damage (Averill, 1982; Ferguson and Rule, 1983). Insults trigger a strong retaliatory action (Baumeister and Boden, 1998) because they inflict psychological harm called ego threat on the victim. Such psychological threats can have the same effect on intergroup relations as interpersonal relations, especially in intergroup conflicts. In particular, social unfairness can cause psychological harm as well as physical harm. Social unfairness is therefore a significant problem that can lead to intergroup conflicts.

Social unfairness is defined as a certain act or decision which treats a person in a way that is not befitting of his or her entitlements and rights (Ohbuchi, 2007a). According to the group-value model proposed by Lind and Tyler et al. (Lind and Tyler, 1988; Tyler, Degoey and Smith, 1996; Tyler and Lind, 1992), people perceive unfair treatment to be a sign of disrespect to themselves. As this sense of disrespect threatens peoples' psychological state (De Cremer and Tyler, 2005), it becomes a motivation for retaliatory attacks (Lickel, Miller, Stenstrom, Denson and Schmader, 2006). For example, Skarlicki and Folger (1997) report that the more strongly employees feel that they are treated unfairly within the company, the more they take retaliatory action against the company (stealing office supplies, slacking off etc.). Further, Branscombe, Schmitt and Harvey (1999) report that African-Americans who consider discrimination to be illegitimate (in other words, their relationship with white people is unfair) tend to have strong hostility toward white people. These examples indicate a process by which ingroup unfairness motivates aggression against the group.

A similar condition can occur between groups. In an experiment by Kumagai and Ohbuchi (2009) with Japanese participants, the participants who witnessed other ingroup members being harmed by the outgroup exhibited stronger retaliatory behavior when harm was unfair (being punished in spite of good task performance) than when harm was fair (appropriate punishment for poor task performance) even though the same physical harm was suffered in either case. This suggests that unfair treatment triggers retaliation in intergroup relations as well.

Group identification

As mentioned above, the unfair treatment of one's own group can lead to a reaction to correct it and that reaction can cause intergroup conflict. Yet, people do not always take collective retaliatory action against unfair treatment. What regulates the potential for such retaliatory behavior is group identification. According to social identity theory (Hogg and Abrams, 1995; Tajfel, 1982; Tajfel and Turner, 1986), a social identity is a collective self, a 'we' who define ourselves as members of a group rather than a personal 'I' (Turner, Oakes, Haslam and MacGarty, 1994; Turner and Onorato, 1999). People categorize themselves in the same way that they categorize others. Turner, Hogg, Oakes, Reicher and Wetherell (1995) posit that social identity is a type of self-categorization according to one's social attributes. People define themselves not only by their individual traits (e.g., I am a kind person) but also by the social groups they belong to (e.g., I am Japanese). People thereby order the world to satisfy individual and social needs for structure, simplicity and predictability.

Group identification is thus a process in which one's sense of self transforms from an individual to a group as a whole (Brewer, 1991). Consequently, it is possible to think that the degree of group identification represents a relative strength of social identity compared with individual identity. Lickel et al. (2006) argue that the more strongly one identifies with a group, the more prone one is to perceive a threat to the group as a threat to oneself and hence the more strongly one reacts to the perceived threat. In fact, the aforementioned intergroup aggression experiment by Kumagai and Ohbuchi (2009) found that retaliation for intergroup unfairness intensified only in those participants whose group identities were strengthened by cooperative experiences within the group. This demonstrates that the effect of group identification on intergroup interaction is the same for Westerners and the Japanese.

Group identification and the effect of national identity on intergroup unfairness

Unfair treatment by the outgroup and group identification

In the process of intensifying group identification, people develop a similarity to other members of the ingroup, group values and rules, and group authority (Tyler, Boeckmann, Smith and Huo, 1997) and modify their behavior as a result. Previous empirical studies have shown that members who identify strongly with a group exhibit higher levels of bias and discrimination against outgroups due to the effect of increasing group identification on intergroup relations (Branscombe and Wann, 1994; Feather, 1994; Jetten, Spears and Manstead, 1996,

1997; Lindemen, 1997). For example, Branscombe and Wann (1994) found that American participants who were subjected to ego threat criticized Russians more severely than participants not subjected to ego threat, but this tendency was observed only among those who identified strongly with the US.

According to intergroup emotions theory (Mackie, Devos and Smith, 2000, Mackie and Smith, 2002), people experience negative emotions toward outgroups when social identity is salient. These emotions are, however, not uniform and are strongly influenced by the cognition of intergroup relations, or one's own group's position in relation to other groups, that is, the cognition of conditions that regulate group identity. For example, a study by Mackie et al. (2000) had American participants express their opinions for and against giving same-sex couples the same legal rights as heterosexual couples and categorized the participants based on their opinions. Then, participants were given information about the level of public support for the human rights of same-sex couples which had been manipulated by researchers (numbers in supportive newspaper articles were manipulated). Finally, their negative emotions (anger and fear) toward outgroups with opposing views, the degree of identification with their own group, and the degree of behavioral tendency (move against and move away) in relation to outgroups were measured. Results showed that the participants who perceived strong support for their own group's view identified more strongly with their own group and intensified their anger and tendency to move against dissenting outgroups compared with the participants who perceived the level of support as low. Thus people with strong group identity tend to show strong emotional reactions against outgroup threats and intensify negative attitudes.

It appears that by simply forming a group, people become more prone to perceive intergroup unfairness. For example, Guimond and Dube-Simard (1983), in a study on relative deprivation, report stronger discontent in intergroup comparisons than in intragroup comparisons. Others have reported that a sense of relative deprivation is stronger when group membership is salient (Kawakami and Dion, 1993; Smith, Spears and Oyen, 1994). In a scenario experiment by Kawakami and Dion, for example, Canadian participants read either a scenario emphasizing the 'individual' (emphasizing individual contributions to a task and the dissimilarity of members' views by using expressions such as 'you' and 'individual') or a scenario emphasizing the 'group' (emphasizing the term 'Group A', collective contributions to a task, and the similarity of members' views). Researchers also manipulated inequalities in intragroup and intergroup assessments. They found that participants in the group-emphasis group had a stronger sense of intergroup relative deprivation than those in the individual-emphasis group. This effect was not found in relation to a sense of intragroup relative deprivation.

Furthermore, group identification is expected to impact on perceptions of intergroup unfairness. Troppe and Wright (1999) report that not only the increasing salience but also the degree of ingroup identification intensify people's sense of relative deprivation. In their experiment in the US, Latino and African-American participants were asked how strong their sense of relative deprivation was when comparing their own group with other minority and majority (whites) groups. Results indicated that their sense of relative deprivation was regulated by each participant's degree of ingroup identification. In other words, those who identified strongly with their ingroup reported a stronger sense of relative deprivation than those with weak ingroup identification. This suggests that people perceive intergroup unfairness more strongly when group salience is strong or group identification is strong.

National identity

I have so far discussed the possibility that group identification intensifies a sense of intergroup unfairness. In this section, I shall transpose the issue into Japanese society and discuss whether people who identify strongly with Japanese society and Japanese people feel strongly that they are treated unfairly by foreign nations.

As a precondition for verifying whether identification with Japan regulates the cognition of unfair treatment by outgroups, participants must perceive Japan to be treated unfairly in the international community. Even though Japan is highly respected as an economic power, there are various sources of discontent with Japan's international standing such as its exclusion from permanent membership on the UN Security Council despite contributing the second largest share of the UN budget (265 million dollars, 12.5 per cent as at 2010; from the MOFA web page) and the crimes committed by American soldiers at the US military bases in Japan. Consequently, many Japanese people may not be completely satisfied with their country's current international standing and will have some sense of unfairness.

One possible process by which national identification influences perceptions of international unfairness is as follows. As people intensify their group identification with the state of Japan, their loyalty, their interest in the country's history and culture, their attachment to their own society and their pride in their international standing become stronger. Favoritism for their own country can be divided into emotional and cognitive dimensions, that is, patriotism and nationalism.

Mummendey, Klink and Brown (2001) have argued that these two dimensions are distinguishable both theoretically and empirically. Karasawa (2002) confirmed by factor analysis in a study of the Japanese people that they are distinct factors. Patriotism is a strong emotion toward one's country, especially in the form of commitment. Nationalism, in contrast, is a belief that one's country is superior to other countries. People with strong patriotism consider their country's living environment and policies as desirable. People with strong nationalism consider that their nation and race have a relative advantage over others in terms of its relationships with neighboring countries and its immigration policy.

If patriotism and nationalism are distinct factors, it may be possible to discover a process by which group identification causes various international problems by studying how these factors intensify intergroup unfairness, or a sense of international unfairness toward Japan. If patriotism alone intensifies a sense of intergroup unfairness, we can surmise that the effect of group identification is based on emotional discontent with outgroups. If nationalism alone intensifies a sense of international unfairness, then we can surmise that cognition of the superiority of the ingroup and the motivation to maintain it, not an emotion, are the cause of intergroup conflicts.

We conducted a survey study in Japan in order to verify this hypothesis (Kumagai, 2009; Kumagai, Kawashima and Asai, 2009). We mailed out a questionnaire to people living in the Tokyo metropolitan area randomly selected from the basic residents' register and asked them to return completed forms by post at a later date. The questionnaire included six Japanese identity items, which were adapted from Doosje, Branscombe, Spears and Manstead (1998) by replacing the ingroup identification items with 'Japan' (e.g., 'I am happy to be Japanese', 'Being Japanese is important to me' etc.), and six patriotism items (e.g. 'If I am to be reborn, I want to be born in Japan again', 'In view of law and order, I do not want to live in other countries' etc.) and four nationalism items (e.g., 'The Japanese is one of the best races in the world', 'Japan's amazing postwar growth is attributable to the brilliance of the Japanese people' etc.) from Karawasa's (2002) national identity scale. Two items were added to measure a sense of international unfairness—'The international recognition given to Japan is unjust' and 'Japan deserves to be given higher recognition by the world'. The average score was calculated for each of the identity, patriotism, nationalism and international unfairness items and taken as a measure.

We performed a multiple regression analysis with Japanese identity, patriotism and nationalism as explanatory variables and international unfairness as an objective variable in order to elucidate a psychological process by which national identity intensifies unfair attitudes toward outgroups. We repeated the multiple regression analysis with Japanese identity as an explanatory variable and patriotism, nationalism and international unfairness as objective variables. Results were very simple. Japanese identity significantly increased both patriotism and nationalism. However, nationalism alone significantly increased a sense of international unfairness whereas patriotism had no such effect. Therefore it is possible to say that the level of attachment to Japan is irrelevant to the perception that Japan is unfairly treated in the international community, at least based on the survey results. However, the stronger one's belief in Japan's superiority over other countries is, the stronger one feels that Japan's current international standing is unfair. This implies that not all aspects of group identification intensify a sense of unfairness toward outgroups equally in intergroup relations. Only certain aspects, especially nationalism, which is cognitive rather than emotional, intensify the tendency to feel that one's group is unfairly treated by outgroups.

Unfairness against outgroups and group identification

I have so far discussed a sense of unfairness and group identification on the part of 'victims'. However, social fairness from the perspective of 'perpetrators' is the more important issue in discussing intergroup social fairness. Treating outgroups unfairly is a direct cause of intergroup conflicts. In fact, there have been many social psychological studies on intergroup relations that report various cases of unfair outgroup treatment by people in the form of intergroup discrimination or prejudice (e.g. Hewstone, Rubin and Willis, 2002).

As mentioned earlier, the minimal group experiment by Tajfel et al. (1971), a classic study on social identity, actually measured unfair distribution against outgroups although its aim was to study ingroup favoritism. In the experiment, participants were randomly divided into two groups and later asked to decide how to distribute gratuity money to other participants. Distribution methods were provided in the form of a matrix with equal distribution at the center and more unequal distribution towards either end. Tajfel et al. found that participants chose to distribute equally when the other two participants were both ingroup members or outgroup members. When one of them was an ingroup member and the other was an outgroup member, however, participants chose unequal distribution by allocating more money to their ingroup member.

This ingroup favoritism is observed not only in relation to physical benefits but also in judging the fairness of levels of punishment. Judging the levels of punishment given to criminals is an act that clearly manifests the effect of a psychological process concerning social fairness. In an experimental study by Van Prooijen (2006) about the relationship between group membership and punishment determination, Dutch participants played the role of a court judge and determined the level of punishment for a suspect. The suspect was either an ingroup member (a Dutch person) or an outgroup member (a German person) and the probability of the guilty verdict was manipulated (100 per cent vs. 50 per cent) as information for decision making. It was found that heavier punishments were handed down to the offender who was an outgroup member rather than an ingroup member when the suspect's guilt was uncertain. This result demonstrates that fairness judgments tend to be biased against outgroups, albeit limited to highly uncertain situations.

While the experiments by Tajfel et al. (1971) and Van Prooijen (2006) demonstrated that the mere formation of a group promoted unfair behavior toward outgroups, they did not consider the regulatory role of group identification in it. However, the effect of group identification on a decision to support prejudice against other groups has been studied by Struch and Schwartz (1989). Their study measured the attitudes of ordinary Jews in Israel toward the abolition of the country's policy giving privileges to the ultra-orthodox Jews (e.g., exemption from military service, etc.) by way of questionnaire survey. It found that the more strongly the participants identified themselves as modern Israelis, the more strongly they saw a conflict and value gaps between themselves and the ultra-orthodox Jews and the more they were opposed to policies which privilege the ultra-orthodox.

These findings suggest that discriminatory attitudes toward and unfair treatment of outgroups are engendered by group membership and enhanced by group identification. As shown by Struch and Schwartz (1989), this seems to manifest more clearly in an indirect manner. Nonsupport for welfare benefits and student aid for foreigners is a pertinent example of this. We (Kumagai, Cakal and Hewstone, 2010) conducted a survey of Japanese people regarding the effects of patriotism and nationalism on the process by which identification with a state promoted unfair treatment of outgroups. The survey assessed the attitudes of Japanese participants toward an outgroup of Chinese people who were 'legally' residing in Japan. Unlike Kumagai's (2009) findings on a sense of international unfairness, this survey found that a negative attitude toward an outgroup was increased not only by nationalism but also by patriotism. However, the ways patriotism and nationalism influenced the negative attitude (nonsupport for outgroup aids) appeared to differ. On the one hand, patriotism seems to instill a lack of trust in the outgroup and thus weaken support for policies to aid it. On the other hand, nationalism increased both the real and symbolic forms of threat, which concurs with Kumagai's (2009) findings. Furthermore, this study found that nationalism intensified nonsupportive attitudes toward outgroup aid policies based on real threat alone (symbolic threat did not affect a nonsupportive attitude toward Chinese).

Intergroup unfairness, patriotism and nationalism

I have so far discussed the relationship between intergroup unfairness and group identification. I have addressed intergroup unfairness in terms of two types of psychological process, namely, the cognition of unfair treatment by outgroups and unfair attitudes toward outgroups. I have also discussed the effects of group identification on intergroup unfairness mediated by emotional and cognitive processes called patriotism and nationalism, focusing on identification with a social group called 'Japan' by the Japanese.

While one study cited earlier (Kumagai, 2009) found no relationship between the cognition of unfair treatment by outgroups and the level of patriotism, another study (Kumagai et al., 2010) demonstrated that patriotism reduced people's trust in outgroups, which in turn weakened their support for policies to remedy injustices against outgroups. Since patriotism is a positive feeling towards one's ingroup, it is likely to increase one's favoritism for ingroup members.

Such a person has a strong sense of trust in Japanese people, and has a relatively low level of trust in others. As a result, such a person is less trustful of foreigners (e.g., Chinese residents in Japan) and exhibits a less cooperative attitude toward policies that may favor them.

A similar tendency was discovered by our study on imagined intergroup contact (Kumagai and Crisp, 2010), although it was not about attitudes toward social fairness. It has been reported that positive attitudes toward outgroups are increased by simply imagining positive contact between groups (Crisp and Turner, 2009) but this effect is suppressed in the presence of strong group identification (Stathi and Crisp, 2008). Accordingly, we turned our attention to the effect of group identification that weakened the effect of contact and the effect of national identity as a mediation process and studied the effect of imagined intergroup contact using Japanese participants. The study found that the Japanese participants who had experienced imagined intergroup contact exhibited a more positive and cooperative attitude toward British home-stay students as outgroup members than did those who had no such experience. However, this effect disappeared in the case of the participants with high patriotism scores. This also suggests that patriotism probably suppresses cooperative and friendly attitudes toward and a sense of trust in outgroups (this effect was not found with nationalism).

In contrast, Kumagai (2009) found that nationalism had the effect of increasing the cognition that one's group was treated unfairly by outgroups. Kumagai et al. (2010) also found that nationalism intensified the perception of both real threat and symbolic threat and that the former weakened support for policies intended to increase fairness for outgroups. Nationalism is an attitude based on the cognition of superiority over outgroups. It is likely that participants with a stronger sense of nationalism perceived threats more strongly because improving an outgroups' standing would clearly threaten their superiority. And they intensified their opposition to policies favoring outgroups in order to diminish the threat.

It has come to light through discussions in this chapter that patriotism is a suppressor of positive emotions and cognitions toward outgroups. Patriotism aggravates intergroup relations indirectly by making it difficult to form cooperative relationships which positive emotions and cognition toward outgroups are supposed to engender. By contrast, nationalism aggravates intergroup relations more directly. Because nationalism is the cognition of the ingroup's superiority, it is likely to stimulate people to consider that privileged and favorable treatment received by their ingroup is 'fair'. Consequently, people with strong nationalism may think that 'we are treated unfairly' even though the treatment is considered to be fair by a third party. Moreover, nationalism increases a tendency to perceive outgroups as a threat and this perception intensifies negative attitudes towards the fair treatment of outgroups. It is considered that this will actually promote unfair treatment of outgroups. The difference between the influence processes of patriotism and nationalism raises one problem with respect to intergroup conflict resolution. As nationalism tends to result in explicit prejudices and unfair reactions, it is easily identifiable and therefore easy to direct efforts to address it in trying to improve intergroup relations. Patriotism, in contrast, is a 'suppressor of positive effects' which exerts an indirect effect on intergroup conflicts that is neither obvious nor urgent. Although this effect of patriotism tends to be overlooked for this reason, it needs to be taken into account in trying to resolve intergroup conflicts or to form cooperative relations from a long-term perspective.

Conclusion

I have looked at the effects of group identification on fairness in intergroup relations. In particular, I have clarified the psychological process which explains why group identification aggravates intergroup unfairness by analyzing the effects of group identification mediated by patriotism and nationalism. Considering that intergroup conflicts mostly occur between groups with strong identities and that intergroup unfairness is a major cause of intergroup conflicts, analysis of the relationship between these factors is of great significance in the study of intergroup conflict resolution. Particularly in Japan, patriotism and nationalism have been considered taboo since the Second World War for the reason that war-time patriotism encouraged *kamikaze* and other suicide attack tactics and nationalism was used to justify a war of aggression. As a result, the amount of social psychological research into the effect of national identity in intergroup relations, especially international relations, has been small in Japan. However, it is expected to become an important issue in Japanese society from now on in view of a rise in patriotism and nationalism in today's Japan, especially among young people. This chapter can make up for a deficit in research-based knowledge on Japanese people by offering these findings about contemporary Japanese society. The effects of group identification are of course not limited to the aspects of patriotism and nationalism. This is an oversimplified argument and I am well aware of this weakness in the above discussion. Yet, I believe that this detailed analysis of the effects of group identification, albeit only in two categories, will pave the way for more precise discussions of the psychological processes involved in intergroup conflicts and contribute to advancing the study of the intergroup conflicts that are troubling many countries in the world, including Japan, and perhaps contribute to their resolution.

7 Maintaining the gender gap and benevolent sexism

Takehiro Yamamoto and Ken-ichi Ohbuchi

Introduction

Two types of sexism

The typical manifestation of sexism is founded in malice towards women, but it is most definitely not the case that that is all it comprises. The fact that sexism and the gender stereotypes on which it is based are not founded solely in such negative emotions as malice towards women has been known since the 1960s (Rosenberg, Nelson and Vivekananthan, 1968), but many researchers have focused only on discrimination arising from malice towards women and have not seen discrimination against women based on good intentions and gentleness as a subject for research. That is because whereas the former has been deemed abhorrent, giving rise to ostracism of women, the latter has been considered desirable, being based on positive feelings about women. Glick and Fiske (1996), however, advocated the concept of ambivalent sexism and pointed out that sexism has two different aspects: hostile sexism and benevolent sexism. They also identified that these two types of sexism exhibit similar harmful effects above and beyond their qualitative differences.

Hostile sexism is a prototype sexism (Glick and Fiske, 2001) incorporating clear hostility and antipathy toward women who defy the social ascendancy of men. Specifically, this typically manifests as ostracism of women in the labor market and unfair assessment of women's abilities and manner of working. Most of the behavior we are able to recollect as sexism corresponds to this hostile sexism. In modern day society, with its strongly egalitarian climate, opportunities to observe clearly malicious hostile sexism have declined, but that does not mean that such discriminatory behavior has completely disappeared. Hostile sexism manifested against women continues to exist in no small measure. For example, differences in the speed at which men and women are promoted, known as 'the glass ceiling', and pressure on women associated with marriage and birth to resign from work, are typical of hostile sexism.

In contrast, there is a conceptual line between benevolent sexism and our image of discrimination. Unlike traditional sexism, exemplified by hostile sexism, benevolent sexism does not include clear hostility or antipathy toward women. Rather, it manifests as paternalistic concern for and preferential treatment of women, and admiration of feminine characteristics. Its intent is interpreted as something positive, founded in chivalrous ideology (Viki, Abrams and Hutchison, 2003). For that reason, benevolent sexism is not recognized as a form of sexism that has harmful effects on women; it still manifests in daily life, and we see it frequently. For example, keeping women from dangerous work is a typical example of benevolent sexism (Moya, Glick, Exposito, de Lemus and Hart, 2007). However, there are probably few who would be prepared to deem this discriminatory toward women and would try to suppress its manifestation. As evidence, even now that revision of the Equal Employment Opportunity Law has removed the prohibition against women working late at night, from the perspective of preventing victimization from crime, staff in convenience stores late at night are typically men, and it is very rare to see a solitary woman engaged in late night work. Further, society is replete with behavior that could be deemed benevolent sexism, such as paying for a woman's meal at a restaurant, or offering assistance to a woman carrying heavy items (Dardenne, Dumont and Bollier, 2007). In an egalitarian climate it may be described as a phenomenon that contrasts with hostile sexism, of which opportunities for observation are in decline.

As mentioned, benevolent sexism is perceived as gentlemanly behavior replete with gentleness toward women, and almost no one interprets it negatively. Further, encounters with benevolent sexism typically afford women some type of benefit, such as economic assistance. As a result, our attention is taken up with the beneficial aspects of benevolent sexism and we typically do not notice its harmful nature. There are even those who may harbor doubt about how such behavior could be discriminatory. The hidden fear with benevolent sexism is exactly that: that people are unable to recognize it as harmful.

The aims and an outline of this chapter

The aims of this chapter are to identify the nature of this benevolent sexism which people are unable to recognize, and to discuss the harmful effects that encounters with it have on women. In order to understand benevolent sexism and its harmful nature, we will first discuss the socio-cultural context that has given rise to it. The socio-cultural context is an important variable in predicting gender stereotyping and the discrimination gender stereotyping manifests (Caprariello, Cuddy and Fiske, 2009). The socio-cultural factor that gave rise to benevolent sexism is the male-dominant social system based on traditional gender roles (Jackman, 1994). Nearly all societies existing in the world—albeit with slight cultural differences—maintain a male-dominant social structure in accordance with traditional gender roles (Baxter, 1994; Yamaguchi and Wang, 2002). Because women in such social systems are restrained in low socio-economic status, they may experience strong dissatisfaction with the status quo and begin to harbor doubts about maintaining the system. In reality, and in support of this prediction, women have complained about the status quo and have resisted it. For example, the women's lib movement from the latter half of the 1960s, and the continuing strong tendency to gender equality, is probably part of women's complaints about the status quo. At the same time, however, there were those who conspired to maintain the status quo; both men and socially successful women. To protect their own privilege, they desire to maintain the status quo, the social system which constitutes the foundation of existing society (Glick and Fiske, 2001). Essential to fulfilling that desire is suppressing the dissatisfaction of the many socially repressed women, and encouraging their assumption of traditional roles (Barreto and Ellemers, 2005). It is our hypothesis that people wanting to maintain the status quo created benevolent sexism as a means of encouraging women to engage in traditional gender roles, without discontent. Based on this hypothesis, we will consider the relationship between the motivation to maintain the social status quo and benevolent sexism, with reference to knowledge gained from earlier research.

Second, we will investigate the psychological mechanism whereby exposure to benevolent sexism causes harmful effects in women. Specifically, we will point out that the discriminatory messages inherent in benevolent sexism are at the root of the harmfulness, and we will investigate the process by which harmful effects are manifested via two different routes: the mental intrusion model and the motivation reduction model. The harmful effects of benevolent sexism are extensive, ranging from a decline in an individual woman's performance, to rationalization of gender inequality and the gender gap. We will also provide an explanation, with reference to specific research results, of the types of harmful effects that are linked to each of the models—mental intrusion and motivation reduction.

In this chapter we will also investigate factors that increase the harmful effects of benevolent sexism. Humans are equipped with defensive psychological barriers which as much as possible reduce harmful effects and protect self-esteem from discrimination. Benevolent sexism, perceived as gentlemanly behavior towards women, nevertheless sneaks easily through those barriers. That then encourages ready acceptance by women of benevolent sexism, and even gives rise in women to a sense of dependence on assistance and protection. The clever traps that infallibly disseminate these harmful effects are spread layer upon layer throughout benevolent sexism. The aims of this chapter are to show that benevolent sexism is difficult for women to oppose and is used to maintain the social system, and to further the discussion on the harmfulness of benevolent sexism.

What gives rise to benevolent sexism?

What is at the root of sexism: maintaining the status quo

When considering the context that gives rise to benevolent sexism, it is not possible to ignore the socio-cultural context. We cannot explain the reasons that gave rise to benevolent sexism as simple calculations of gain or loss at the level of the individual. If we re-visit benevolent sexism without taking into account the socio-cultural context, it should become readily apparent that for men it is no more than irrational behavior requiring self-victimization. For example, a man paying for a woman's meal on a date certainly appears to be engaging in behavior that is replete with concern for making the woman's economic burden smaller. However, it means that the man's economic burden becomes bigger. If we posit that human behavior is decided on the basis of rational judgment (calculation of short-term gain or loss), then we must ask if a man would really spontaneously choose to behave in the benevolently sexist manner that involves that type of self-victimization. The likelihood is probably extremely low. What is inferred by this discussion is that in order to understand the mechanism that gives rise to benevolent sexism, there is a need to consider a macro level factor above and beyond calculation of gain or loss at the level of the individual.

What then, is that factor? It is our assertion that the social status quo, in other words, the male-dominant social structure, is the socio-cultural context that gives rise to gender stereotypes and the benevolent sexism founded in them. We posit that humans are equipped with a universal cognitive tendency to desire the maintenance of the social status quo (Jost and Hunyady, 2002). This tendency has lead people to assume benevolent sexism in order to maintain the status quo, above and beyond calculation of gain or loss at the level of the individual (Jost and Kay, 2005). As an understanding of the male-dominant social structure is essential to understanding benevolent sexism, we will discuss the process by which that social structure arose.

Traditional gender roles and male-dominant social structures

If we ascribe to Eagly (1987), it was the traditional gender roles assigned to men and women as being responsible respectively for work and home that caused the emergence of the male-dominant social structure. In traditional gender roles men are generally depicted as strong and dependable, and women as physically weak and incompetent, but personally warm (Eagly and Mladinic, 1989). This view of gender difference is, of course, no more than gender stereotyping, in other words, preconceptions about men and women. Hence there is no need for a man to fill a work or authority role in a manner that obeys the stereotypical view of gender difference, nor is there any need whatsoever for a woman to assume the subordinate status of an auxiliary role or doing housework. The view of gender difference and its associated traditional gender roles are nevertheless perceived as role expectations by which men and women should abide, and are internalized in individuals via the socialization process (Rudman and Happen, 2003). As evidence, people possess an implicit association that links men to work and women to the home, which is not influenced by approval or disapproval of the visible gender role of the individual (Rudman, McGhee and Greenwald, 2001). This gender role view, which is internalized at a latent level, can be predicted to motivate men and women to choose roles that will be in accord with traditional gender roles. As evidence, and in support of this prediction, it has been discovered that men will pursue high-class occupations, while conversely women will unconsciously show interest in roles that relate to helping the weak, in accord with traditional gender roles (Pratto et al., 1997). This preference by women for supportive roles is not only apparent in western society, but is similarly observable in Japanese society. For example, in occupations that require 'emotional labor'—known as 'pink collar' jobs—the number of women workers

Table 7.1: Proportion of women in Japan's pink collar sector

	Women	Total	Proportion
Nurses	810,157	848,185	95%
Kindergarten teachers	99,223	106,859	93%

Sources: Statistical Data on Nursing Services in Japan 2008 (Japan Nursing Association, 2009). Statistical survey of school teachers (Ministry of Education and Science, 2007)

is significantly higher than the number of men workers, and women continue to have a monopoly (Table 7.1).

The fact that this inherent preference for and assumption of occupations and roles founded in traditional gender roles has continued to be reproduced across generational divides is probably why a social structure in which men occupy higher status and women are subordinate to them has widely permeated society. According to the Global Gender Gap Report 2009 (Hausmann, Tyson and Zahidi, 2009), which ranked the gender gap according to nation, the country assessed as being the one in the world in which men and women are most equal is located in northern Europe: Iceland. However, even Iceland's gender equality index was in the order of only 0.82, which, if compared to perfect gender equality represented by 1.0, can still be seen to be small. This figure shows that even in Iceland, where men and women are the most equal in the world, society is still male-dominant. It goes without saying, but at 101st in the world (among 134 countries), Japan is a thoroughly male-dominant society. In fact, the gender equality index is a very low 0.64. These results suggest that the male-dominant social system is a universal structure that supersedes borders and cultures. This fact further suggests that the mechanism that seeks to maintain this (the desire of people wanting the social status quo maintained) is also a universal psychological process that supersedes cultural difference.

A sweet trap to maintain the status quo

Well then, why did the desire of men wanting to maintain a male-dominant social system give rise to benevolent sexism? That is without doubt due to the fact that it was difficult to maintain the status quo, in other words, to hold women down in a socio-economically low, subordinate status, by simply cracking the whip of hostile sexism, redolent as it is with malice (Glick and Fiske, 2001). Held down in a low status within a social structure based on traditional gender roles, the latent dissatisfaction and rage of women toward the social status quo was relatively significant. To maintain this social system, women's dissatisfaction and rage needed to be alleviated (Barreto and Ellemers, 2005). It was here that men began to offer a sweet inducement to eliminate women's dissatisfaction and get them to accept traditional gender roles. That inducement was benevolent sexism. For example, men would frequently act in a gentlemanly manner toward women who had assumed a traditional gender role and treat them with deference. This is classic benevolently sexist behavior, designed to encourage women to engage in traditional gender roles (Glick and Fiske, 1996). Men would heap praise on feminine features replete with warmth and love, and at times even dangle the carrots of protection and economic assistance. All this behavior is part of an obdurate male strategy to alleviate women's dissatisfaction with the social system and cause women to assume traditional gender roles. Jackman (1994), who conducted research into paternalistic beliefs comprising the belief foundation for benevolent sexism, also theorized that men had waved gentleness around in order to convince women to accept the status quo, and suggested the possibility that benevolent sexism arose as part of a stratagem designed to maintain the status quo.

From the perspective of gain-loss calculation at the level of the individual, benevolent sexism may appear for men to be burdensome, irrational behavior. However, if the perspective of maintaining a male-dominant social structure is taken into account, men proffering benevolent sexism can be understood as rational behavior, not at odds with self-interest. For men, there is sufficient value in maintaining the social status quo, even paying the cost of benevolent sexism, because that is what guarantees the stability of men's higher socio-economic status.

Men create benevolent sexism and women conspire in it

Those who are in receipt of big benefits from maintaining a male-dominant social structure are, of course, men. Hence, it can be surmised that it will be mainly men who will desire the maintenance of the social status quo and who will partake in manifesting benevolent sexism. That expectation is not wrong. In fact, comparative international research completed in 16 countries revealed that men are more positive toward benevolent sexism than women and possess a more accepting attitude (Glick et al., 2000). However, not only men, but women also can cooperate in sending the message of benevolent sexism. A classic example is socially successful women. To preserve their own status, it can be predicted that socially successful women will, just as do men, desire the maintenance of the male-dominant social status quo, and will hope that other women will assume traditional gender roles. The reason being that for women like that, a fellow woman active in the same domain becomes an inherent threat to their own status. In support of this prediction, there is research that points out that socially successful women manifest sexism towards other women (Ellemers, van den Heauvel, de Glider, Maass and Bonvini, 2004). The researchers administered a questionnaire to female university professors to measure their attitudes toward male and female university students. The result was that female educators assessed female post graduate students more negatively than male post graduate students. At the time the researchers also had the students do their own self-assessment, but no significant difference was found in self-assessment between male students and female students. In other words, the negative assessment of female students was not due to actual lack of power or competence in female students, it was quite simply due to the hostile preconceptions of female educators. This series of phenomena, in which socially successful female educators handed down negative, discriminatory assessments of female students, is called the 'Queen Bee Syndrome' and may be cited as evidence that women seeking to protect their own status will manifest discriminatory behavior towards other women. It is generally surmised that most manifestations of benevolent sexism is due to men, but not all can be attributed to men. We must not ignore the possibility that a portion of women, in order to maintain the status quo, will manifest benevolent sexism.

Why is benevolent sexism harmful?

On what exactly are the harmful effects of benevolent sexism based? The consistent view of researchers is that they are due to the inherently discriminatory messages contained within benevolent sexism (Dumont, Sarlet and Dardenne, 2010). Benevolent sexism typically manifests as assistance to and protection of women, but the flip side is that these behaviors simply deem women to be weak and needing of assistance and protection. Exposure to benevolent sexism and the discriminatory messages contained therein give rise in women to a negative assessment of their own abilities, and this low self-assessment by women is revealed to be harmful via two different psychological mechanisms (mental intrusion and motivation reduction). We will now describe these two mechanisms in detail, with reference to knowledge gained from earlier research.

The mental intrusion model

The mental intrusion model is a theory which asserts that exposure to benevolent sexism reduces cognitive resources. The theory posits a mental mechanism by which women who encounter benevolent sexism are induced to negative self-assessment, and the resulting insecurity about ability leads to harmful effects (Dardenne et al., 2007). Insecurity wipes out people's cognitive resources, weakening their attentiveness to immediate problems and working to make effective courses of action difficult (Beilock and Carr, 2005). As a result, it has been identified that exposure to benevolent sexism causes a range of harmful effects, including decline in performance (Cihangir, Barreto and Ellemers, 2010). In an experiment conducted by Dardenne et al. (2007), female participants underwent job interviews as applicants for a fictional company. Female participants in the benevolent sexist condition, wherein they were told they would be given the assistance necessary for them to adapt to the workplace by male staff, achieved lower scores in problems on an 'entrance test' than women participants in the control condition, who were told they would not be given assistance. Dardenne et al. (2007) interpreted these results to mean that the exposure to benevolent sexism in the form of assistance gave rise to feelings of discomfort, and cognitive resources thereby declined. In this way, in the mental intrusion model the assertion is that benevolent sexism has the harmful effect of causing the performance of female participants to decline through the intervention of reduced cognitive resources.

The motivation reduction model

In contrast, the motivation reduction model posits that the exposure to benevolent sexism causes a decline in motivation to achieve among women. People are equipped with a universal motivation to achieve the highest possible social status (Rudman and Happen, 2003), but benevolent sexism works to reduce this (Vescio et al., 2005). The reason being that benevolent sexism contains discriminatory messages that women are incompetent and powerless, and this forms a self-assessed incompetence in women which gives rise to a sense of helplessness that they really cannot do something anyway, and causes women's performance to decline (Vescio et al., 2005).

In an experiment conducted by Vescio et al. (2005), female participants were required to take on the challenge of a group task on which prize money was riding (a masculine, stressful task). However, it was not the case that all participants could undertake the challenge. Only those participants assessed as being highly able and chosen in advance by the leader with reference to answers to a questionnaire could undertake the challenge. Participants not chosen were to take on the challenge of a separate task to which no remuneration was attached. The leader assigned the participants to the non-stressful task condition in terms of paternalism. Paternalism is the ideology at the root of benevolent sexism (Viki et al., 2003), and so, for the female participants, receiving paternalistic treatment was synonymous with being exposed to benevolent sexism. It was reported that as a result of the experiment, the participants assigned according to this paternalistic condition experienced intense rage. However, the rage did not heighten the motivation of the female participants towards the task. Rather, they lost confidence and fell into a type of learned helplessness (reduced self-efficacy).

Self-efficacy is an important predictor of individual performance (Bandura, 1977) and its decline means a decline in performance. In fact, a decline in the performance of female participants was observed. As the results of this experiment demonstrate, the motivation reduction model asserts that loss of the sense of self-efficacy and a decline in motivation through exposures to benevolent sexism induce a decline in performance. Declining motivation does not only stop at declining performance, but hides other risks that additional harmful effects will be induced. The reason being that loss of the sense of self-efficacy and associated reduced motivation are likely to heighten the erroneous perception that, based on ability, women deem their inferior status to be justified. Taking this factor into account, the motivation reduction model suggests the possibility that as a result of exposures to benevolent sexism, an additional harmful effect may be induced, in the form of women themselves seeing the gender gap as justified.

Factors that increase the harmfulness of benevolent sexism

One feature of benevolent sexism that has been cited is the difficulty of rejecting it (Fehr and Sassenberg, 2009). That is because both within and without, benevolent sexism contains layer upon layer of clever traps that increase harmful effects. In this section we will look at four topics: the benefits that arise from benevolent sexism and reliance on them; synergistic effects with hostile sexism; poorly functioning defensive psychological barriers; and support from the social system, and we will look at the process by which each encourages acceptance of benevolent sexism.

Women's dependence on benevolent sexism

Sexism is behavior that arose to maintain the male-dominant society. Hence there is a strong tendency to attribute responsibility for its harmful effects to men (Kilianski and Rudman, 1999). For example, men with a tendency to sexism tend to be negatively evaluated by women (Barreto and Ellemers, 2005). However, it is impossible to lay the blame for the harmfulness of benevolent sexism entirely on men. That is because factors that increase the harmful effects of benevolent sexism also exist in the psychological mindset of women (Glick and Fiske, 2001). One of those is the desire of women to depend on assistance and protection (Jackman, 1994). Superficially, benevolent sexism is behavior that provides the benefits to women of assistance and protection, and is typically perceived positively by women themselves. Hence, women frequently depend on benevolent sexism from men and seek to enjoy its benefits. However, the object of benevolent sexism is women who assume traditional gender roles; women who pursue social achievement are excluded and cannot participate in its benefits.

If women want to continue to enjoy the benefits of benevolent sexism, they must dispense with pursuing social achievement. This sense of dependence by women on benevolent sexism deprives them of the motivation to achieve and gives rise to harmful effects that hold women down in low socio-economic positions. In fact, in support of this view, it has been identified that the woman who deems her male partner to be a knight on a white horse providing assistance and support is more likely to spontaneously abandon social achievement (Rudman and Happen, 2003). Further, Yamamoto and Ohbuchi (2010) have proven women's desire for dependence in experimental research. Female participants who worked overtime with same sex or different sex colleagues expected they would receive more assistance when working overtime with male colleagues than with female colleagues. Further, women felt dissatisfaction when they did not receive the expected assistance from colleagues, but the degree was greater for male colleagues. These results indicate that women see men as providers of benevolent sexism, in other words, a useable 'resource' that brings benefit, or phrased another way; they depend on benevolent sexism from men. Our results revealed not just that women do not reject benevolent sexism; they desire it to be provided. For as long as women expect benevolent sexism, the class structure wherein men provide assistance and women are provided with it will likely be maintained and not change. This suggests, in other words, that at least one of the causes of inequalities between men and women going unremedied may lie within women themselves who expect assistance and seek to remain at a low status.

The synergistic effects of benevolent and hostile sexism

As has so far been discussed, even alone, benevolent sexism manifests enough harmful effects. However, if packaged with hostile sexism, those effects are further enhanced. The reason is that hostile sexism redolent with malice enhances the erroneous perception that benevolent sexism is behavior replete with gentleness (Fischer, 2006).

Men cannot turn a blind eye to women who jolt the social status quo by refusing to assume traditional gender roles. It may seem obvious, but men exclude such women from the set of objects of benevolent sexism and do not proffer assistance or protection to them. However, although women who raise objections to male society are removed from the set of objects of benevolent sexism, they are not forgiven. As may be understood from the high correlation between hostile sexism and negative attitudes to women who are not in accord with traditional gender roles (Glick et al., 1997), such women are seen as objects of hostile sexism and are subject to discriminatory action, including ostracism and insults (Greenwood and Isbell, 2002).

Raising objections to male-dominant society and seeking gender equality are acts that from the perspective of all women's groups are in their interests. At the level of the individual, however, such behavior by women is associated with the fear and insecurity of becoming an object of hostile sexism (Fischer, 2006). At the least, for an individual woman, becoming an object of hostile sexism is entirely bad. Under these circumstances the sweet inducement effect of benevolent sexism may appear conspicuously bright. It is possible that a woman may more positively evaluate benevolent sexism, in which—while it may include a certain amount of harmful effect—they are treated gently by men and even provided assistance and protection. From the foregoing, it can be expected that women who harbor strong fear or uncertainty toward hostile sexism may have their motivation to achieve equality between the sexes at the level of society suppressed, and may become accepting of benevolent sexism. In fact, in countries where hostile sexism is strong, accepting attitudes from women toward benevolent sexism have been reported in earlier research (Glick and Fiske, 1999; Barreto and Ellemers, 2005). Further, Fischer (2006) has identified that women who were engaged in interactions with men having hostile sexist tendencies and interacting women participants become accepting of benevolent sexism. These results suggest that by its existence, hostile sexism makes women more accepting of benevolent sexism and that in turn perpetuates the reproduction of disadvantage for women.

Benevolent sexism that pierces psychological defenses

Factors that enhance the harmful effects of benevolent sexism also exist within our poorly functioning defensive psychological mechanisms. People are equipped with defensive psychological reactions that protect self-assessment and self-esteem (Crocker and Major, 1989), and when we encounter discrimination and prejudice containing clear malice, we are able to minimize that negative influence (McCoy and Major, 2003). If we are able to recognize discrimination as discrimination, the defensive psychological reaction is activated and no damage is sustained as a result of an encounter with discrimination. That is because the cause of discriminatory damage is attributed to the discriminatory intent of the person manifesting discrimination, and we are able to reject attribution to internal factors (Mendoza-Denton et al., 2009). For example, failing in a job test is an event that could injure the average person's self-esteem, but how would it be if it becomes known that the company that administered the exam is discriminatory in its employment and almost never hires women? A female job applicant will probably not attribute the cause of not being hired to her lack of power or lack of competence, but to the company's discriminatory employment criteria. In other words, it means that there will be no harmful effects from the intervention of a lowered assessment of ability. In accord with this thinking, it has been pointed out that, compared to members of majority groups, the self-esteem and sense of their own efficacy of people from minorities, including African Americans, who are the object of prejudice and discrimination, are not very low (Crocker and Major, 1989).

However, because benevolent sexism is not readily perceived as discrimination, it easily breaks through women's psychological defenses (Moya et al., 2007). For example, what if the company proffered to the woman who was not hired in the employment test, 'concern for women' as the reason for not hiring her? In that instance it becomes difficult for the woman to attribute the negative result of not being hired to the company's employment criteria (an external factor). The reason proffered by the company contains absolutely no words that contain a nuance that is negative towards women. In situations like this, where external attribution is difficult, it is relatively likely that the cause of the unfavorable treatment will be attributed to internal factors (one's own ability, for example) (Croker et al., 1991). This means the woman acknowledging her own lack of competence, and contributes indirectly to maintaining and perpetuating the male-dominant society. However, the woman does not notice the cunning trap that benevolent sexism has laid. Women therefore even now accept benevolent sexism without hesitation and continue to contribute to maintaining the harmful social system that is the male-dominant society.

A social system that supports benevolent sexism

It is important not to forget the social system as a factor that enhances the harmful effects of benevolent sexism, just as in the very strong connection identified by Allport (1954) between maintaining prejudice and the social system. Many of Japan's social systems and practices inherently encourage the assumption of traditional gender roles (Dainiji Danjo Kyōdō Sankaku Kihon Keikaku: Gender Equality Bureau, 2005) and the possibility cannot be denied that these have encouraged sexism and the maintenance of the sexist gender gap. Preferential taxation treatment typified by the spousal exemption is one example.

The spousal exemption is a preferential system that alleviates the tax paid by the primary income earner of a household (the man) where the income of their spouse (the woman) does not reach a stipulated level. If a woman works in a regular job and her income exceeds the upper limit, this exemption will not apply, and the female spouse must also then pay tax commensurate with her income. That is, if—in the pursuit of high income—a woman works in a regular job, not only is she not able to participate in the benefits of the spousal exemption, she is subject to double torture through being levied tax on her own income. In other words, considering the major burden on women from housework, for a woman to work full time is highly disadvantageous behavior. As invited by such a taxation system, many women see marriage and childbirth as opportunities to terminate their working career and either become homemakers, or in many cases return to work in an atypical job (Statistics Bureau, 2001). Specifically, among women with a spouse, only 20.3 per cent of the total work in a regular job, and it is apparent that even in the modern egalitarian society they remain in the minority. Further, another report identified that more than half of women who work are engaged in an atypical job (Statistics Bureau, 2007). Hence, it is incontrovertible that even now the social system continues to follow exactly the same vector as benevolent sexism, seeking to maintain the male-dominant society. It is also possible that this type of social system became a social structure factor that encourages women to depend on male protection and assistance. In reality, it has been identified that married women who engage in traditional gender roles for economic reasons place high value on benevolent sexism such as economic assistance and protection from their male spouse, and demonstrate an accepting attitude toward benevolent sexism (Moya et al., 1999; Yamamoto and Ohbuchi, 2011). It is possible that social policies which support a male-ascendant society, in combination with micro level effects like benevolent sexism, niggle at women's sense of dependence and encourage stronger legitimization of the status quo and reproduction of inequality.

Conclusion

Benevolent sexism is a by-product created by people to maintain a social system based on traditional gender roles. It is not only men, thereby able to protect their high socio-economic status, who contribute to maintaining the status quo. Women held down at lower status by traditional gender roles, also display a positive attitude and are accepting of benevolent sexism (Barreto and Ellemers, 2005) and may contribute to maintaining that status quo (Jost and Kay, 2005). The fact that benevolent sexism, with its assistance and protection, is perceived as attractive behavior, is the greatest factor in motivating women to maintain the system (Moya et al., 2007), but that is not all. If women object to the status quo, they face the threat of becoming a target of hostile sexism (Fischer, 2006). To avoid this risk, it is possible that women are pushed to maintain the system by the economically rational decision to participate in the benefits of benevolent sexism. In reality, many women in a situation where they could expect to be provided with benevolent sexism have desired its provision (Yamamoto and Ohbuchi, 2010). Focusing on this point opens up new pathways to the problems associated with sexism. The reason being that for a long time it has been claimed that in problems associated with gender, such as discrimination and difference, the cause of inequalities is men (Glick and Fiske, 1999). However, as discussed in this chapter, while not to the same degree as men, women have also had an active role in maintaining inequality.

Glick and Fiske quote Virginia Woolf, the British woman literary writer, when they say "true gender equality will happen only when 'womanhood has ceased to be a protected occupation.'" In using this quote, they are invoking ambiguous sexism and commenting on the role of women in maintaining sexism. If inequality between the sexes is to be remedied, we must take the next step. It cannot be expected that it is possible to achieve perfect gender equality only through implementation of affirmative action policies and lobbying men, as has been done so far. Bearing in mind that expectations of benevolent sexism heighten women's motivation to maintain the status quo, it is also important to work on women to not expect assistance behavior, such as from benevolent sexism, and to not depend on it.

8 Strategies for Coping with Discrimination: How Do Disadvantaged Group Members Explain Their Experience of Discrimination?

Nobuko Asai

Recently in Japan, members of groups that were formerly considered to be disadvantaged have become able to actively participate in society, as a result of the development of new laws and the government's social support programs. However, social disparities and prejudices have not been eliminated completely; even today, members of several social groups (e.g., women, physically or mentally handicapped persons, patients with specific diseases, such as HIV or leprosy, ethnic or racial minorities, foreign residents in Japan, and the minority group known as '*Dowa*') are prone to suffer unreasonable disadvantages or discrimination in broad aspects of social life, including employment, housing, education and medical services (e.g., Kōsei Rōdō Shō [Ministry of Health, Labor and Welfare], 2010; the United Nations Committee on the Elimination of Racial Discrimination, 2001). Prejudice against these groups can also lead to disadvantages and problems in terms of personal relationships, such as neglect, exclusion, disregard or violence by others.

This chapter will discuss, based on empirical evidence, how members of disadvantaged groups cope with discrimination. We especially focus on the causal explanation process about discriminatory events, i.e., the causal attribution strategy, which is a strategy for coping with discrimination at the cognitive level. Causal explanation for events is closely related with the state of mental health of disadvantaged group members. In the following, I will first review theoretical findings and empirical studies accumulated in Western countries where active research has been conducted on strategies to cope with discrimination. This will be followed by a further discussion based on data from our recent research on disadvantaged groups in Japanese society.

Converting the image of victim: From weak and passive beings to resilient and active agents

Members of groups with low social status are likely to be targets of discrimination at the individual level as well as the group level and are susceptible to negative personal and economic treatment. I summarize the psychological impacts of discrimination on a target before entering a specific discussion of the process for coping with discrimination.

A number of theories proposed in the area of social psychology predict that experiences of discrimination undermine the target's mental health (Crocker and Major, 1989). Cooley's (1902) 'looking glass self' theory is representative of these theories, arguing that people use the others' behavior toward themselves as a clue to infer how they are recognized and evaluated by others and then reflect these inferences in their self-concept. According to this theory, discrimination can be expected to develop negative self-concepts and self-evaluations of the targets of discrimination and thus deteriorate their mental health. Social acceptance by others is essential for human life and is a basic human need (Maslow, 1954). The sociometer hypothesis and related studies (e.g., Baumeister and Tice, 1990; Leary, Tambor, Terdal and Downs, 1995) have pointed out that once a person experiences discrimination and no longer feels socially accepted, the victim may experience low self-esteem or negative emotions such as anxiety that alerts him/her of a potential crisis affecting his/her survival.

Interestingly, however, contrary to the theories generally accepted in social psychology, empirical studies on psychological aspects of disadvantaged group members have demonstrated that they do not always suffer mental damage. For instance, despite the fact that women generally work under employment conditions inferior to those for men and bear a greater load of housework than do men, most women feel as satisfied and happy with their lives as do men (Crosby, 1982). It has also been shown that, while members of disadvantaged groups, such as those with mental illness, African-Americans and lowest-income groups, experience discrimination in their daily lives (e.g., low wages, housework and neglect), they often report positive levels of well-being (Diener and Diener, 1996). Furthermore, Crocker and Major (1989) reviewed studies on members of a number of disadvantaged groups, including ethnic minorities, women, people with disabilities, and homosexuals, and revealed that their self-esteem is not lower but, in fact, often higher than that of members of higher-status groups. These findings demonstrate that members of disadvantaged groups are not weak or passive beings who suffer mental damage from discrimination but are resilient or active agents who have the potential to protect their mental health from the negative impacts of discrimination (Major, Quinton and McCoy, 2002). This change in the understanding of disadvantaged group members or, more specifically, the conversion from the image of weak and passive victims to that of resilient and active agents, prompted studies of strategies used for coping with discrimination in Western countries.

Explanation of discriminatory events and mental health

In this section, the issues of how members of disadvantaged groups maintain their mental health despite often suffering negative treatments in their daily life from members of higher-status groups are discussed. Causal attribution studies have shown that the impact of a certain event on a person's mental health is not determined in an unambiguous manner by the nature of the event but is moderated by the person's explanation of the cause of the event (i.e., their construction of the psychological meaning and value of the event; e.g., Bradley, 1978; Stevens and Jones, 1976). For instance, if a person attributes his/her low salary to poor ability, the low salary will represent an event signifying his/her poor ability, which would undermine their self-confidence in ability and self-esteem. By contrast, if the person blames his/her low salary on the poor economy, the low salary will represent an event signifying the economic conditions of the society at large, which reduces perceptions of self-responsibility for the low salary and enables him/her to maintain self-esteem and positive self-regards. Human beings are motivated to maintain and improve his/her self-esteem and, in terms of causal attribution, tend to cognitively construct an explanation that will satisfy this motivation (e.g., Bradley, 1978; Weiner, 1979; Zuckerman, 1979). The key to disadvantaged group members' successful maintenance of their mental health at high levels seems to lie in the causal attribution strategies used when faced with negative events.

Self-protective causal attribution strategy: Whether or not to attribute negative treatments to discrimination

Regarding disadvantaged group members' causal attribution strategies to maintain their mental health, the discount hypothesis proposed by Crocker and Major (1989) has been widely accepted in the field of social psychology. Crocker and Major predicted that disadvantaged group members maintain positive self-esteem and self-image by actively attributing negative treatments to discrimination. The discount hypothesis argues, for instance, that a woman who was rejected as a result of an employment examination can maintain her mental health by constructing an explanation that she was rejected due to the examiner's prejudice against women and nothing was wrong with her. The discount hypothesis regards attributing a negative treatment to discrimination as an attribution of the cause to others' prejudices, or to factors other than themselves (i.e., external attribution), consistent with a perspective widely accepted in conventional attribution studies. In other words, as its name suggests, the discount hypothesis takes the position that a person can discount perceived responsibility for negative events by recognizing the influence of discrimination, an external factor, as the plausible cause of the events, and thus maintain the view that there is no problem with his/her personal factors, such as ability or character (Kelley, 1972; Major et al., 2002). Furthermore, in their argument on the discount hypothesis, Crocker and Major (1989) and Major et al. (2002) have pointed out that disadvantaged group members can maintain their self-esteem by actively suspecting that prejudice and discrimination is the cause of the negative treatment, even if the treatment actually reflects personal or internal factors (such as ability or effort).

Empirical studies have consistently demonstrated that where a perpetrator obviously has discriminatory beliefs, members of disadvantaged groups have a tendency to attribute a negative treatment to discrimination. These results support the discount hypothesis. However, if there is no information on whether or not the perpetrator has such beliefs, then they do not usually attribute their treatment to discrimination (e.g., Dion and Earn, 1975; Major, Quinton and Schmader, 2003). If, as predicted by Corker and Major (1989), the attribution of a negative treatment to discrimination maintains one's mental health, members of disadvantaged groups must attribute any negative treatment received to discrimination, regardless of the circumstances or context. Thus, it is difficult to say that the results of empirical studies strongly support the prediction derived from the discount hypothesis.

We consider that this inconsistency between the predictions of the discount hypothesis and the results of some empirical studies lies in the discount hypothesis' oversimplification of the psychological meanings of the attribution to discrimination. We (Asai, 2006; Asai, Karasawa, Kumagai and Kawashima, 2010; Asai, Karasawa and Ohbuchi, 2010) and Schmitt and Branscombe (2002a) have pointed out that, considering the social situation surrounding disadvantaged group members and their self-conceptions, the attribution of a negative treatment to discrimination does not simply signify attribution to prejudiced others. When disadvantaged group members attribute a negative treatment from others to discrimination, they are also recognizing that the treatment is in part caused by an unjust social system and their negative social identity (i. e., membership of a disadvantaged group). From this perspective, attributions to discrimination may not necessarily work to maintain the disadvantaged group members' mental health. Proponents of this view argue that, contrary to the discount hypothesis, it is important for disadvantaged group members to cognitively avoid acknowledging that they suffered discrimination at all, in order to maintain their mental health. This perspective is known as the 'minimizing hypothesis'.

As we can see, there are two competing hypotheses concerning strategies of disadvantaged group members for protecting their mental health. The points of difference between these hypotheses lies in the psychological meanings and effects of the attribution to discrimination. Below this issue is discussed from the viewpoint of disadvantaged group members to demonstrate the negative impact of the attribution to discrimination on mental health and to clarify problems with the discount hypothesis based on our perspective. This will be followed by a reconsideration of causal attribution strategies that contribute to maintain the mental health of disadvantaged group members.

Attributions to discrimination as attributions to society

If a person experiences discrimination from someone who is the only person with specific prejudice against the target's group, the target is able to prevent any further discrimination by avoiding this particular person. However, prejudices are deeply rooted and commonly shared within a society. Furthermore, prejudice is widely embedded in social systems in the form of norms and customs (e.g., 'a woman should leave her job when she marries'). Disadvantaged group members tend to be well aware of the nature of prejudice (e.g., Kobrynowicz and Branscombe, 1997; Shelton, Richeson and Salvatore, 2005). More specifically, for the members of disadvantaged groups, an individual who (or a group which) directly discriminates against him/her works to ensure the existence of socially shared prejudice and unjust social systems. Hence, the victim's acknowledgment of negative treatments as discrimination leads to a recognition that socially shared prejudices and unjust social systems will permanently affect him/her across all circumstances (i.e., regardless of the specificity of the other party or of the place, context, issue, etc.) and at any time. Even if the victim has no further encounters with the person who once treated him/her negatively, his/her attribution of the discrimination to prejudice leads to expectation that he/she will be the target of further negative treatment (i.e., discrimination) from other people and groups (i. e., expectation of future failure; Weiner, 1979). This expectation should induce negative emotions such as a sense of helplessness and resignation, and threatens disadvantaged group members' mental health (Asai, 2006; Branscombe, Fernández, Gómez and Cronin, in press; Weiner, 1979). Furthermore, recognition that the shared beliefs and social systems cannot be changed by their personal efforts is expected to damage their sense of control and self-efficacy (Ruggiero and Taylor, 1997).

Thus, considering the social situation in which the members of disadvantaged groups live, explaining a negative treatment from others as discrimination means that the treatment is attributed to three factors: the prejudiced agent (whether an individual or organization) who gave the treatment; people who share discriminatory beliefs; and discriminatory social systems. It follows that a disadvantaged group member's explanation that he/she suffered discrimination damages his/her mental health because it has the latter two psychological meanings as well as the first one. Schmitt, Branscombe, Kobrynowicz and Owen (2002) and Kobrynowicz and Branscombe (1997), for example, have shown that the perceived discrimination against women undermined psychological well-being among women. In contrast, perceptions of discrimination were unrelated to well-being among men. These findings support the hypothesis that the perception of discrimination harms the mental health of disadvantaged groups by promoting perceptions not only of the existence of prejudiced others but also of the disadvantaged social situations of one's group.

Needless to say, as the discount hypothesis (Croker and Major, 1989) argues, if the disadvantaged group members explains that negative treatment he/she received can be attributed to external factors (i.e., prejudiced others and unjust social systems), it is then expected that his/her own responsibility for the events is considered to be low by the target, which will help to maintain their self-esteem, at least in terms of abilities. Consistent with this argument, Ruggiero and Taylor (1997) have demonstrated a positive correlation between the degree of attribution to discrimination and the level of state self-esteem in the performance domain. However, as long as the disadvantaged group members are in a social environment in which their group is discriminated against, it will remain difficult to receive fair evaluations or treatment (Branscombe et al., in press; Kobrynowicz and Branscombe, 1997; Schmitt and Branscombe, 2002a). Even if the disadvantaged group members maintain confidence in their own ability or qualifications, failure to feel that society will fairly evaluate the ability will, conversely, pose a strong threat to the sense of controllability and self-efficacy. In other words, it is predicted that the disadvantaged group members' capacity to maintain self-esteem in their ability—which is a psychological benefit of the attribution to discrimination—will be offset by the following psychological costs of the attribution strategy: recognition of the unjust social environment; and the resulting loss of a sense of controllability and self-efficacy. Therefore, the attribution to discrimination serves to maintain the mental health as predicted by Croker and Major's (1989) discount hypothesis, only if the discrimination against the own group is not widespread in people or the social system.

Attributions to discrimination as attributions to group membership

Schmitt and Branscombe (2002a) have pointed out that external factors (i.e., individuals directly discriminating against the victim, shared discriminatory beliefs, and discriminatory social systems) are not sufficient causes of discrimination. Certainly, it is the prejudiced person or society that discriminates. However, discrimination is triggered by (conditioned upon) the group membership of its target (Schmitt and Branscombe, 2002a; Major et al., 2002). If the person were not a member of a vulnerable group, he/she would seldom suffer discrimination. Therefore, when the target explains negative treatment from others as discrimination, he/she must admit that such treatments were triggered by his/her own negative or disadvantaged group membership.

A person's group membership, i.e., the disposition, social status and history of the person's group is an important aspect of the self-concept (i.e., social identity; Hogg and Abrams, 1988; Tajfel and

Turner, 1979), comparable to his/her ability and personality. Thus, consciousness that one's group membership functions as a stigma that triggers discrimination poses a threat to his/her positive self-regards and prompts emotional reactions, such as anxiety or desolation (e.g., Baumeister and Tice, 1990; Leary et al., 1995). In fact, Ruggiero and Taylor (1997) have shown that when making an attribution to discrimination, disadvantaged group members experienced a threat to their state self-esteem in the social dimension.

Consistent with the above argument, Schmitt and Branscombe (2002b) have also demonstrated by experimental study that the attribution to discrimination has a meaning of self-blaming. In their experiment, undergraduate students were asked to read a scenario in which their request for a closed class was rejected by a professor of the opposite sex (Schmitt and Branscombe, 2002b, Experiment 1). They used two types of scenarios in this experiment. In one scenario, the professor rejected all students who requested to add a closed class ('Everyone excluded' condition). In the other scenario, the professor systematically rejected all of the students of the participants' gender, including the participant, but accepted the requests of about 10 students of the other gender ('Prejudice' condition). The most plausible explanation for the former scenario is that the participants were rejected due to purely external factors, such as the professor's personal disposition or trait. As for the latter scenario, the most plausible explanation is that the students were rejected due to the professor's prejudice against the opposite sex. After reading a scenario, participants were asked to complete measures of the causal explanation of their rejection. The results indicated that, the extent to which participants thought the rejection was due to something about the professor did not differ by condition. However, in the 'Prejudice' condition, participants were more likely to attribute the rejection to something about themselves. These results indicate that an attribution to purely external factors and an attribution to prejudice (= attribution to discrimination) have different psychological meanings from one another. The latter case does partly have a meaning of an internal attribution, that is attributions to themselves.

From these theoretical arguments and empirical studies, the following conclusion is drawn: for a member of a disadvantaged group, explaining negative treatment from others as discrimination means being forced to acknowledge their involvement (i.e., their group membership) in the evaluation, which, as such, poses a threat to their social identity.

The discount hypothesis also pointed out that an attribution to discrimination entails an attribution to their own group membership as an internal factor (Crocker and Major, 1989; Major et al., 2002). However, advocates of the discount hypothesis have focused only on the meaning of the attribution to discrimination as an external factor, i.e., the attribution to prejudiced others. As we have seen, group membership plays an important role as a trigger of discrimination against an individual and is an important element of one's self-concept. We therefore cannot ignore the fact that an attribution to discrimination means an attribution to group membership.

Self-protective attribution strategy of disadvantaged group members

For members of disadvantaged groups, attributing a negative treatment to discrimination means both of the following: (i) an attribution of the cause to three external factors, i.e., the prejudiced actor, people who share the prejudice, and unjust social systems; and (ii) an internal attribution to their own group membership. Considering these components, it is predicted that the perception of discrimination will damage the target's mental health, by promoting their awareness of people who, and social systems which, reject them and their group, and of the fact that he/she is a member of the vulnerable group. Consistent with this prediction, Schmitt, et al. (2002) and Goodwin, Williams and Carter-Sowell (2010) have shown that disadvantaged group members' self-esteem and self-valuation were threatened by attribution of their experience of exclusion to discrimination. Similarly, Herek, Gillis and Cogan (1999) have demonstrated that, when a person suffers physical violence, they are more likely to show symptoms of depression, anxiety or PTSD if they perceive the violence to be due to prejudice against their sexuality (i.e., a hate crime) than if they perceives it to be unrelated to prejudice (i.e., an ordinary crime). As predicted by the minimizing hypothesis, it is useful for members of disadvantaged groups to avoid explaining negative events as discrimination to prevent damage to their positive social image and self-regards.

Vorauer and Kumhyr (2001) have shown that even when an Aboriginal Canadian felt uncomfortable communicating with a White Canadian with high prejudices, they did not recognize the other as prejudiced. This indicates that if a member of a disadvantaged group encounters another person's negative behavior, he/she avoids labeling the behavior as discrimination. Similarly, Crosby (1984) and Taylor,

Wright, Moghaddam and Laloned (1990) have shown that women and immigrants reported that they had not had much experience of discrimination against themselves personally on the basis of their group membership, despite recognizing that their groups were discriminated against. These results are consistent with the arguments that members of disadvantaged groups use a strategy to maintain their mental health by cognitively refusing to acknowledge any discrimination against themselves, even when they are actually discriminated against in their daily life.

With more meticulous insight, the psychological costs involved in an attribution to discrimination may change depending on the controllability of group membership.[1] For instance, if a person suffers discrimination due to their group membership and if the group membership is changeable, then they can escape the influence of discriminatory people or social systems by moving to another group. Additionally, even if the perception of discrimination against one's group reduces the value of their own group membership and damages their social identity, people are able to achieve a positive social identity by moving to another high-status group. Thus, the degree to which one's mental health is affected by their attribution to discrimination is smaller when the group membership is controllable than otherwise. It is also likely that the strategy of avoiding an attribution to discrimination is used less often in this case. However, it is usually difficult for members of disadvantaged groups to change their group membership by personal effort, since the membership in most disadvantaged groups is defined by permanent, personally uncontrollable factors and characteristics, such as gender, race or medical history (Goffman, 1963; Fine and Bowers, 1984). Furthermore, it is not easy to move from a disadvantaged group to a higher-status group. It can be predicted that members of disadvantaged groups will generally be susceptible to damage to their mental health as a result of the perception of discrimination against themselves. Therefore, as a strategy to minimize such damage, members of disadvantaged groups are likely to avoid the perception of such discrimination.

Cognitive coping with discrimination among Japanese

The discussion thus far has been based on the results of Western theoretical and empirical studies. This section will discuss whether or not the predictions drawn from Western studies apply to members of disadvantaged groups in Japan.

As mentioned at the beginning of this chapter, efforts to develop laws and systems to eliminate discrimination in order to realize a fair society are currently under way in Japan, including the enforcement of the Equal Employment Opportunity Law for Men and Women, the abolition of the Leprosy Prevention Law, and discussions concerning the enactment of a law prohibiting discrimination against people with disabilities. However, the social power of groups with traditionally low social status still remains less than higher-status groups. Take women, for example. As of 2009, the proportion of women in managerial positions in Japanese companies is only 10.2 per cent, suggesting that it is mainly men who construct and change corporate systems and cultures (Sōmu Shō [Ministry of Internal Affairs and Communications], 2009). In politics, women's participation has not progressed much; women comprise only 11 per cent of the members (52 of the 480 members) of the House of Representatives and 18 per cent (44 of the 242 members) of the House of Councillors (as at the end of July 2010). Many other disadvantaged groups are in a similar situation. It is therefore easy to imagine that if members of disadvantaged groups in Japan suffer discrimination and acknowledge the discrimination inherent in Japan's social systems, they will have a sense of uncontrollability, or a sense of helplessness over their own rights, share in social distribution, evaluations, etc., and will feel that their future aspirations are threatened.

It is widely believed that, compared to Westerners, Japanese people tend to define themselves by focusing on their relationships with others, such as social roles and group memberships (Kitayama, 1998). Cousins' (1989) has shown that, when Japanese and Americans were asked to write 20 statements about themselves, the Japanese participants' statements contained a higher percentage of descriptions of their group membership or the social categories that they belonged to than the American participants' statements. In particular, an analysis of the five sentences picked out by each participant as the most important statements about themselves found that 27 per cent of the Japanese participants' statements were of this type, compared to only nine per cent for the American participants. Considering the tendency that Japanese people pay more attention to their relationships with others, they are likely to be more susceptible to threats to their self-concept if they are made aware that their group membership is socially stigmatized than are Westerners.

Based on the arguments above, it is predicted that members of disadvantaged groups in Japan are at least as, if not more, susceptible to damage their mental health due to the perception of discrimination as are Westerners. In other words, we can assume that avoiding the perception of discrimination is an effective strategy for maintaining positive mental health for Japanese people, too.

Empirical study of causal attribution strategies among Japanese people

In this section, we discuss the causal attribution strategies used by the members of disadvantaged groups in Japan and their psychological impact, based on our study (Asai 2006, Experiment 2). The findings of this study are very important not only because the participants were Japanese, but also because the study empirically investigated the association between the self-defense motivation and the causal attribution strategy. Specifically, we introduced comparative conditions in which participants were asked to make an attribution about a negative treatment toward an in-group other and attribution of a positive treatment toward the participant. These attributions would have relatively weak or no negative impacts on participants' mental health and, as such, are unlikely to be influenced by participants' self-defense motivation. By comparison to the causal attributions in comparative conditions, this study attempted to highlight the feature of the disadvantaged group members' causal attribution strategy for coping with a discriminatory treatment.

In an experiment, 204 Japanese female undergraduate students (mean age: 18.51 years) were asked to imagine a specific scenario in which either the participant herself or another woman took a job interview and received a successful or unsuccessful result. After reading a vignette, each participant rated the extent to which they thought the result was due to discrimination / favoritism against women. Then, they also reported the current state of their self-esteem (Heatherton and Polivy, 1991). As shown in Figure 8.1, the causal attribution to discrimination was not increased unless the interviewer was obviously sexist (if the population of biased people in potential interviewers was 5/5, 3/5 and 0/5, $M = 5.89 > M = 4.65$, and $M = 3.90$, respectively). In other words, even if the possibility that the interviewer was sexist was moderate, the degree to which participants attributed their own failure to discrimination remained at the same level as in the case where the interviewer was unlikely to be sexist. In contrast, as for the causal attribution of another woman's failure, even if it was unclear whether or not the interviewer was sexist, participants attributed the result to

Figure 8.1: Mean attribution ratings as a function of the target, outcome and the population of biased people in potential interviewers

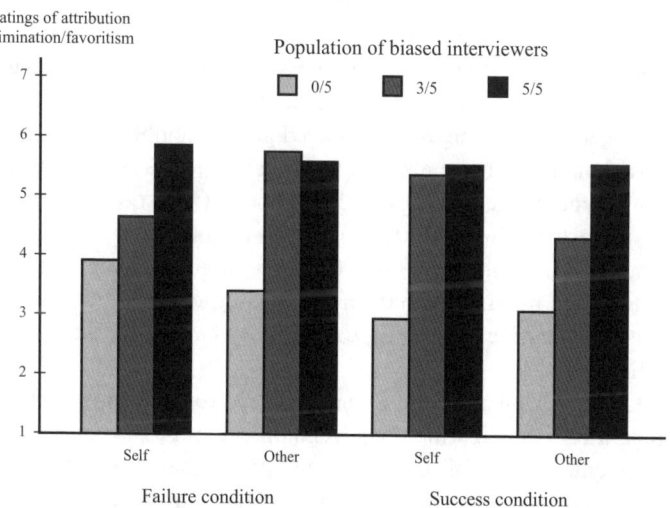

Note: The population of biased interviewers was controlled by varying the number of persons who tend to give discrimination/favoritism to women included in the five male potential interviewers. We described that one of the five interviewers conducted the interview of the protagonist in the scenario.

discrimination to the same degree as in the case where the interviewer was undoubtedly sexist (if the population of biased people in potential interviewers was 5/5, 3/5 and 0/5, $M = 5.77$, $M = 5.57 > M = 3.40$, respectively). These results suggest that female participants avoided the perception of themselves as a target of discrimination, as indicated by: the nonlinear association between the objective likelihood of suffering discrimination and the degree of the attribution of their own result to discrimination; and a comparison between the causal attribution pattern of their own result and that of another woman's result. Furthermore, although attribution to discrimination and that to favoritism both represent a causal attribution to interviewer's biased beliefs against the group, participants were more willing to attribute their own success to favoritism towards women, in contrast to their tendency to avoid attribution to discrimination[2] (if the population of biased people in potential interviewers was 5/5, 3/5 and 0/5, $M = 5.55$, $M = 5.40 > M = 2.98$, respectively). These results indicate that disadvantaged group members have some psychological mechanisms intended to deny the influence of discrimination on themselves. In addition, this study showed a negative association between perceptions of discrimination and state self-esteem on the social dimension ($r = -.35, p < .05$). Another study using almost identical scenarios demonstrated that an attribution to discrimination damages a person's sense of control (Asai, 2006; Asai, 2009, Experiment 1). Our results provide further evidence that avoiding an attribution to discrimination is effective at maintaining disadvantaged group members' mental health.

Although further empirical analysis of groups other than women is warranted, the findings outlined above (Asai, 2006, Experiment 2) suggest that, as with their Western counterparts, disadvantaged group members in Japan also attempt to maintain their mental health in the face of discrimination, by strategically belittling the fact that the negative treatment was actually caused by discriminatory beliefs.

Our experiment (2006, Experiment 2) provides another important insight for investigating the psychological processes for maintaining the mental health of disadvantaged group members: the existence of a cognitive bias (i.e., Self-Other Discrimination Discrepancy: hereinafter collectively referred to as "SODD") due to which these members tend to avoid attributing negative treatment received by themselves to discrimination while tending to attribute negative treatment received by others in their in-group to discrimination. The bias is also observed in our previous experiment (2006; Experiment 1). This cognitive bias between attribution of negative treatment of oneself and that of in-group others provide relative gratification and enhancement of the self-esteem based on comparison with others in the same group (Taylor and Brown, 1988), such as 'You are a target of discrimination, but I'm not'. This finding gives rise to a new hypothesis: that members of disadvantaged groups maintain and enhance their mental health not only by avoiding an attribution to discrimination but also by assuming that they are less likely to be a target of discrimination than others in their group.

Social impacts of avoiding perception of being a target of discrimination

If we focus on its psychological effects, the avoidance of an attribution to discrimination seen in disadvantaged groups can be regarded as a self-protective causal attribution strategy. We next try to elucidate the impact of members' avoidance of the perception of being a target of discrimination on the disadvantaged group or society.

When a person receives negative treatment from another person due to discrimination, the target tends to refrain from taking any immediate reactions against the discriminatory person if they do not feel the treatment to be discrimination (Ruggiero and Taylor, 1997). This is also considered to result in lack of awareness of the discrimination and lack of a sense of ownership in the discrimination against their own group, as well as in poor commitment to collective actions intended to eliminate the discrimination (Ruggiero and Taylor, 1997). Moreover, Asai (2006) has shown that members of a disadvantaged group not only avoid the perception that they have been discriminated against, but they also tend to perceive that other members of their group have been discriminated against. This bias in the perception of discrimination suffered by oneself and others provides a feeling of gratification to people as compared to other members of their in-group. The person's intention and action to improve the current status of the in-group is suppressed when people feel such satisfaction with their own status or situation (Foster and Matheson, 1999).

Thus, it is predicted that the avoidance of an attribution to discrimination works to maintain the prejudice and discrimination within the society and social system. In other words, even though the avoidance of acknowledging discrimination helps to maintain the mental health of individual members of a disadvantaged group, it ironically results in the maintenance of the social environment that threatens their mental health and standards of living. Seen from the perspective of its influence on society, the avoidance of an attribution to discrimination cannot be regarded as the best strategy for disadvantaged group members. Rather, without a correct understanding of the impacts of discrimination on themselves, members of disadvantaged groups will not be able to eliminate prejudice and discrimination against their group and ensure a truly stable social life and mental health.

Disadvantaged group members' mere perception of discrimination against themselves will not always result in their active response to discrimination. Activities opposing discrimination involve the risks of giving a negative impression to others, such as being overly sensitive or emotional, or of seeking retaliation. It has been shown that these psychological costs involved in active behavior against discrimination leads to people avoiding any expression of experiences of discrimination, much less protesting against it (e.g., Asai and Karasawa, 2009; Swim and Hyers, 1999). Furthermore, as has been repeatedly discussed in this chapter, the perception of being a target of discrimination is likely to have a negative impact on the mental health of the victim. In order to promote a tranquil social life and stable mental health for disadvantaged groups, it is necessary to find a strategy that will promote taking action against discrimination as well as maintaining their mental health.

Conclusion and future directions

Individual members of a disadvantaged group are likely to be targets of prejudice and often suffer discrimination. It has been argued that these individuals attempt to maintain their mental health through two different cognitive processes. Figure 8.2 is a diagram of the relationship between these processes and the mental health of disadvantaged group members.

The first process of the cognitive strategy of maintaining mental health is the avoidance of acknowledging the discrimination one faces (Figure 8.2, the left column). Acknowledgment that one has been the target of discrimination threatens positive self-regards by prompting a perception of one's own stigmatized group membership. Acknowledging discrimination also reminds the disadvantaged group members of the fact that they are evaluated and (mis-) treated by others who share discriminatory beliefs against their group as well as by discriminatory social systems, and can result in a loss of their sense of control and expectation of future failures. Disadvantaged group members would protect themselves from these psychological costs by avoiding the recognition of discrimination. While psychological costs involved in recognizing discrimination may vary from culture to culture, it is likely that the aforementioned cognitive strategy for coping with discrimination is common to all cultures.

We would also have to pay attention to the fact that identification of the cause of a negative event is important for maintaining mental health. When disadvantaged group members cannot subjectively identify the cause of the negative treatment by others, it is difficult for them to expect or control the others' treatment and evaluations that may be given in the future. Lack of a sense of predictability and control can make one feel helpless and lead to maladaptive reactions, damaging one's mental health (e.g., Seligman, 1975; Weiner, 1979). Specifically, in order for

Figure 8.2: Cognitive strategies for coping with discrimination used by members of disadvantaged groups

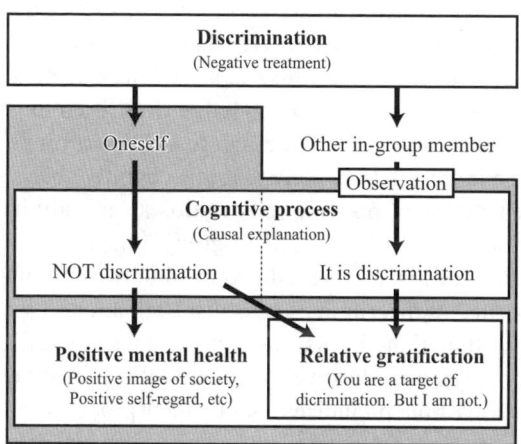

Note: The left column indicates the process used to cope with one's own experience of discrimination. The right column indicates the process of the attribution of discrimination against an in-group other.

disadvantaged group members to truly maintain their mental health, it is necessary not only to avoid an attribution to discrimination but also to attribute the cause of a negative event to any specific factor. In an experiment demonstrating that disadvantaged group members avoid an attribution to discrimination, Asai (2006) also demonstrated that individuals often attribute the cause of a negative treatment to their personal factors, such as ability and effort. It may be important for their mental health to actively recognize the association between negative treatment and their personal factors in order to maintain a feeling that they might be able to succeed in the future by self-improvement. It may be that personal factors are seen as easier to change than a prejudiced society. There could be other possibilities. Studies on causal attribution of failure have also shown that people can maintain their expectations of future success and their positive self-regards by attributing the cause of their own failure to unstable and temporary factors, such as luck, physical condition or the environment (Weiner, 1979). Disadvantaged group members may also attempt to self-protect by making an attribution to temporary factors. Future studies are needed to investigate the disadvantaged group members' causal attribution strategies against discrimination in detail.

A second process that members of disadvantaged groups use for maintaining their mental health lies in the cognitive bias (i.e., Self-Other Discrimination Discrepancy) in the perception of discrimination received by oneself and others (Asai, 2006, Figure 8.2, the right column). This bias is a tendency of disadvantaged group members to hardly acknowledge their own experience of discrimination, while making it easier to see discrimination against others in the in-group. It is likely that this cognitive bias contributes to the construction of positive self-regards as an individual who is more accepted by the society than in-group others.

If members of disadvantaged groups do not acknowledge their own experience of discrimination as discrimination, it would be not surprising if they thought that their group does not suffer from discrimination anymore. However, members of disadvantaged groups are well-aware of the prejudices against their group even if they feel that they themselves are not a victim of prejudice and discrimination (cf., Crosby 1984; Taylor et al., 1990). The "SODD" cognitive bias may work to remind people of the prejudices and discrimination against their group. For instance, even if a woman does not acknowledge being discriminated against, she confirms that women are discriminated against by her recognition of discrimination against other women. Further studies are necessary to clarify the effects of the "SODD" cognitive bias on the confirmation of discrimination against their group and its psychological impact.

As described above, disadvantaged group members are likely to protect their mental health from the negative impact of discrimination through both: cognitive processes used to cope with personal experiences of discrimination; and causal attribution processes to explain prejudicial treatment against other members of the in-group. While this chapter has focused on cognitive strategies for coping with discrimination, it is necessary that future studies address behavioral coping strategies as well in order to clarify the overall strategies for coping with discrimination that are used by members of disadvantaged groups.

9 Local Cooperation and Social Inequalities

Hiroyuki Hikichi

Much has been said of the breaking down of local communities in contemporary Japan. In the past, local communities such as *chōnai-kai* (neighborhood association) and *jichi-kai* (residents' association) in Japan performed self-governing functions such as public security, public health and protecting the weak, which contributed greatly to the maintenance of the country's living environment. The origin of these local tie-based small social groups can be traced back to the *gonin-gumi* (five-household neighborhood unit) system of the Edo period (1603–1867). Under this system, five or so householders were organized into a group, which became jointly responsible for paying land taxes and mutual surveillance for crime prevention. The shogunate government used this system to control local residents and achieve political stability. The *gonin-gumi* served not only as the lowest branch of administration but also as the unit for providing mutual assistance to residents in arranging marriages and adoptions, farming and petitioning authorities (Nakagawa, 1980). While this system was abolished by the new government of the Meiji period (1868–1912), the activity of mutual aid organizations such as *ujiko shūdan* (shrine parishioner group), *wakamono-gumi* (young men's association) and *chōnai-kai* continued in local communities (Kurasawa and Akimoto, 1990). However, the advance of industrialization and globalization as well as the development of the market economy after the Second World War both increased mobility in local communities and reduced the need of local residents' for mutual aid, weakening the ties between them (Yamashige, 1998).

Yet, many people today believe that local communities must be brought back to life. The nuclearization of the family weakened family relationships in postwar Japan. An increase in the number of elderly people living alone has led to an upsurge of problems such as poverty and solitary death. Local community-based welfare for the elderly appears to be needed in order to support the lives of these people (Kurasawa and Akimoto, 1990). In the old days, residents were acquainted with one another and often knew their neighbor's family composition and lifestyle. Now that residents rarely socialize with each other, people often do not know what kind of life or family their neighbors have. In view of a spate of child abuse cases being reported in the media almost daily, it is important to strengthen the community's mutual surveillance function in order to facilitate early detection of such crimes.

The mutual aid function of the local community cannot be simply or easily replaced by public or private services. Provision of public services imposes a large tax burden on residents and private services can only be provided to those who can pay for them. It is therefore difficult for low-income earners to receive sufficient services.

In order to revive local communities, it is essential to increase exchange between residents. One way to do this is to promote the participation of residents in local events such as neighborhood cleanups. Participants can become acquainted with and feel friendly toward one another.

However, this is not easy in practice. Because community activities incur costs in the form of personal time or labor, people are faced with a conflict, or a social dilemma, between the acquisition of a social benefit (an improved living environment) and the loss of a short-term private benefit before deciding whether to participate or not.

The first objective of this chapter is to theoretically analyze the determinants of intra-community cooperation using a social dilemma structure. The second objective is to examine empirically how intra-community cooperation is influenced by social inequalities that have become problematic in recent years.

Factors of cooperation

This section will discuss the main factors of intra-community cooperation by reference to preceding studies. They can be divided into two categories—the economic factors for the maximization of self-interest and the socio-psychological factors that motivate people toward psychological connection with the local community.

Economic factors

Recognition of costs and benefits
If we assume that people act to maximize their self-interest, then residents can be expected to decide to participate in community ac-

tivities if, after comparing the costs of participation and the benefits of participation, they conclude that the latter will be greater. However, Andō and Hirose (1999) measured the levels of recognized costs and benefits of participation among members of the Japan Youth Ecology League as factors promoting participation in activities such as collecting disposable plates and cutlery at school festivals, conducting environmental surveys at supermarkets and providing environmental education for children and found that benefit recognition was not a significant factor in the participants' decision to participate. Similarly, Hashimoto, Tanishita and Kashima (2003) found that the levels of recognized benefit were the same between the participants and nonparticipants of a participatory town planning project to design a park. These studies demonstrate that benefit recognition is not a major factor in deciding whether to participate in collective action or not.

One possible reason for this is as follows. Collective activities such as community cleanups produce greater results when a large number of residents participate. In other words, the benefit becomes greater than the cost to individual participants when the number of participants reaches a certain level in these activities. Accordingly, residents are more inclined to decide to participate when they can expect a good turnout. However, it is difficult to accurately forecast the number of potential participants when deciding whether to participate in collective action because individuals do not know all of the other members in the case of a large group such as a local community. By contrast, it is relatively easy to assess personal costs such as the time required and transport expenses to the venue. Since people tend to avoid more uncertain choices in their decision making (Ellsberg, 1961), residents are likely to focus on the cost more than the benefit in making the decision to participate.

Personal interests
In the payoff structure of a common social dilemma, the benefit of cooperating is smaller than that of not cooperating. In the case of intra-community cooperation, residents gain the benefit of habitat improvement from participating in a participatory community development project. However, it makes more economic sense not to participate and simply live in the habitat that has been improved by other people's work. In other words, an individual gains a greater benefit if he or she is the only person who chooses not to cooperate.

However, the payoff structure varies between individuals who are faced with an issue. In the above example, those who are unlikely to be saddled with some direct burdens (such as house relocation) due to the project will not suffer a personal loss regardless of the direction of the project. Therefore it is most economically rational for them not to participate. However, the direction of the project determined by the participatory activity may dramatically change the daily lives of those who are likely to be directly affected by the project in various ways. In this case, the cost of non-participation may be greater than the cost of participation. In other words, residents who have strong interests in the project tend to show an increased desire to participate because their participation in a participatory community project no longer constitutes a social dilemma situation. In fact, Maekawa, Takayama and Rachi (2003) reported that in the case of public involvement-type road planning the rate of participation tended to be higher among residents who operated retail shops along the existing road and landowners along the proposed new road.

One's relationship with the issue must be assessed not only from the perspective of personal interests but also from the perspective of a benefit or loss to society as a whole. According to Andō and Hirose (1999), one of the motivating factors for involvement in conservation groups is the recognition that current environmental problems will take their toll on future generations. Lubell, Zaharan and Vedlitz (2007) found that participants in the fight against global warming were driven by concerns that the problem might adversely affect the entirety of the states in which they lived.

In practice, cooperation for community activities must be sought from a broad range of local residents, including those who have few personal interests in the issue. It is possible that these people are not motivated to participate because of their perception of the cost involved. In this case, it is important to make them aware of how the issue will impact on present society as a whole or how it will affect future generations.

Recognition of the effectiveness of activity
While it is important for people to assess their personal interests in the issue accurately, it is also important in achieving intra-community cooperation that they believe that they can resolve the issue by themselves. Cocking and Drury (2004) reported that participants' confidence in the effectiveness of action and their active involvement were strongly correlated in the case of a campaign against road construction. Manzo and Weinstein (1987) demonstrated that active members of community groups involved in conservation movements

strongly recognized the effectiveness of their own activities. As mentioned earlier, it is difficult for individuals trying to decide whether to participate in collective action to assess the benefits that they may be able to derive from participating. However, they can be more certain about acquiring some benefit if they can strongly believe that community action is effective in resolving the issue. And they are motivated to participate when they estimate that the benefit will outweigh the cost of participation.

While the recognition of the effectiveness of action can be a determinant of participation in campaigns that can produce results in a relatively short period of time such as a labor movement, it has been suggested that it may not be a strong promoter of participation in actions that take a long time to produce tangible results such as a peace movement (Andō and Hirose, 1999). The possible reason for this is that people tend to focus more on the cost of participation rather than the benefit and tend to decide not to participate because it is difficult for them to imagine the outcome of an action with a long to medium term perspective for the resolution of the issue. Based on this tendency, the recognition of effectiveness may promote participation in activities that produce immediate results such as local community cleanups but it may not be an important determinant for activities that produce few short-term results such as community planning. The impact of this factor therefore varies depending on the issue in question.

Trust

In a social dilemma situation such as local community action, the benefit to the individual is increased when he or she chooses not to cooperate and simply live in a better environment built by others' cooperation. Everyone wishes to behave in this manner. However, the local environment would deteriorate and everyone would lose if everyone behaved in this manner. Consequently, the actualization of mutual cooperation is the way to maximize one another's self-interest in the long term. In order to actualize this, it is important to build one's sense of trust that others will cooperate and not try to exploit one's participation. In fact, a study of several companies has found that mutual trust is a factor promoting cooperation among employees (Lyon, 2006). Tanishita (2001) reports that one's expectations toward the participation of other residents are an important factor in deciding to participate in community activities.

However, the effect of this factor is considered to be limited. Local community is a large-scale group and individual residents usually do not know all of the other residents. Since it is not easy to put one's trust in strangers, it is difficult to trust that the other residents will participate (Hirose, 2008). For this reason, the cooperation promoting effect of trust is expected to be most potent in the case of small-scale activities in which participants know one another.

Socio-psychological factors

Subjective norms
Subjective norms are the perceived social pressures as to whether one is expected by others to take certain action or not. They are considered to be a major factor in one's decision-making (Hirose, 2008). It has been suggested that this factor even promotes behavior that is not economically rational. For example, it was found that the reason for households to agree to the installation of water saving devices (to the toilet) under the condition of tight water supply was the householder's perception that his/her family expected him/her to take that course of action (Lam, 2006). And those who participate in a boycott campaign against particular corporations were driven by the belief that many other people expected them to join the campaign (Farah and Newman, 2010).

The effect of subjective norms has been reported by a study of residents' participation in local community activities. According to Nonami, Katō, Ikeuchi and Kosugi (2002), the activities of members of a river conservation group such as reducing the use of synthetic detergents at home to maintain water quality and gathering information from local authorities for the appropriate implementation of river management were prompted by their perception that nearby residents and other members regarded these activities as desirable. It is therefore considered that emotional connection with local community is a determinant of people's action.

The more significant the person who expects one to take certain action is, the stronger the effect of subjective norms on one's decision-making. Consequently, those who are connected to a large social network and have close relationships within it are more prone to be strongly influenced by their subjective norms in decision-making. Yet, local community is a large-scale group and cannot be fully covered by individual residents' social networks. This is why the effect of subjective norms varies among individuals depending on the size of their network and the interests of their significant others.

Community commitment

Many researchers have pointed out that a strong commitment to local areas is a common trait among residents who are interested in the local environment and actively involved in community activities (Lewicka, 2005; Manzo and Perkins, 2006; Tanaka, Todoroki, Nakajima and Tawada, 2008, for example). Community commitment entails one's awareness of membership in the local community and attachment to or pride in one's local area.

Many concepts similar to community commitment have also been reported. For example, Kasarda and Janowitz (1974) proposed 'community attachment' as a sense of belonging to the local area or an intention to settle permanently. Hummon (1992) suggests 'sense of place', which entails attachment to and a sense of satisfaction with community. Hidalgo and Hernandez (2001) described these core characteristics as the 'affective bond of people to places', while Proshansky (1978) argued that such an attitude developed as 'place identity' emerged out of one's relationship with the local environment. It is considered that one's attachment and pride develop as one begins to identify with one's local community.

What is the process in which community commitment promotes participation in community activity? Organizational commitment elicits one's awareness of being a member of an organization, that is, group identity. According to Brewer (1979), the realization of a group identity in members promotes intra-group cooperation because they have a sense of psychological closeness to other members and identify collective interests with self-interests. On the other hand, Reicher (1984) argues that members who strongly identify with their group act in compliance with group norms, i.e., cooperative behavior, because they internalize the group norms. These findings suggest that residents with a strong community commitment attach importance to their status as members of local community and choose to behave in an appropriate manner.

I have raised six factors of intra-community cooperation so far and found that their effectiveness is limited by the estimated likelihood of success or the size of community.

How about the effect of community commitment? The rationale behind it can be found in organizational and industrial psychological studies on organizational commitment. Many researchers have studied organizational commitment as the source of employees' attachment to and pride in their company and awareness of being one of its members. Organizational commitment was defined as 'an individual's identification with or involvement in a particular organization' by Porter, Steers, Mowday and Boulian (1974) and it has been found that employees with strong organizational commitment deal with tasks unrelated to their duties in earnest (organizational citizenship behavior) and devote themselves to the organization (Randall, 1990; Becker and Billings, 1993; Lavelle, Brockner, Konovsky, Price, Henley, Taneja and Vinekar, 2009).

Just like organizational commitment, community commitment must promote spontaneous and voluntary cooperation. In recent years, people who contribute to the promotion of local tourism have been given the title *kankō karisuma* (charismatic tourism promoter) and their activities are publicized widely. The *kankō karisuma* did not necessarily have a strong prospect of success or many supporters in the early stages of their activity. Yet, they dedicated themselves to their local communities at their own expense. This indicates that a strong community commitment promotes cooperation even when there is no firm prospect of success (Suminaga, Hatori and Fujii, 2009).

According to Hogg (1992), group cohesiveness arises from the recognition of shared membership of the same group rather than the mere accumulation of social networks between individuals. This means that community cohesiveness is increased when individual members identify strongly with the group even in the absence of strong relationships between them. This suggests that community commitment can promote voluntary cooperation even in a large-scale group such as a local community.

In view of the above, community commitment can be considered a more effective factor among various cooperation promoters in that it can promote cooperation for a wide range of activities.

Factors of community commitment

Community commitment can promote intra-community cooperation but what are its determinants? These factors are divided into three types in the following discussion: personal attributes, environmental factors and social factors.

Personal attributes
Many studies have identified the length (years) of residency as a determinant of community commitment. Mesch and Manor (1998) argue that this is because the size of temporal cost spent in the local

area determines the level of community commitment. Hikichi, Aoki and Ohbuchi (2009) consider that it is because people get to know the positive aspects of their local area and feel proud of it as they reside there longer. However, attachment can be formed even within a short period of residency and attachment may not be formed by people who have negative feelings toward their local community even if they have lived there for many years (Twigger-Ross and Uzzell, 1996). These studies suggest that long-term residency alone does not increase attachment to the local community. In fact, Hikichi et al. (2009) demonstrated that the effect of the length of residency was not particularly great compared with other factors.

Age has also been regarded as a factor relating to community commitment. In fact, Fujikawa (1994) and Lewicka (2010) demonstrated that older residents tended to have a stronger community commitment. However, Mesch and Manor (1998) found that the effect of age was not significant. This suggests that the effect of age is not consistent either. Manabe (1996) and Lewicka (2010) suspect that older residents have generally lived in the community for longer periods and therefore have a stronger community commitment. These findings suggest that the relationship between age and community commitment may be a spurious correlation mediated by the length of residency.

It has been reported that home ownership consistently strengthens community commitment (Takahashi, 1982; Fujikawa, 1994; Brown, Perkins and Brown, 2003; Mesch and Manor, 1998). Because home is a large financial investment in the local area, one's intention to settle down in the area becomes stronger, and as a result one has more opportunities to communicate with neighbors and learn the positive aspects of the local habitat. And purchasing a home increases the length of residency and hence community commitment also intensifies according to the level of associated temporal cost.

Although there have also been studies on the relationship between educational background and community commitment, their findings have been inconsistent. Some studies have found that residents with lower education levels exhibit a stronger community commitment (Takahashi, 1982; Williams, Patterson and Roggenbuck, 1992; Lewicka, 2005). Lewicka (2005) argued that highly educated residents tended not to develop a strong community commitment because they were less likely to settle in one area due to job transfers and they were more committed to their workplace rather than local community. Other studies have found that residents with higher education levels have a stronger community commitment (Taylor,

Gottfredson and Brower, 1985; Mesch and Manor, 1998). Mesch and Manor (1998) reported that the higher the social status of the resident was, the broader his or her social network was within the local community. This suggests that highly educated residents have more social contacts in the neighborhood and through communication with them develop a strong community commitment compared with less educated residents.

Physical environmental factors
A habitat consists of the physical environment and the social environment, both of which have impacts on the formation of community commitment (Hikichi et al., 2009). With regard to the physical environment, Watanabe (2006) has found that safe playgrounds, well-equipped hospitals and kindergartens, and shopping convenience are factors of community commitment. Other factors include the natural environment (Manabe, 1996), well-developed parks, playgrounds and car parks (Mesch and Manor, 1998). By contrast, street graffiti signifying poor public security and dilapidated houses reduce community commitment (Brown et al., 2003). One of the reasons for the effects of these factors on the level of community commitment is that a well-managed physical environment enhances the convenience and comfort of the habitat which increase the life satisfaction level of residents. It is conceivable that residents' self-esteem increases when they recognize the advantages of their local area and their awareness of being community members intensifies (Hikichi et al., 2009). In view of these, factors which reduce residents' life satisfaction and the local area's social value weaken community commitment.

However, there are factors that cannot be explained by the abovementioned mechanism. Lewika (2008) reports that historical heritage is effective for the development of community commitment. Having tourist attractions that receive publicity in the media and famous cultural assets that capture the interest of many people creates pride in the local area which translates to an individual's sense of pride as a member of the local community. Historical heritage is seen to increase residents' community commitment because it symbolizes a high value of the local area (Hikichi, Ohbuchi and Aoki, 2010). Besides these honorable historical assets, it has also been suggested that tragic assets which tell of the scars of past disasters and wars also strengthen residents' community commitment. Hayden (1995) suggests that local industrial heritage promotes an understanding of the historical development of the local area among its residents and enhances their sense of belonging and pride regardless of how widely it is known. According to Devin-Wright and Lyons (1997), historical buildings symbolizing the Irish War of Independence evoke unpleasant feelings such as anger and sadness in the Irish people but at the same time they intensify a sense of belonging to their country. These historical assets do not strongly symbolize a high social value of the local area because they do not help improve the fame of the area or they represent ignominious experiences of the past.

This mechanism has been demonstrated by Hikichi et al. (2010). The historical heritage of the local area not only symbolizes the social value of the area but also reminds residents through historical buildings and ceremonies that their ancestors and past local residents were engaged in the same activities. This sense of commonality with past residents is one of the factors reinforcing community commitment.

Social environmental factors
The intra-community social network is an important social environmental factor for the development of community commitment. Intra-community support networks (Manabe, 1996) and the number of friends living in the neighborhood and the number of times one is invited to their homes and parties (Mesch and Manor, 1998) are promoters of community commitment. Sugimoto, Narumi, Sawaki and Oka (2003) report that new residents become familiar with and develop attachment to the local community through participation in traditional local festivals. These findings suggest that having social ties within the local area is a factor to promote community commitment regardless of the length of residency.

In contrast, poor public security weakens community commitment. Being aware of drug dealings, violence and gang activity in the neighborhood (Brown et al., 2003) and fears of crime (Adams, Rohe and Arcury, 2005) reduce community commitment.

The problem of growing social inequalities, which has been drawing attention in recent years, is also likely to reduce community commitment. While personal possessions such as a house and a car and lifestyle choices such as how to spend a holiday vary according to an individual's economic circumstances, economic inequalities are making consumption patterns more diverse. As a result, residents tend to perceive distances from other residents whose possessions or consumption patterns are very different from their own (Phan, 2008). The increase in psychological distance from others due to economic inequalities may weaken one's sense of unity with or attachment to the local community. In other words, economic inequalities weaken community commitment and hence reduce residents' intentions to cooperate with community activities.

Since there were no preceding studies on the effect of economic inequalities on community commitment, we decided to conduct a social survey by ourselves. A total of 2,400 respondents were randomly chosen from the electoral rolls of Naka Ward (Hiroshima City, Hiroshima Prefecture), Nara City (Nara Prefecture), Sumida Ward (Tokyo), Bunkyō Ward (Tokyo), Aizuwakamatsu City (Fukushima Prefecture) and Matsushima Town (Miyagi Prefecture) (400 respondents from each area). The number of valid responses was 931 (male 415, female 510, unknown 6), the response rate was 38.8 per cent, the average age was 52.8 years (SD = 15.58) and the average length of residency was 27.6 years (SD = 19.00). The survey questionnaire asked respondents to rate their community commitment, sense of relative deprivation in the community and intention to cooperate with community activities (three items each) using a six point scale before asking their personal attributes such as annual household income and education level.

Our analysis of the relationship between the social strata and the sense of relative deprivation in the community found that the sense of relative deprivation was stronger among residents with a lower education level and household income (education, β = -.12, household income, β = -.39, both ps < .01, R^2 = .21). Consequently, social inequalities appear to increase the sense of relative deprivation among community residents. An analysis of the formation mechanism of cooperative intention toward community activities confirmed our hypothesis about the causal relationship (χ^2 = 249.87, p < .01, GFI = .937, CFI = .953), meaning that community commitment is a determinant of cooperation with community activities but it is weakened by the sense of relative deprivation in the community (Figure 9.1). Accordingly, the sense of relative deprivation appears to reduce both community commitment and participatory intention among residents.

Conclusion

This chapter has discussed the determinants of intra-community cooperation with a special focus on the effect of community commitment. While community commitment is considered to be an effective factor in promoting the participation of residents in

Figure 9.1: *The effect of the sense of relative deprivation in the community on community commitment and the intention to participate in community activity*

Notes:
** p < .01.
Observed variables and error variables are omitted.

community activities, the effectiveness may diminish with the growing inequalities in society today.

However, it is suggested by various studies that the physical environment of the local community can sufficiently intensify community commitment as well. Japan's prolonged recession and dwindling public works budgets will make the implementation of large-scale works for infrastructure improvement and development difficult in the future. Nevertheless, we believe that community commitment can be strengthened by utilizing the existing community assets. The utilization of historical heritage is one example. It would be cheaper to maintain and manage the existing local historical assets than redeveloping or developing new facilities. More specifically, local government agencies can provide information about historical heritage through their web pages and other publications so that residents in non-historical heritage areas and relatively new residents can learn the history of their local area. For festivals and other community events, strengthening a sense of commonality with past residents by publicizing the fact that local residents have run and participated in these events throughout the ages is considered to be effective.

10 Pro-social Behavior and Fairness Studies: A Review and Perspective

Toshiaki Aoki

It is necessary for a lot of people to act in pro-social ways to construct a better social environment. However, because most pro-social behaviors bring 'social dilemmas' by simultaneously giving rise to both social benefits and individual losses, even though their importance may be understood, they are not often put into practice. The importance of recycling is, for example, something that most people understand, but few people actually practice. This is because individual costs to segregate trash could be greater than either the social or individual benefits gained from recycling. Meanwhile, however, there are also people who are enthusiastic about recycling. If the main factors separating the behavior of both types of people and the mechanisms involved in recycling behavior could be clarified, then effective policies for promoting recycling could be developed. In other words, if the determinants of and the mechanisms giving rise to pro-social behavior could be established, then this would contribute to resolving social dilemmas through enabling discussion of policies for promoting pro-social behavior. In this chapter, the research regarding cooperative behavior within social dilemmas is reviewed, focusing on the determinants of and mechanisms behind cooperative behavior. Then research devoted to the theoretical analyses of the processes giving rise to cooperative behavior is introduced. Finally, the future prospects of pro-social behavior research are discussed.

Studies on cooperative behavior in public problems and fairness studies

The problem

Public problems raise issues that require cooperation by the people living in the affected area to increase the area's social benefits. This problem is a kind of social dilemma, characterized by its emphasis on residential areas and their participation in local activities such as regional or school events. If the word 'region' is interpreted widely, it would also include activities, such as recycling, which aim to reduce the load on the global environment. The cooperative behavior of individuals towards these types of problems will be examined in terms of both 'social/regional benefits' and 'individual benefits'.

Solutions to public problems have been discussed in field studies such as environmental psychology and urban engineering (civil engineering, architecture and the like).While research in the field of environmental psychology has progressed around the central theme of cooperative behavior in recycling, in the field of urban engineering, research has centered on consensus building in public development projects. Accordingly, after introducing representative studies from both fields, this chapter will consider these studies from the perspective of 'fairness'. Finally, the future prospects of cooperative behavior research are discussed.

Research on pro-environmental behavior

Due to the small amount of research in this field in Japan, this chapter will mainly introduce research that was conducted in the United States and Europe. Cooperative behavior which aims to reduce the burden on the environment, such as recycling behavior, is called pro-environmental behavior. Studies on the determinants of cooperative behavior using actual recycling projects as case studies have revealed that monetary rewards are not sufficient to induce strong cooperative behavior (Thøgersen, 1996) and that the impact of monetary rewards is limited (Porter, Leeming and Dwyer, 1995). At present, although there are no additional studies looking into the efficacy of other types of rewards, earlier studies suggest that rewards are not strong determinants of cooperative behavior.

Aside from rewards, many reports have emphasized the importance of norms and morals as determinants of cooperative behavior (Thøgersen, 1996; Bamberg and Möser, 2007). Norms can be divided into social norms and personal norms. Social norms refer to behavior and standards for decision making that are expected by one's society and social groups. Personal norms refer to behavior and standards for decision making that the individual considers desirable for others and for his or her own group, and as such are practically synonymous with moral consciousness. These morals and norms increase in importance as the costs of cooperative behavior also increase (Andersson and Borgstede, 2010).

The importance of morals and norms is also emphasized in some theories of cooperative behavior. In *Theory of Planned Behavior*, Ajzen (1991) argues that the intention behind behavior is a strong determinant of behavior, and is dependent upon attitudes to behavior (whether it is liked or disliked), perceived behavioral control, and subjective norms. Additionally, the Norm Activation Model (Schwartz, 1977) assumes that an awareness of both the necessity for action and a sense of personal responsibility can activate moral obligations, thus giving rise to altruistic behavior. These ideas have been applied to various cooperative behaviors and verified their validity. Hence it is concluded that morals and norms are indispensible factors for considering the mechanisms of pro-social behavior.

Although Thøgersen's (1994) conceptual model structurally resembles the theory of planned behavior, it is characterized by its explicit consideration of the impact of rewards besides consideration about impacts of morals and norms. That is, this model considers that pro-social behavior is not determined only by morals and norms, but also by public benefits, individual benefits and behavioral costs. This conceptual model has not been empirically verified, but its comprehensive framework is helpful in examining pro-social behavior.

These theories assume that moral obligations are more important factors than rewards in determining one's cooperative behavior regarding public problems such as recycling. Hence, their validity suggests that motives based on morals are more fundamental than utilitarian motives for pro-social behavior. This finding is extremely important in thinking about policies to promote pro-social behavior, because a majority of public policies have been grounded in rational choice theory and public choice theory, both of which are founded upon utilitarian premises. Rational choice theory regards the maximization of expected utility based on monetary rewards as the overriding determinant of behavior, and public choice theory analyzes cooperative behavior in public problems by applying the concepts of rational choice theory. This perspective leads to the conclusion that providing incentives should render people cooperative, but this turns out not to be the case in practice. A prime example of this in Japan is the inspection of the suitability of sites for the disposal of radioactive waste. Under this inspection system, local governments need only provide the national government with local geographical information (without actually considering the construction of a local disposal site) to receive one billion yen (about US$ 8.5 million) in assistance. From a utilitarian perspective, most local governments should be jumping at the chance to receive such funding, but to date, none have done so. This case demonstrates that rewards are not crucial determinants of cooperative behavior. However, because the impact of rewards is nevertheless significant (Hikichi et al., 2006; Thøgersen, 1996), encouraging cooperative behavior appears to require consideration of rewards as well as morals and norms.

Searching for other factors that encourage cooperative behavior, Hikichi, Aoki and Ohbuchi (2006) focused on fair treatment as a primary factor. They analyzed why residents do not participate in meetings to discuss problems and countermeasures in their community; i.e., what are the reasons for non-cooperation? Employing the Group Value Model (Tyler, 1989), they found that in cases where residents have no expectation of fair procedures such as information disclosure and opportunities to voice their opinions, the residents feel that the administration does not respect them, and therefore withhold their cooperation. That is, Hikichi et al. showed that grievances about unfair treatment is a factor that can restrict or limit cooperative behavior every bit as much as negative utilitarian judgments that 'it is not worth it'.

Another study pointed out the importance of group identity, i.e., a sense of unity with one's own group. Ando and Hirose (1999) surveyed members of environmental conservation groups, and found that the social desirability of action and the personal rewards attained through participation heighten volunteers' intentions to act. Importantly, the personal rewards here are not monetary gain but affective, such as pride in group membership or psychological benefits (self-growth or the expansion of friendships). Hence the greater the feeling of pride in one's group is, the greater one's cooperative intent is. Baron reported similar findings (Baron, 2001). Maeda and Hirose (2009) developed this idea even further showing that a strong sense of unity with one's group can enhance cooperative intent for the group. They show that group identity can also be a determinant of cooperative behavior. Although these studies analyze cooperative behavior from other perspectives than the egotism-altruism dimension, considering that the more a sense of solidarity with one's group increases, the more likely one is to perceive group gains as personal, these findings are also understandable within the framework of utilitarianism.

The literature on pro-environmental behavior introduced thus far analyzes cooperative behavior with a relatively low burden as its focus. There are, however, also considerable numbers of public problems that need solutions which have serious burdens, such as relocation or job change. The cooperative behavior accompanying these types of heavy burdens is mostly to be found in large-scale projects that tend to generate tremendous social benefit. Hence, studies into how cooperative behavior accompanied by serious burdens can be promoted are an important issue for future study.

Consensus building studies in public development

There are also numerous Japanese studies on consensus building in public development issues. These studies began with accumulating knowledge about the experiences of consensus building between administrative authorities and citizens. Initially, studies focused on cases in which there were few stakeholders, and which had minor social influence, such as streetscape improvements and participation in community events. However, since the primary emphasis in these studies was the accumulation of practical skills to encourage cooperative behavior, there was little theoretical consideration. Consequently, although there are many case studies, it remains unclear what processes produce particular consequences (see, for example, Ito, 2001).

Later, as the conflict surrounding large development projects was taken up as a serious social problem, the focus of research into consensus building shifted to finding practical techniques for reaching agreement. However, the conventional approach remained strong, and thus the majority of the research has produced case studies without clear theoretical frameworks (see, for example, Yai et al., 2000). At the same time, however, not being bound by any particular theoretical framework, a variety of research perspectives have developed. Aoki and Nakai (2004), for example, analyzed the comments at explanatory meetings for citizens concerning subway developments, and found that if the citizenry possesses basic knowledge about regional planning, citizens' comments can decrease by around 20 per cent, and they are able to spend much more time discussing more important topics. Usuda et al. also found that the time constraints imposed by Japanese administrative systems act as a barrier to reaching agreement (Usuda, Fujimoto, Yamashita, Aoki and Matsuda, 2000). In other words, because of Japan's budgetary system based on single year accounts, at large-scale consensus building processes accompanied by budgetary provisions, it is difficult to achieve agreement within the fiscal year. In such situations, the inability to secure adequate time for discussion due to time pressures could be evaluated as an unfair process. Consequently, serious conflict could occur due to the governmental budgetary system. Thus, studies in this field have been developed for the purpose of improving public developments by discussing the problems from several points of view. The prevalence of such unique studies could be regarded as a feature of research in this field.

The research approach to consensus-building underwent considerable change when public involvement (PI), which had been implemented in the United States, was introduced into Japan. PI is a system to discuss plans and practical direction for public development projects with stake holders, such as land owners, inhabitants, citizens, and environmental groups. Before that, generally speaking, public opinion had not been taken into consideration when determining public policies in Japan. After Yai and Terabe (1996) introduced the PI system from the United States, projects including public involvement increased in Japan. Consequently, the approach to case studies significantly changed and factors for consensus building came to be explicitly discussed. For example, both Matsuda and Ishida (2002) and Maekawa et al. (2002) point out the importance of providing citizens with information for consensus building. However, they do not refer to the theoretical mechanisms of their findings. This change in research interest led to demands for explanation about the consequences of consensus-building along theoretical lines. Accordingly, new research which employs a social psychology framework was inspired in the field of public development. One pioneer of such studies was Fujii, Takemura and Kikkawa (2002).

They had students discuss the locations of rubbish disposal facilities, on the hypothesis that fair procedures would increase satisfaction with policy making. They also conducted psychological experiments manipulating decision making approaches (three ways: lottery, majority rule and discussion) and individual costs (two levels: with and without). The results showed that satisfaction with outcomes was highest in conditions where participants were given opportunities for discussion, and that this impact was strongest in the conditions with the highest cost. Fujii et al. further found that the focus of discussions shifted to social benefits, and that utilitarian motives could be restricted in cases that provide opportunities for discussion.

Fujii (2006) also conducted experiments using college students while manipulating government intentions for disclosing information. In experiments based on the theory that voluntary disclosure of information could increase trust in government (Nakayachi and Watabe, 2005), Fujii established four categories of government motives for openness of information—'voluntary', 'forced', 'utilitarian' and 'undescribed'—and measured trust of government in virtual development projects. The results showed that voluntary openness of information did not necessarily have a significant effect in improving trust. Furthermore, Fujii (2006) also showed that explaining the necessity for projects led to increased levels of trust. Obana and Hirose (2008) also discussed the issue of trust in relation to public developments. They divided trust into two types: trust in the government's intentions and trust in its practical abilities (technical abilities), and showed that fair procedures increase trust regarding intentions. These works are important for the introduction of theoretical approaches and attempts to theorize consensus building processes in the public development field.

Aoki (2007) has constructed the Fairness-oriented Information Processing Model, which combines the Elaboration Likelihood Model (ELM) (Petty and Cacioppo, 1986)—a famous theory for persuasion—with theories in fairness studies, and analyzed stakeholder's psychological processes in forming attitudes regarding public development projects. Under this model, in cases in which stakeholders can feel high levels of self-interest in a project, they form their views of the project after careful consideration of both social and personal benefits. Under those conditions, if fair procedures are employed, then projects are more likely to be seen as valid, and favorable attitudes are more readily formed in deliberations about the project information that has been presented. However, in cases where the information provided is not sufficient and the processes employed are deemed to be unfair, evaluation of project validity does not increase, and negative attitudes are more likely to be formed. In this regard, as with ELM, in cases where stakeholders are not in a normal situation due to something like strong affection, attitudes tend to be formed without deliberation using peripheral information like affection, even though the project has much relevance to stakeholders. Meanwhile, it is assumed that when stakeholders feel that a project has little relevance to them, they also form their attitudes heuristically, on the basis of peripheral information, such as the proponents' trustworthiness and personal impressions of the project. This model was applied to the conflict in the Isawa Dam construction project, and explained the mechanisms by which the opponents' attitudes changed to supportive (Aoki and

Suzuki, 2008). The model and process is discussed in detail in the following section.

Ohbuchi et al. analyzed the influence of the respondents' attributes (demographic variables) on their evaluations of the validity of public development projects (Ohbuchi, Kawashima and Aoki, 2008). The result shows that supporters of the government party at that time, the Liberal Democratic Party (LDP), emphasized project benefits and the government's priorities in decision making and had few concerns about fairness, whereas those who did not support the LDP held quite different views. Ohbuchi et al. also found that compared to low educated people, those with higher education emphasized not only project benefits but also fairness, and reached their evaluations from a variety of perspectives. Their research found that the determinants of attitude formation were dependent on individual attributes, and showed that in public developments affecting a variety of people, it is necessary to have a flexible response which takes account of the circumstances.

There have also been studies with mathematical approaches to consensus building in the public development field. Using game theory, Hatori et al. (2008) describe the process of consensus building among a three-member group of citizens, a third party committee and the government, and analyze the process of the formation of trust in the government. This approach has shown that it is difficult for governments to win the trust of citizens simply by disclosing information via the establishment of a third party committee, and that what is needed is the disclosure of information expressed in plain words. Sakakibara (2006) examined the efficacy of third party mediation for consensus building using experiments based on game theory. He found that when third parties communicated the individual benefits predicted from the present situation to game participants, the participants had an objective understanding of the circumstances in the discussions and were willing to compromise. These studies can be evaluated as favorable for their creation of a clear hypothesis regarding the process of consensus building, and for their description of psychological processes using mathematical formulation.

Yai (2006) has comprehensively reviewed studies on consensus building in public developments, and concluded that the legitimacy of the project plan and of the project process are the conditions governing the acceptance of public development projects. The legitimacy of the project plan, Yai suggests, relies on the public development project being recognized as contributing to improve social welfare. The reasonableness of the goals and of the means for improving social welfare is a primary factor of the legitimacy of a project plan. Yai argues that the legitimacy of the project process lies in the favorability of the process for making judgments about the legitimacy of the development project, and suggests six primary factors in this process: validity, fairness, objectivity, rationality, sincerity, and legality. Yai's summarization has provided a theoretical perspective for the real work of consensus building, thereby making it possible to discuss the pros and cons of the various communication methods used in practice.

More recently, studies have begun to appear that focus on the secondary effects brought by consensus building, such as increases in social capital and commitment to a community (Hikichi et al., 2009). The concerns of consensus building studies are shifting away from building cooperative attitudes to projects towards improving the Quality of Life of citizens via consensus building activities. Such change could be linked to changing social needs caused by factors such as the aging of society and the prolonged recession. The development of these additional studies could be accounted for in terms of people's strong appeals for higher levels of well-being in response to current, austere social circumstances.

Fairness theories and cooperative behavior research

Recently, 'fairness' has become an important key word in studies on pro-environmental behavior and on consensus building. This section is devoted to an attempt to reinterpret these studies using a fairness theory framework. This will be followed by an exploration of the possibilities of constructing a unified theory of cooperative behavior.

Fairness theories

In fairness theory, it is assumed that the fair allocation of resources via the conduct of fair process will be likely to encourage the formation of favorable attitudes. Fairness in resource allocation is called distributive fairness, and can be classified into two concepts: micro-fairness, meaning fairness of individual benefit, and macro-fairness, meaning fairness of social or group benefit (Brickman et al., 1981). Fairness of the decision making process is called procedural fairness, and its effectiveness and determinants have been discussed. The early research addressed the efficacy of voice opportunity (Tyler et al.,

1997) and other primary factors such as consistency, the suppression of bias, accuracy, possibilities for correction, representativeness and ethics (Leventhal, 1980). There have been criticisms of these factors, but such factors are also regarded as helpful in practice.

Some theories have been put forward regarding the impact of fair process. For example, the Self-interest Model, which is also referred to as the Instrumental Model, holds that people value fair procedures as a means of gaining self-benefit (Thibaut and Walker, 1975). The Group Value Model hypothesizes that people emphasize fair process as a way of confirming the positive evaluations of important others such as the members of one's own group or authorities (Lind and Tyler, 1988). The Fairness Heuristic Model emphasizes that fairness judgments are used as a means of gauging the trustworthiness of a negotiating partner under uncertain circumstances (van den Bos and Lind, 2002). The next section will be an attempt at reinterpreting theories on cooperative behavior, using the framework of fairness studies.

A reinterpretation of cooperative behavior research

The main findings of pro-environmental behavior studies are that not only rewards but also morals, norms, group identity and fairness can prompt cooperative behavior. Some of these elements are also included in fairness theories. For example, the importance of appropriate rewards is argued in studies on distributive fairness (Tyler et al., 1997) which emphasizes the importance of appropriate resource allocation. The reason why people are more cooperative when they have a stronger sense of belonging towards their group can also be explained by the Group Value Model, which holds that fair treatment can encourage cooperative behavior via identification with one's own group. Thus some aspects of the findings of pro-environmental behavior studies can be explained by fairness theories. However, the idea that morals and norms encourage cooperative behavior does not form part of fairness theories, because fairness theories describe responses to extraneous influences, and do not deal with spontaneous motives. Hence, the efficacy of morals and norms can be seen as a finding specific to pro-environmental behavior studies.

The findings of consensus building studies in public developments can be similarly interpreted. The finding that fair procedures help citizens to understand the validity of a project, and prompts the formation of positive attitudes to a project, is an application of procedural fairness studies. These studies in the public development field, however, do not merely highlight the importance of procedural fairness in practice, but offer more practical knowledge and techniques regarding consensus building processes with stakeholders in practice (Fujii, 2002; Aoki and Suzuki, 2008). Furthermore, while most fairness studies pay attention to either distributive fairness or procedural fairness, consensus building studies concerning public developments use a theoretical framework that includes both aspects of fairness simultaneously (Aoki, 2007), and this is a feature that characterizes these studies. There are also aspects which cannot be found in fairness studies, such as discrepancies in points of view in evaluating policies due to attributes of citizens. Accordingly, consensus building studies regarding public development can be interpreted as practical applications of fairness theories.

The possibility of theoretical integration

Applying a theoretical framework that integrates both distributive fairness and procedural fairness, most of the findings presented in the preceding section can be organized in that framework. Furthermore, if that framework could be expanded to include morals and norms, then its applicability would be even greater. Accordingly, how to incorporate morals and norms into a fairness framework is an important matter when considering theoretical integration regarding cooperative behavior. Unfortunately, there is, to my knowledge, no theory which has such an integrated framework. Instead, the following section introduces research which uses a similar framework that integrates only two concepts of distributive fairness and procedural fairness, to analyze the process of conflict resolution regarding the Isawa Dam construction project.

Case study:
Conflict resolution in the Isawa Dam construction project

History

The Isawa Dam construction project was proposed around 1982 as a Japanese Ministry of Land, Infrastructure and Tourism (MLIT) initiative. Since approximately 150,000 people live along the lower reaches of the Isawa River, the Isawa Dam was planned with the aim of providing both flood control and irrigation. At a cost of around

244 billion yen, the Isawa Dam would bring immense social benefits. Meanwhile, having the largest capacity (13.5 million cubic meters) of any dam in Japan, it would also have considerable impact on both the natural and social environments and result in the relocation of numerous households. Consequently, the Isawa Dam project can be regarded as a construction project that would have a tremendous impact on both society and the natural environment.

In 1953, the Ishibuchi Dam was built on the Isawa River. The compensation offered for the site, at that time, was unfairly low, which led to strong landowners' anger towards the government, but the government forced them to agree. Subsequently, since the Ishibuchi dam proved to be insufficient to control for either water shortages or floods, the Japanese government planned the construction of an even bigger dam, the Isawa Dam. The 73 landowners affected by the Isawa Dam construction site formed an opposition movement. Among them were nine households which previously had been forced to relocate for the construction of the Ishibuchi Dam and continued to feel strong animosity. Thus consensus building for the Isawa Dam was a significant challenge.

In the attempt to build consensus, Iwate Prefecture, the local government, was central in the formation of a negotiating body, which mediated negotiations between locals and the national government. This negotiating body began the task of mediation with a policy of respect for the locals. In concert with this policy, the national government also set up an advisory office which locals could visit at any time to consult about their future lives after relocation. Although this office dealt with a considerable amount of close questioning by and long consultation sessions with locals, as the government officials continued to deal with the locals thoughtfully and politely, little by little, a more positive mood gradually developed among the locals.

It was under these conditions that the government announced plans to establish another works site in the vicinity of the dam construction area. The additional 22 households that would be required to relocate to provide this site also formed a landowner group, and began negotiations with the national government. This meant that the government was now negotiating with two bodies representing locals; one for the dam construction site and another for the works site. The locals in the area of the works site also, initially, displayed unyielding opposition. However, the government strove to be fair and sincere in its interactions with them and, eventually, was able to win this group's trust as well. The government subsequently decided on a policy of purchasing the dam construction site and leasing the works site. As a result of its continued negotiations with both groups, in 1992, the government was able to conclude an agreement on the bases of compensation, thus bringing to an end nine long years of efforts for consensus building.

The mechanism behind the locals' change of attitude

Changes in trust towards, and attitudes for and against, the government
In an attempt to elucidate the process that lead to a change of attitude among the locals, in 2003, we conducted interviews with the relevant government authorities, including the MLIT, and representatives of the groups of landowners, as well as surveying the landowners (79 were approached and 38 responded). In interviews and a questionnaire survey, questions were asked about how landowners currently feel and about their feelings at the time when negotiations began. As can be seen in Figure 10.1, the results show that trust in the government increased significantly from the time of negotiations starting to the period following negotiations ($t(37) = 3.21, p < .004$). A similar change was observed in levels of approval attitude ($t(54) = 5.48, p < .001$). These changes could be described in terms of the efficacy of procedural fairness brought about through negotiation.

The structure of attitudinal change
A path analysis based on multiple regression analysis was conducted in order to clarify the main cause of the landowners' change of attitude. Figure 10.2 shows that it was only trust that determined approval at the time of negotiations beginning. Given also that some landowners opposed the dam construction out of strong resentment, the source of opposition to construction can be interpreted as having been mistrust of the government. This can be explained by the Fairness-oriented Information Processing Model, which regards the formation of negative attitudes as arising from strong negative feelings. Figure 10.3, which shows the attitude structure after negotiations, suggests that the disclosure of information increased the positive evaluation of the social validity of the dam. Simultaneously, it can be confirmed that respectful treatment by the government increased the landowners' sense of social validity via enhancing their sense of individual validity (ratings on benefit). The sincerity demonstrated by the government in the course of negotiations produced a feeling in the landowners of having been respected, and this feeling

Figure 10.1: Changes in trust of the government and intention to approve the dam construction

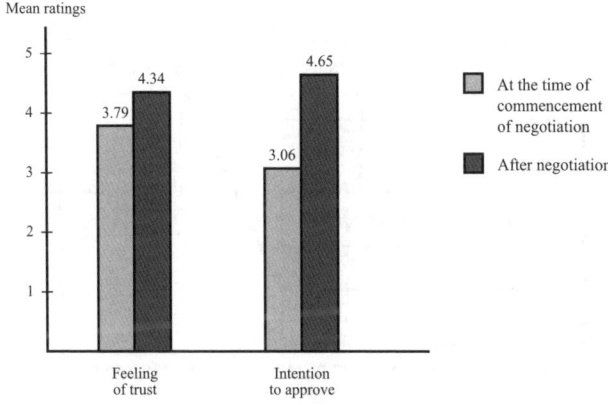

Figure 10.2: Structure of attitude formation at the commencement of negotiations

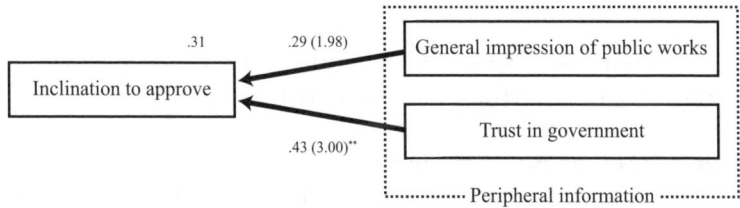

Notes:
** p < .01
The numerical value near an arrow is the ß value.
The numerical value on a box is the coefficient of determination.

served as an emotional reward for them. This can be seen as having resulted in the landowners being able to consider matters calmly. Consequently, the landowners noticed the benefit that they could live in a convenient area after they aged. In other words, it could be argued that fair procedures had the dual effect of prompting an assessment of personal benefit and bringing about an understanding of the social necessity for the dam, thus leading to approval for its construction. Therefore, it can be concluded that in the construction

Figure 10.3: Structure of attitude formation after negotiations

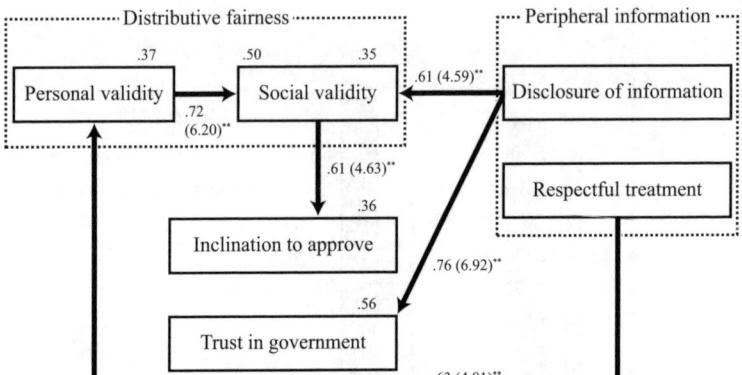

Notes:
** p < .01
The numerical value near an arrow is the ß value.
The numerical value on a box is the coefficient of determination.

of the Isawa Dam, two procedural fairness factors, disclosure of information and respectful treatment, were the keys to success.

Disclosure of information and respect: Important motives
Following the utilitarian explanations for procedural fairness, the landowners can be seen as having used fair procedures in order to sell their land in advantageous conditions. However, it is difficult to think of respectful treatment as being applied in a utilitarian manner. Nor is the voice opportunity, a variable closely linked to utilitarian motives, significant. Utilitarian explanations also differ from the interview results. For this reason, it is considered unlikely that the disclosure of information and respectful treatment were stressed from utilitarian motives.

Then again, from the perspective of the Fairness Heuristic Theory, the landowners sought fair procedures in an attempt to gauge the government's credibility. In this case, in addition to being able to gauge trustworthiness of the government from its responses to the unexpected circumstances, the landowners could also estimate potential risks from the disclosed information. Consequently, the disclosure of information and respectful treatment may have provided important clues for the landowners to avoid risks that might occur after relocation. Furthermore, the Group Value Model assumes the existence of a motive to enhance self-esteem by having one's membership acknowledged by the other group members (Lind and Tyler, 1988). According to this view, the landowners would have hoped for respectful treatment by the government. It is evident, on the above assumptions, that respectful treatment is important. The disclosure of information is considered to be a behavior that reflects respect for the individual, and thus becomes a barometer of respectful treatment. Accordingly, it is possible to conclude that the disclosure of information and respectful treatment were important in the sense that they acted to enhance depressed self-esteem.

In addition to the above interpretations, this case also provides a new perspective in considering the effects of procedural fairness; the 'recognition of a cause' by fair process. In Japan, land is not only considered to be an asset belonging to an individual but is also a symbol of the family that has been handed down from the ancestors. This notion is particularly common in rural areas, and when people do part with their land, they can feel pangs of conscience. In such cases, although one may receive some monetary compensation, the feelings of guilt do not go away. However, if it is considered to be a just cause that contributes to society, then the feelings of guilt can be reduced, facilitating acceptance of the offer for land acquisition. This reasoning suggests that the disclosure of information was successful in conveying to the landowners the social contribution that they were making by supplying the site, which tapped into their morals and norms and brought about the cooperative behavior of giving up their land. In other words, it is conjectured that through tapping into morals and norms, the disclosure of information increased the landowners' micro distributive justice (evaluation of personal benefit). This reasoning assumes that the evaluation of fairness is in part dependent on morals and norms, which was increased by the disclosure of information. This hypothesis that morals and norms mediate fairness evaluation creates a need for future investigations to look at this anew.

Based on the above discussion, it can be said that the Isawa Dam project is not only a rare case of conflict resolution with attitude change, but one that suggests important implications for the theoretical framework of cooperative behavior.

Beyond clarification of the mechanism of pro-social behavior

This chapter has discussed both the theoretical integration of and future prospects for research into theoretical models of cooperative behavior with regard to public issues, focusing on the environmental psychology field and the public development field. Furthermore, a case study on the Isawa Dam project, has confirmed the validity of fairness theories in stimulating cooperative behavior, and has suggested adopting morals and norms into fairness theory frameworks. Both are concerned with the modeling of pro-social behavior, however, these discussions have not referred to the influence of the social environment on pro-social behavior.

In the case of the Isawa Dam, the beneficiaries held an event to show the appreciation of the whole society for those on whom the burden fell, and to show that they actually cared about the burdens on the landowners. The chain of events in the Isawa Dam project suggests that highly developed social capital in this area encouraged the national government and the beneficiaries to show sufficient consideration toward the landowners, and which developed emotional compensation for the landowners and prompted them to accept the burden. If this was the case, then even though problems with government communication skills may explain the uncooperative behavior displayed by considerable numbers of people towards public problems, the level of maturity of a community may be considered as an even more important factor. In other words, low levels of social capital can be a factor preventing pro-social behavior. Consequently, in order to prompt pro-social behavior, it would be essential to increase the public spirit that makes people want to contribute to their community or society, which includes developing mutual trust amongst citizens. Public spirit and mutual trust, however, would not increase spontaneously. Hence, in current situations where utilitarian behavior is rampant, a social environment needs to be built in which people with strong mutual trust and public spirit can easily engage in pro-social behavior. However, there are still not enough of such studies. Therefore, in order to prompt pro-social behavior, research should not be limited to expanding theoretical models but must expand to exploring sociological factors that will prompt pro-social behavior.

Notes

Chapter 1

1. In fairness to Van den Bos and his coauthors (2010), they probably would have conducted the study in the same way if they had not had recourse to the Hofstede masculinity-femininity distinction. The point is that in traditional approaches to cross-cultural studies of fairness now it is more difficult to justify studying cultural distinctions that do not align with some cultural distinction like those proposed by Hofstede and that may limit our exploration of differences in fairness across cultures. The point of this chapter is to suggest that we might find interesting cultural differences—or interesting cultural similarities—if we begin our search by looking at how fairness might be expected to work in various socio-historic contexts.
2. Thanks to Leigh Tost for pointing out the need to examine the consequences of negative fairness judgments. System Justification Theory accounts typically begin with the assumption that almost all members of an organization or society will hold positive attitudes toward the social entity in question, because such attitudes provide reassurance and psychological protection. It can happen, however, that a person or group experiences repeated bad treatment or processes and outcomes that are so manifestly unfair that they cannot bring themselves to support the social system.

Chapter 2

1. Researchers have used the words, 'justice' and 'fairness', as interchangeable, though some regard 'justice' as more formal. In this chapter we primarily use 'fairness', but use it synonymously with 'justice'.
2. The SSM Survey (Social Stratification and Mobility Survey) is a leading public opinion survey about social stratification which has been conducted at ten year intervals since 1955.
3. JIS (The Japan Survey on Information Society) is a multidisciplinary study of cultural, social and psychological effects of the information technology (IT) revolution (Naoi and Sugano, 2004). JIS2002 was conducted in October and November 2002 with 1256 valid responses.

Chapter 3

1. This chapter is an English translation of an article originally published in Japanese: Ohbuchi, K. (2010). Nihon ni okeru shakai kaiso to kachikan. *The Annual Reports of Graduate School of Arts and Letters Tohoku University*, Vol. 60.

Chapter 4

1. The term was used in the 1995 SSM survey.

Chapter 5

1. Hirano, Kamemoto and Hattutori (2002: 157) cite as examples of problems with distributive justice in present day Japan: imbalances in the value of votes cast in different electorates; sexual inequalities in employment or family relationships; the issues of political suffrage and social welfare for foreign nationals; disparities in inheritance between legitimate and illegitimate children in the family system; and the issue of criminal defendants and prisoners.
2. The following quote from Robbins summarizes the economists' justifications for drawing a sharp line between efficiency matters and fairness matters: "it does not seem logically possible to associate the two studies [ethics and economics] in any form but mere juxtaposition. Economics deals with ascertainable facts; ethics with valuation and obligations." (Robbins, 1932: 132)
3. The literature generally uses the term *utilitarianism*, but in this chapter we use welfarism. According to Sen (1979a), utilitarianism comprises three elements: *consequentialism*, *sum-ranking*, and welfarism. Consequentialism is a criterion for judging the good or evil of an action and the good or evil of a situation arising from that action. Sum-ranking is a criterion that deems social welfare to be the sum of individual welfare. In this chapter, therefore, welfarism is considered to be an element of utilitarianism.
4. An associated discussion is the example of women who live in societies where discrimination is rife: what are known as the so-called 'domesticated housewives'. For these women to survive in such societies there is no other recourse than to limit their natural preferences and adapt their preferences to find significant satisfaction in the smallest things. What is known as the concept of adaptive preference formation was posed by Elster (1983). Chapter 2 of Nussbaum (2005) discusses adaptive preference and related issues in detail.
5. This table is based on Sen (1979b: 547), and has been rearranged by the author.
6. This figure was drawn by the author with reference to Bojer (2004: 26).
7. Another example of the relationship between goods and characteristics is: 'the possession of food gives the owner access to the properties of food, which can be used to satisfy hunger, to yield nutrition, to give eating pleasure and to provide support for social meetings' (Sen, 1985a: 6).
8. The following discussion was constructed with reference to Yoshihara (2003).
9. For an explanation of the theory of equality of resources, see Roemer (1996), Matsui (1999), Yoshihara (2003), and Satō (2005). In particular, Yoshihara (2003) explains in detail *the hypothetical insurance market*, not addressed in this chapter.
10. According to Dworkin, damage sustained in a natural disaster such as an earthquake is known as *brute bad luck* (natural misfortune); while he calls loss due to gambling etc. *optional bad luck*.

11. Dworkin implicitly assumes that preferences are formed autonomously. Critical investigation of this point has been undertaken by Arneson (1989) and Cohen (1989), and each has developed theories of egalitarianism; *equality of opportunity for welfare* and *equality of access to advantage*, respectively. In their discussions, preference is not only formed autonomously, but also is socially prescribed. Consequently, only situations that have arisen as a result of preferences formed by factors beyond the control of the individual are subject to compensation.
12. The problem of stigma is related to real life. Tachibanaki and Urakawa (2006) point out the problem of stigma as one of the reasons for the low take-up rate in Japan's livelihood protection system. Take-up rate here is the proportion of households actually receiving livelihood protection among households with incomes less than the minimum cost of living determined by the government. Looked at in comparative terms, the take-up rate in Japan is low: They estimate it at 19.7 per cent in 1995, 16.3 per cent in 1998 and 16.3 per cent in 2001. They cite as one reason for the low take-up rate the sense of stigma experienced by people receiving livelihood protection.
13. This section relies on Suzumura and Gotoh (2001: Chapter 9).
14. According to Barberá et al. (2004), this method is called the indirect-utility ranking.
15. Pattanaik and Xu (1990) axiomatically characterized the cardinality criterion. Barberá et al. (2004) conducted a detailed survey of set ranking. See also Farina et al. (2004) and Gaertner and Xu (2008).
16. See Nussbaum (2005) for detail.
17. As may be understood from these research efforts, interdisciplinary research, especially including ethics, economics and sociology have been created. See Kawamoto (1995), Gotoh (2002), Shionoya (2002), Shionoya et al. (2004), Doba and Seiyama (2006), and Grusky and Kanbur (2008).

Chapter 8

1. In this context, controllability of group membership refers only to whether or not the person can move from one specific group to another by him/herself, and not to whether or not the person is controllable and responsible for getting in the group.
2. As for the causal attribution of another woman's success, the degree to which participants attributed the result to favoritism were increased with the population of persons who have favorable beliefs about women in potential interviewers (if the population of biased people in potential interviewers was 5/5, 3/5 and 0/5, $M = 5.57$, $M = 4.33$ and $M = 3.10$, respectively). In addition, there was no significant effect of the population of biased persons on the degree of the attribution to interviewee's personal factor, such as ability or effort. Participants highly attributed the cause of success and failure to personal factors ($M = 5.09$). Furthermore, there was no discount relationship between the degree of causal attribution to discrimination/favoritism and that to personal factors.

Bibliography

2003 Nen Kaisō Chōsa Kenkyūkai (The 2003 Social Stratification Research Group) (2007). *2004 nen kankoku shokugyō ni kansuru zenkoku chōsa (shokugyō ishin) kōdo bukku kiso shūkei hyō shūsei ban* (The 2004 national occupational survey in Korea [occupational prestige]: Codebook and basic spreadsheets, modified version).

Abe, A. (2008). *Kodomo no hinkon: Nihon no fukōhei wo kangaeru* (The poverty of children: Scrutinizing Japan's inequality), Tokyo: Iwanami Shoten.

Adams, J. S. (1965). Inequity in social exchange. In L. Berkowitz (Ed.). *Advances in experimental social psychology* (Vol. 2, pp. 267–299). New York: Academic Press.

Adams, R. E., Rohe, W. M., and Arcury, T. A. (2005). Awareness of community-oriented policing and neighborhood perception in five small to midsize cities. *Journal of Criminal Justice*, 33, 43–54.

Ajzen, I. (1991). The theory of planned behavior. *Organizational Behavior and Human Decision Processes*, 50, 179–211.

Allport, G. W. (1954). *The Nature of Prejudice.* Cambridge, MA: Perseus Books.

Anderson, E. S. (1999). What is the Point of Equality. *Ethics*, 99, 906–944.

Andersson, M., and von Borgstede, C. (2010). Differentiation of determinants of low-cost and high-cost recycling. *Journal of Environmental Psychology*, 30(4), 402–408.

Andō, K., and Hirose, Y. (1999). Kankyō borantia dantai ni okeru katsudō kēzoku ito sekkyokuteki katsudō ito no kiteiin (Determinants of continuous involvement and active involvement in environmental volunteer groups). *Shakai shinrigaku kenkyū* (Japanese journal of social psychology), 15(2), 90–99.

Aoki, T. (2007). Consensus-building in Japanese public development: The application of fairness theory and the creation of a new field of research. In K. Ohbuchi (Ed.). *Social justice in Japan: Concepts, theories and paradigms* (pp. 211–238). Melbourne: Trans Pacific Press.

Aoki, T., and Nakai, Y. (2004). Shakai shihon seibi ni kansuru shimin kōza no hitsuyōsei (Necessity of open citizen information fora on infrastructure development). *JSCE Journal of Construction Management*, 11, 427–432.

Aoki, T., and Suzuki, Y. (2008). Isawa dam kaihatsu ni miru gōi no kōzu (The structure of consensus building in the Isawa dam construction project). *JSCE Journal of Infrastructure Planning and Management D*, 64(4), 542–556.

Arneson, R. J. (1989). Equality and equal opportunity for welfare. *Philosophical Studies*, 56, 77–93.

Asai, N. (2006). Shozoku shūdan ni taisuru sabetu/yūgū ga gen'in kizoku ni ataeru eikyō (Causal attribution of discrimination and favoritism in a

disadvantaged group). *Shinrigaku Kenkyū* (Japanese Journal of Psychology), 77, 317–324.
Asai, N. (2009). Sabetsu kara no jikobōei hōryaku to sono shinri/shakaiteki eikyō. (Self-defensive strategy against discrimination and its psychological and social effects). *Gunma Daigaku shakai shinrigaku seminā hōkoku* (Report of the Gunma University Seminar of Social Psychology), 61–78.
Asai, N., and Karasawa, M. (2009). Influence of perceived social support on reporting discrimination. Poster presentation at the 8th Biennial Conference of the Asian Association of Social Psychology, New Delhi, India.
Asai, N., Karasawa, M., and Ohbuchi, K. (2010). Causal explanation of discrimination: Impact of perceived immutability of belief. Poster presentation at the 8th Biennial Conference of the Society for the Psychological Study of Social Issues, New Orleans, Louisiana, USA.
Asai, N., Karasawa, M., Kumagai, T., and Kawashima, N. (2010). Recognizing personal experiences of discrimination: Impact of essentialist beliefs of group differences and social structure. Poster presentation at the Society for Personality and Social Psychology 11th Annual Meeting, Las Vegas, Nevada, USA.
Averill, J. R. (1982). *Anger and aggression: An essay on emotion.* New York: Springer-Verlag.
Balkwell, J. W., Bates, F. L., and Garbin, A. P. (1982). Does the degree of consensus on occupational status evaluations differ by socioeconomic stratum?: Response to Guppy. *Social Forces*, 60(4), 1183–1189.
Bamberg, S., and Möser, G. (2007). Twenty years after Hines, Hungerfold, and Tomera: A new meta-analysis of pro-social determinants of pro-environmental behavior. *Journal of Environmental Psychology*, 27(1), 14–25.
Bandura, A. (1977). Self-efficacy: Toward a unifying theory of behavioral change. *Psychological Review*, 84, 191–215.
Barberá, S., Bossert, W., and Pattanaik, P. K. (2004). Ranking sets of objects. In S. Barberá and C. Seidl (Eds). *Handbook of Utility Theory, Vol. 2: Extensions* (pp. 893–978). Dordrecht: Kluwer Academic.
Baron, J. (2001). Confusion of group interest and self-interest in parochial cooperation on behalf of a group. *Journal of Conflict Resolution*, 45(3), 283–296.
Barreto, M., and Ellemers, N. (2005). The burden of benevolent sexism: How it contributes to the maintenance of gender inequalities. *European Journal of Social Psychology*, 35, 633–642.
Baumcister, R. F., and Boden, J. M. (1998). Aggression and the self: High self-esteem, low self-control, and ego threat. In R. G. Geen and E. Donnerstein (Eds). *Human aggression: Theories, research, and implications for social policy* (pp.111–135). San Diego: Academic Press.
Baumeister, R. F., and Tice, D. M. (1990). Anxiety and social exclusion. *Journal of Social and Clinical Psychology*, 9, 165–195.
Baxter, J. (1994). Is husband's class enough? Class location and class identity in the United States, Sweden, Norway, and Australia. *American Sociological Review*. 59, 220–235.
Becker, T. E., and Billings, R. S. (1993). Profiles of commitment: An empirical test. *Journal of Organizational Behavior*, 14(2), 177–190.

Befu, H. (1980). A critique of the group model of Japanese society. *Social Analysis*, No. 5/6, 29–43.
Beilock, S. L., and Carr, T. H. (2005). When high-powered people fail: Working memory and "choking under pressure" in math. *Psychological Science*, 16, 101–105.
Benedict, R. (1946). *The chrysanthemum and the sword: Patterns of Japanese culture*. Boston: Houghton Mifflin.
Blau, P. M. (1957). Occupational bias and mobility. *American Sociological Review*, 22, 392–399.
Blau, P. M., and Duncan, O. D. (1967). *The American occupational structure*. New York: John Wiley & Sons.
Bojer, H. (2004). *Distributional Justice: Theory and measurement*. London and New York: Routledge.
Bradley, G. W. (1978). Self-serving biases in the attribution processes: A reexamination of the fact of fiction question. *Journal of Personality and Social Psychology*, 36, 56–71.
Branscombe, N. R., and Wann, D. L. (1994). Collective self-esteem consequences of out-group derogation when a valued social identity is on trial. *European Journal of Social Psychology*, 24, 641–657.
Branscombe, N. R., Fernández, S., Gómez, A., and Cronin, T. (in press). Moving toward or away from a group identity: Different strategies for coping with pervasive discrimination. In J. Jetten, C. Haslam, and S.A. Haslam (Eds). *The social cure: Identity, health and well-being*. New York: Psychology Press.
Branscombe, N. R., Schmitt, M. T., and Harvey, R. D. (1999). Perceiving pervasive discrimination among African Americans: Implication for group identification and well-being. *Journal of Personality and Social Psychology*, 77, 135–149.
Brewer, M. B. (1979). In-group bias in the minimal intergroup situation: A cognitive-motivational analysis. *Psychological Bulletin*, 86, 307–324.
Brewer, M. B. (1991). The social self: On being the same and different at the same time. *Personality and Social Psychology Bulletin*, 17, 475–482.
Brickman, P., Folger, R., Goode, E., and Schul, Y. (1981). Microjustice and macrojustice. In M. J. Lerner and S. C. Lerner (Eds). *The justice motive in social behavior* (pp. 173–202). New York: Plenum.
Brosnan, S.F., and De Waal, F. B. M. (2003). Monkeys reject unequal pay. *Nature*, 425, 297–299.
Brown, B., Perkins, D. D., and Brown, G. (2003). Place attachment in a revitalizing neighborhood: Individual and block levels of analysis. *Journal of Environmental Psychology*, 23, 259–271.
Cabinet Office (2009). *Heisei 21-nendo nenji keizai zaisei hōkoku* (Annual report on the Japanese economy and public finance). Retrieved 31 July 2010, from http://www5.cao.go.jp/j-j/wp/wp-je09/09p00000.html
Caprairiello, P., Cuddy, A. J. C., and Fiske, S. T. (2009). Social structure shapes cultural stereotypes and emotions: A causal test of the stereotype content model. *Group Processes and Intergroup Relations*, 12, 147–155.
Chanley, V. A. (2002). Trust in government in the aftermath of 9/11: Determinants and consequences. *Political Psychology*, 23, 469–483.
Cihangir, S., Barreto, M., and Ellemers, N. (2010). The dark side of ambiguous

discrimination: How state self-esteem moderates emotional and behavioral responses to ambiguous and unambiguous discrimination: Men's and women's responses to old-fashioned and modern sexist views. *British Journal of Social Psychology*, 49, 155–174.

Cocking, C., and Drury, J. (2004). Generalization of efficacy as a function of collective action and intergroup relations: Involvement in an anti-roads struggle. *Journal of Applied Social Psychology*, 34(2), 417–444.

Cohen, G. A. (1989). On the currency of egalitarian justice. *Ethics*, 99, 906–944.

Cooley, C. H. (1902). *Human nature and the social order*. New York: Scribner's.

Counts, G. S. (1925). The social status of occupation. A problem in vocational guidance. *School Review*, 33, 16–27.

Cousins, S. D. (1989). Culture and self-perception in Japan and the United States. *Journal of Personality and Social Psychology*, 56, 124–131.

Coutu, W. (1936). The relative prestige of twenty professions as judged by three groups of professional students. *Social Forces*, 14, 522–529.

Crisp, R. J., and Turner, R. N. (2009). Can imagined interactions produce positive perceptions?: Reducing prejudice through simulated social contact. *American Psychologist*, 64, 231–240.

Crocker, J., and Major, B. (1989). Social stigma and self-esteem: The self-protective properties of stigma. *Psychological Review*, 96, 608–630.

Crocker, J., Voelkl, K., Testa, M., and Major, B. (1991). Social stigma: The affective consequences of attributional ambiguity. *Journal of Personality and Social Psychology*, 60, 218–228.

Crosby, F. J. (1982). *Relative deprivation and working women*. New York: Oxford University Press.

Crosby, F. J. (1984). The denial of personal discrimination. *American Behavioral Scientist*, 27, 371–386.

Dalbert, C. (1999). The world is more just for me than generally: About the Personal Belief in a Just World Scale's validity. *Social Justice Research*, 12, 79–98.

Dalbert, C. (2002). Beliefs in a just world as a buffer against anger. *Social Justice Research*, 15, 123–145.

Dardenne, B., Dumont, M., and Bollier, T. (2007). Insidious dangers of benevolent sexism: Consequences for women's performance. *Journal of Personality and Social Psychology*, 93, 764–779.

De Cremer, D., and Tyler, T. R. (2005). Managing group behavior: The interplay between procedural justice, sense of self, and cooperation. In M. P. Zanna (Ed.). *Advances in Experimental Social Psychology* (Vol. 37, pp. 151–218). San Diego: Academic Press.

De Waal, F. (1996). *Good natured: The origins of right and wrong in humans and other animals*. Cambridge, MA: Harvard University Press.

Dentsu Communication Institute Inc. (2005). *'Sekai kachikan chōsa 2005' Kokunai repōto: Maruchi sutandādo na shakai bijon wo—sasuteinaburu na seijuku shakai he* ('The World Values Survey 2005' Report on Japanese results: For a multi-standard social vision—toward a mature sustainable society). Retrieved 31 July 2010, from http://www.dentsu.co.jp/di/archive/wvs/pdf/wvs_2005_1.pdf

Dentsu Communication Institute/Nippon Research Center (2008). *Sekai*

shuyōkoku kachikan. (Data book of the values of the world's major countries). Tokyo: Dōyūkan.
Deutsch, M. (1975). Equity, equality, and need: What determines which value will be used as the basis for distributive justice? *Journal of Social Issues*, 31, 137–149.
Deutsch, M. (1985). *Distributive justice: A social-psychological perspective*. New Haven: Yale University Press.
Devin-Wright, P., and Lyons, E. (1997). Remembering pasts and representing places: The construction of national identities in Ireland. *Journal of Environmental Psychology*, 17, 33–45.
Diener, E., and Diener, M. (1996). Most people are happy. *Psychological Science*, 7, 181–185.
Dion, K. L., and Earn, B. M. (1975). The phenomenology of being a target of prejudice. *Journal of Personality and Social Psychology*, 32, 944–950.
Doba, G. (Ed.) (2008). *Kōkyōsei to kakusa* (Publicness and economic inequality in contemporary Japan). 2005 nen SSM Chōsa Kenkyūkai (The 2005 SSM Research Society).
Doba, G., and Seiyama, K. (2006). *Seigi no ronri: kōkyō teki kachi no kihan teki shakai riron* (The logic of justice: Normative social theory of public values). Tokyo: Keisō Shobō.
Doosje, B., Branscombe, N. R., Spears, R., and Manstead, A. S. R. (1998). Guilty by association: When one's group has a negative history. *Journal of Personality and Social Psychology*, 75, 872–886.
Dumont, M., Sarlet, M., and Dardenne, B. (2010). Be too kind to a woman, she'll feel incompetent: Benevolent sexism shifts self-construal and autobiographical memories toward incompetence. *Sex Role*, 62, 545–553.
Duncan, O. D. (1961). Socioeconomic index for all occupations. In A. J. Reiss, Jr., O. D. Duncan, P. K. Hatt and C. C. North (Eds). *Occupations and social status* (pp. 109–138). New York: Free Press.
Dworkin, R. (1981). What is equality? Part 1: Equality of welfare. *Philosophy and Public Affairs*, 10, 185–246.
Eagly, A. H. (1987). *Sex differences in social behavior: A social role interpretation*. Hillsdale, NJ: Lawrence Erlbaum.
Eagly, A. H., and Mladinic, A. (1989). Gender stereotypes and attitudes toward women and men. *Personality and Social Psychology Bulletin*, 15, 543–558.
Ellemers, N., Van den Heuvel, H., De Gilder, D., Maass, A., and Bonvini, A. (2004). The under representation of women in science: Differential commitment or the Queen-bee syndrome? *British Journal of Social Psychology*, 43, 315–338.
Ellsberg, D. (1961). Risk ambiguity and the savage axioms. *Quarterly Journal of Economics*, 75, 643–669.
Elster, J. (1983). *Sour Grapes*. Cambridge: Cambridge University Press.
Farah, M. F., and Newman, A. J. (2010). Exploring consumer boycott intelligence using a socio-cognitive approach. *Journal of Business Research*, 63, 347–355.
Farina, F., Peluso, E., and Savaglio, E. (2004). Ranking opportunity sets in the space of functionings. *Journal of Economic Inequality*, 2, 105–116.
Feather, N. T. (1994). Attitudes toward high achievers and reactions to their fall:

Theory and research concerning tall poppies. In M. Zanna (Ed.). *Advances in experimental social psychology* (Vol. 26, pp. 1–73). San Diego: Academic Press.
Featherman, L. D., and Hauser, R. M. (1976). Prestige or socioeconomic scales in the study of occupational achievement? *Sociological Methods and Research*, 4, 402–422.
Featherman, L. D., and Hauser, R. M. (1978). A refined model of occupational mobility. In D. B. Grusky (Ed.) (2001). *Social stratification: Class, race, and gender in sociological perspective* (pp. 325–335). Colorado: Westview Press.
Fehr, J. and Sassenberg, K. (2009). Intended and unintended consequences of internal motivation to behave unprejudiced: The case of benevolent discrimination. *European Journal of Social Psychology*, 38, 1093–1108.
Ferguson, T. J., and Rule, B. G. (1983). An attributional perspective on anger and aggression. In R. G. Geen, and E. I. Donnerstein (Eds). *Aggression: Theoretical and empirical reviews: Theoretical and methodological issues* (pp 41–74). New York: Academic Press.
Festinger, L. (1957). *A theory of cognitive dissonance*. Evanston, Il: Row, Peterson.
Fine, M., and Bowers, C. (1984). Racial self-identification: The effects of history and gender. *Journal of Applied Social Psychology*, 14, 136–146.
Fischer, A. R. (2006). Women's benevolent sexism as reaction to hostility. *Psychology of Women Quarterly*, 30, 410–416
Folger, R. (1977). Distributive and procedural justice: Combined impact of 'voice' and improvement on experienced inequity. *Journal of Personality and Social Psychology*, 35, 108–119.
Folger, R., and Cropanzano, R. (2001). Fairness theory: Justice as accountability. In J. Greenberg and R. Cropanzano (Eds). *Advances in organizational justice* (pp. 1–55). Stanford: Stanford University Press.
Foster, M. D., and Matheson, K. (1999). Perceiving and responding to the personal/group discrimination discrepancy. *Personality and Social Psychology Bulletin*, 25, 1319–1329.
Fujii, S. (2006). Seifu ni taisuru kokumin no kitai: Taigi aru kokyojigyō ni yoru shinrai no jōsei (The nation's trust in government: Trust development via the implementation of public works with justice). *JSCE Journal of Infrastructure Planning and Management*, 807(IV-70), 29–41.
Fujii, S., Takemura, K., and Kikkawa, T. (2002). Kimekata to gōikeisei: Shakaiteki jirenma ni okeru rikoteki dōki no yokusei ni mukete (Decision making processes and consensus building: A strategy for restraining egoistic motivation in social dilemmas). *JSCE Journal of Infrastructure Planning and Management*, 709(IV-56), 13–26.
Fujikawa, K. (1994). Chiiki he no aichaku to kankyō ishiki: Tomin no mizu kankyō chōsa hōkoku sono 6 (Attachment to community and environmental consciousness: Research report on the consciousness for water environment of residents in Tokyo No. 6). *Sōgō toshi kenkyū* (Comprehensive urban study), 54, 75–87.
Gaertner, W., and Xu, Y. (2008). A new class of the standard of living based on functionings. *Economic Theory*, 35, 201–215.

Gender Equality Bureau (2005). *Dainiji Danjo Kyōdō Sankaku Kihon Keikaku* (The second basic plans for gender-equal society). Cabinet Office.

Glick, P., and Fiske, S. T. (1996). The ambivalent sexism inventory: Differentiating hostile and benevolent sexism. *Journal of Personality and Social Psychology*, 70, 491–512.

Glick, P., and Fiske, S. T. (2001). An ambivalent alliance: Hostile and benevolent sexism as complementary justifications for gender inequality. *American Psychologist*, 56, 109–118.

Glick, P., Diebold, J., Bailey-Werner, B., and Zhu, L. (1997). The two faces of Adam: Ambivalent sexism and polarized attitudes toward women. *Personality and Social Psychology Bulletin*, 23, 1323–1334.

Glick, P., Fiske, S. T., Mladinic, A., Sainz, J., Abrams, D., Masser, B. et al. (2000). Beyond prejudice as simple antipathy: Hostile and benevolent sexism across cultures. *Journal of Personality and Social Psychology*, 79, 763–775.

Goffman, E. (1963). *Stigma: Notes on the management of spoiled identity.* Englewood Cliffs, New Jersey: Prentice-Hall.

Goldthorpe, J. H., and Hope, K. (1972). Occupational grading and occupational prestige. In K. Hope (Ed.). *The analysis of social mobility: Methods and approaches* (pp. 19–79). Oxford: Clarendon Press.

Goodwin, S. A., Williams, K. D., and Carter-Sowell, A. R. (2010). The psychological sting of stigma: The costs of attributing ostracism to racism. *Journal of Experimental Social Psychology*, 46, 612–618.

Gotoh, R. (2002). *Seigi no keizai tetsugaku* (An economic philosophy of justice), Tokyo: Tōyō Keizai Shinpōsha.

Gottfried, R.S. (1983). *The Black Death: Natural and human disaster in medieval Europe.* New York: The Free Press.

Goyder, J. (2005). The dynamics of occupational prestige: 1975–2000. *Canadian Review of Sociology and Anthropology*, 42, 1–23.

Greenwood, D., and Isbell, L. M. (2002). Ambivalent sexism and the dumb blonde: Men's and women's reactions to sexist jokes. *Psychology of Women Quarterly*, 26, 341–350.

Grusky, D. B., and Kanbur, R. (Eds) (2006). *Poverty and Inequality.* Stanford: Stanford University Press.

Guimond, S., and Dube-Simard, L. (1983). Relative deprivation theory and the Quebec nationalist movement: The cognition-emotion distinction and personal-group deprivation issue. *Journal of Personality and Social Psychology*, 4, 526–535.

Guppy, N. L. (1982). On intersubjectivity and collective conscience in occupational prestige research: A comment on Balkwell-Bates-Garbin and Kraus-Schild-Hodge. *Social Forces*, 60, 1178–1182.

Guppy, N. L., and Goyder, J. C. (1984). Consensus on occupational prestige: A reassessment of the evidence. *Social Forces*, 62, 709–725.

Hamaguchi, E. (1982). *Kanjin shugi no shakai Nippon* (Japan, the contexualism society). Tokyo: Tōyō Keizai Shinpōsha.

Hara, J. (1999). Rōdō shijō no henka to shokugyō ishin sukoa (Changes in the labor market and the occupational prestige score). *The Japanese Journal of Labour Studies,* 472, 26–35.

Hara, J. (2008). Shakaiteki fubyōdō to ningen, shakai. (Social inequality and man and society). In J. Hara, Y. Sato and K. Ohbuchi (Eds). *Shakai Kaisō to fubyōdō* (Social stratification and inequality) (pp. 1–14). Hōsōdaigaku Kyōiku Shinkōkai.

Hara, J., and Seiyama, K. (2005). *Inequality amid affluence: Social stratification in Japan.* Melbourne: Trans Pacific Press.

Hashimoto, R., Tanishita, M., and Kashima, S. (2003). Shimin sanka gata kōen ni okeru sanka fusanka kōdō (Participatory behavior in participatory park design). *Doboku keikakugaku kenkyū kōen shū* (Proceedings of infrastructure planning), 28, CD-ROM.

Hatori, T., Jeon, H., and Kobayashi, K. (2008). Dai san sha iinkai no kōkai to shiinrai keisei e no eikyō (Third party open public debate and the impact upon trust formation). *JSCE Journal of Infrastructure Planning and management D*, 64(2), 148–167.

Hausmann. R., Tyson, L. D., and Zahidi, S. (2009). *The Global Gender Gap Index 2009.* Geneva: World Economic Forum.

Hayashi, H. (2008). *Sengo heiwa shugi wo toinaosu* (Redefining post-war pacifism). Kamogawa Shuppan.

Hayden, D. (1995). *The Power of place: Urban landscapes as public history.* Cambridge: MIT Press.

Heathcrton, T. F., and Polivy, J. (1991). Development and validation of scale for measuring state self-esteem. *Journal of Personality and Social Psychology,* 60, 895–910.

Herek, G. M., Gillis, J. R., and Cogan, J. C. (1999). Psychological sequelae of hate crime victimization among lesbian, gay, and bisexual adults. *Journal of Consulting & Clinical Psychology,* 67, 945–951.

Hewstone, M., Rubin, M., and Willis, H. (2002). Intergroup bias. *Annual Review of Psychology,* 53, 575–604.

Hidalgo, M. C., and Hernandez, B. (2001). Place attachment: Conceptual and empirical questions. *Journal of Environmental Psychology,* 21, 273–281.

Hikichi, H., Aoki, T., and Ohbuchi, K. (2006). Machizukuri no keikaku katei ni taisuru sanka kōdō no kiteiin to sono chiikisa (Determinants of and regional differences in participation behavior in planning processes for city planning). *JSCE Infrastructure Planning Review,* 23(1), 237–242.

Hikichi, H., Aoki, T., and Ohbuchi, K. (2009). Chiiki ni taisuru aichaku no keisei kikō: Butsuriteki kankyō to shakaiteki kankyō no eikyō (The formation of attachment to place of residence: Effect of physical and social environment). *JSCE Journal of Infrastructure Planning and Management D*, 65(2), 101–110.

Hikichi, H., Ohbuchi, K., and Aoki, T. (2010). Rekishi shisan ni yoru chiiki comittomento no keisei: Eiyo no rekishi to higeki no rekishi (The formation of community commitment by historical heritage—Honorable history and tragic history). *Nihon Shakai Shinri Gakkai dai 51 kai taikai happyō ronbun shū* (Proceedings of the 51st annual conference of the Japanese Society of Social Psychology), 752–753.

Hirano, H., Kamemoto, H., and Hattutori, T. (2002). *Hō tetsugaku* (The philosophy of law). Yūhikaku.

Hirose, Y. (Ed.) (2008). *Kankyō kōdō no shakai shinri gaku* (Social psychology of environmental behavior). Kyoto: Kitaōji Shobō.

Hochschild, A. R. (1979). Emotion work, feeling rules, and social structure. *American Journal of Sociology*, 85, 551–575.
Hodge, R. W., Kraus, V. E., and Schild, E. O. (1982). Consensus in occupational prestige ratings: Response to Guppy. *Social Forces*, 60, 1190–1196.
Hodge, R. W., Siegel, P., and Rossi, P. H. (1966). Occupational prestige in the United States: 1925–1963. In R. Bendix and S. M. Lipset (Eds). *Class, status, and power: Social stratification in comparative perspective* (pp. 322–334). New York: Free Press.
Hofstede, G. (1980). *Culture's consequences: International differences in work related values*. Beverly Hills, California: Sage.
Hofstede, G. (2001). *Culture's consequences: Comparing values, behaviors, institutions, and organizations across nations* (2nd ed.). Thousand Oaks, CA: Sage.
Hogg, M. A. (1992). *The social psychology of group cohesiveness*. New York: New York University Press.
Hogg, M. A., and Abrams, D. (1995). *Shakaiteki aidentitiī riron. Atarashii shakai shinnrigaku taikeika no tame no ippan riron* (Social identifications: A social psychology of intergroup relations and group processes). M. Yoshimori and Y. Nomura (Trans.). Kyoto: Kitaōji Shobō.
Hogg, M.A., and Abrams, D. (1988). *Social identifications: A social psychology of intergroup relations and group processes*. London: Routledge.
Huddy, L., Feldman, S., Capelos, T., and Provost, C. (2002). The consequences of terrorism: Disentangling the effects of personal and national threat. *Political Psychology*, 23, 485–509.
Hummon, D. M. (1992). Community attachment: Local sentiment and sense of place. In I. Altman and S. M. Low (Eds). *Human behavior and environment: Advances in theory and research* (Vol. 12, Place attachment. pp. 253–278). New York: Plenum Press.
Hunt, M. O. (2000). Status, religion, and the 'belief in a just world': Comparing African Americans, Latinos, and whites. *Social Science Quarterly*, 81, 325–343.
Inkeles, A., and Rossi, P. H. (1956). National comparisons of occupational prestige. *American Journal of Sociology*, 61, 309–334.
Iseda, T. (2003). *Giji kagaku to kagaku no tetsugaku* (Philosophy of science and pseudoscience). Nagoya: The University of Nagoya Press.
Ishida, A. (2008). Shotoku bunpai no fubyōdō to kōfuku sōwa no kanren: Shimyurēshon bunseki no kokoromi (Inequality of income and aggregation of subjective well-being: A simulation analysis by using SSM 2005 dataset). In G. Doba (Ed.). *Kōkyōsei to kakusa* (Publicness and economic inequality in contemporary Japan, 57–70). 2005 nen SSM Chōsa Kenkyūkai (The 2005 SSM Research Society).
Ito, M. (2001). Kenchiku/Machizukuri keikaku ni okeru jūmin sanka shuhō toshite no wākushoppu no kenkyū: komyuniti no jiritsuka o motarasu keikakuron (Workshop research into citizen participation methods in construction and city planning: Planning theories that lead to community autonomy). Doctoral dissertation, Chiba University.
Jackman, M. R. (1994). *The velvet glove: Paternalism and conflict in gender, class, and race relations*. Berkeley: University of California Press.

Japan Nursing Association (2009). *Statistical Data on Nursing Services in Japan 2008.* Japanese Nursing Association Publishing Company.

Jetten, J., Spears, R., and Manstead, A. S. R. (1996). Intergroup norms and intergroup discrimination: Distinctive self-categorization and social identity effects. *Journal of Personality and Social Psychology,* 71, 1222–1233.

Jetten, J. Spears, R., and Manstead, A. S. R. (1997). Strength of identification and intergroup differentiation: The influence of group norms. *European Journal of Social Psychology,* 25, 603–609.

Jonsson, J. O., Grusky, D. B., Carlo, M. D., Pollak, R., and Brinton, M. C. (2009). Microclass mobility: Social reproduction in four countries. *American Journal of Sociology,* 114(4), 977–1036.

Jost, J. T., and Banaji, M. R. (1994). The role of stereotyping in system-justification and the production of false consciousness. *British Journal of Social Psychology,* 33, 1–27.

Jost, J. T., and Hunyady, O. (2002). The psychology of system justification and the palliative function of ideology. *European Review of Social Psychology,* 13, 111–153.

Jost, J. T., and Hunyady, O. (2005). Antecedents and consequences of system justifying ideologies. *Current Directions in Psychological Science,* 14, 260–265.

Jost, J. T., and Kay, A. C. (2005). Exposure to benevolent sexism and complementary gender stereotypes: Consequences of specific and diffuse forms of system justification. *Journal of Personality and Social Psychology,* 88, 498–509.

Jost, J. T., Banaji, M. R., and Nosek, B. A. (2004). A decade of system justification theory: Accumulated evidence of conscious and unconscious bolstering of the status quo. *Political Psychology,* 25, 881–919.

Jost, J. T., Liviatan, I., Van Der Toorn, J., Ledgerwood, A., and Mandisodza, A. (2010). System justification: How do we know it's motivated? In D. R. Bobocel, A. C. Kay, M. P. Zanna and J. M. Olson (Eds). *The Psychology of justice and legitimacy: The Ontario Symposium* (Vol. 11, pp. 173–203). New York: Psychology Press.

Jost, J. T., Pelham, B. W., Sheldon, O., and Sullivan, B. (2003). Social inequality and the reduction of ideological dissonance on behalf of the system: Evidence of enhanced system justification among the disadvantaged. *European Journal of Social Psychology,* 33, 13–36.

Kamijima, J. (1968). Nihonjin no seiji ishiki: Naru yō ni naru no mondaisei (Japanese political awareness: The issue of apathy). In M. Inoki and N. Kamigawa (Eds). *Gendai Nihon no seiji: Bunseki to tenbō* (Modern Japanese politics: Analysis and prospects) (pp. 89–112). Tokyo: Ushio Shuppansha.

Kano, S. (1980). Shūdan nai no bunpai no kōsei (distributive justice) ni kansuru nichibei hikaku (Japan-US comparison of distributive justice in groups). *The Japanese Psychological Association Proceedings of 44th Conference,* 756.

Kanomata, N. (1984). Chii tassei katei bunseki no seika to kadai (The results and tasks of status attainment research). *Japanese Sociological Review,* 35(2), 145–161.

Karasawa, M. (2002). Patriotism, nationalism, and internationalism among Japanese citizens: An etic-emic approach. *Political Psychology*, 23, 645–666.

Kasarda, J. D., and Janowitz, M. (1974). Community attachment in mass society. *American Sociological Review*, 39, 328–339.

Kawachi, I., and Kennedy, B. P. (2004). Fubyōdō ga kenkō wo sokonau (The health of nations: Why inequality is harmful to your health). N. Nishi., T. Nakayama and S. Takao (Trans.). Tokyo: Nihon Hyōron Sha.

Kawakami, K., and Dion, K. (1993). The impact of salient self-identities on relative deprivation and action intentions. *European Journal of Social Psychology*, 23, 525–540.

Kawamoto, T. (1995). *Gendai rinrigaku no bōken* (Adventure of contemporary ethics). Sōbunsha.

Kawashima, N., and Ohbuchi, K. (2009). Nihon ni okeru shakaiteki fubyōdō no seitōka: Taisei seitōka riron no kenshō (Justification of social inequalities in Japan: Verification of the system justification theory). *Nihon shisō kara mita seigi, kosei kannen: Shakai shinrigaku teki kentō* (Justice and fairness in Japanese thought: A social-psychological study) (Heisei 19 nendo–21 nendo kagaku kenkyūhi hojokin (chōsen teki hōga kenkyū) kenkyū seika hōkokusho [kenkyū kadai bangō 19653060; kenkyū daihyōsha Ken-ichi Ohbuchi]) (Grants-in-aid for scientific research FY2007—2009 (challenging exploratory research) research report [project number 19653060; project leader Ken-ichi Ohbuchi]). Pp. 113–125.

Kawashima, N., and Ohbuchi, K. (2010). Shakai teki fubyōdō to shakai ni taisuru chikaku: Makuro kōseikan no yōin (Social inequalities and social perceptions toward Japanese society: Contributing factors of macro fairness). Poster session presented at Tōhoku Shinrigakkai Dai 64 Kai Taikai (The 64th Tōhoku Psychological Association Conference), Miyagi, Japan.

Kawashima, N., and Ohbuchi. K. (2011). Micro fairness mediates the relationship between social inequalities and psychological well-being. Poster session presented at The 12th Annual Meeting of the Society for Personality and Social Psychology. San Antonio, 28 January.

Kawashima, N., Ohbuchi, K., Kumagai, T., and Asai, N. (2009). Shakai kaisō to kosei kan: Tagenteki kosei handan to shakai zokusei no kankei (Social stratification and fairness: Effects of demographic factors on multiple levels of perceived fairness). *Bunka* (Culture), 73, 83–99.

Kawashima, N., Ohbuchi, K., Kumagai, T., and Asai, N. (2010). Perceptions of unfairness and social protests among Japanese: Effects of the immutability belief. Poster session presented at The 11th Annual Meeting of the Society for Personality and Social Psychology. Las Vegas, 30 January.

Kay, A. C., Gaucher, D., Napier, J. L., Callan, M. J., and Laurin, K. (2008). God and the government: Testing a compensatory control mechanism for the support of external systems. *Journal of Personality and Social Psychology*, 95, 18–35.

Kay, A. C., Jost, J. T., Mandisodza, A. N., Sherman, S. J., Petrocelli, J. V., and Johnson, A. L. (2007). Panglossian ideology in the service of system justification: How complementary stereotypes help us to rationalize

inequality. In M. Zanna (Ed.). *Advances in Experimental Social Psychology.* (Vol. 39, pp. 305–358). San Diego, CA: Elsevier.
Kelley, H. H. (1972). Attribution in social interaction. In E. E. Jones, D. E. Kanouse, H. H. Kelley, R. E. Nisbett, S. Valins, and B. Weiner (Eds). *Attribution: Perceiving the causes of behavior* (pp. 1–26). Morristown, New Jersey: General Learning Press.
Kerckhoff, A. C., Campbell, R. T., Trott, J. M., and Kraus, V. (1989). The transmission of socioeconomic status and prestige in Great Britain and the United States. *Sociological Forum,* 4, 155–177.
Kidder, L. H., and Muller, S. (1991). What is fair in Japan. In H. Steensma and R. Verton (Eds). *Social justice in human relations: Social and psychological consequences of justice and injustice* (Vol. 2, pp. 138–152). New York: Plenum.
Kilianski, S. E., and Rudman, L. A. (1998). Wanting it both ways: Do women approve of benevolent sexism? *Sex Roles,* 39, 333–352.
Kimura, K. (1998). Kyōiku, gakureki shakai imēji to fukōseikan (Education, beliefs about educational credentialism and the feeling of fairness). *Riron to Hōhō* (Sociological Theory and Methods), 13, 107–126.
Kitayama, S. (1998). *Jiko to kanjō: Bunka shinrigaku ni yoru toikake* (Self and emotion: Questions from cultural psychology). Tokyo: Kyōritsu Shuppan.
Kitayama, O. (1999). Bunka to kokoro nituiteno minoriaru dialog ni mukete: Takano & Osaka (1997) ronbun no igi to monndaiten (Toward a fruitful dialogue on culture and psychology: Comments on Takano & Osaka (1997)). *Cognitive Studies,* 6, 106–114.
Kobrynowicz, D., and Branscombe, N. R. (1997). Who considers themselves victims of discrimination? Individual difference predictors of perceived gender discrimination in women and men. *Psychology of Women Quarterly,* 21, 347–363.
Kōno, K. (2004). Seiji. (Politics). In NHK Broadcasting Culture Research Institute (Ed.). *Gendai Nihonjin no ishiki kōzō* (Attitude structure of contemporary Japanese people), 6th edition (pp. 71–114). Tokyo: Japan Broadcast Publishing Co., Ltd.
Kōsei Rōdō Shō (Ministry of Health, Labour and Welare) (2010). Henka suru chingin, koyō seido no moto ni okeru danjo kan chingin kakusa ni kansuru kenkyūkai hōkoku (Report of the study group on wage disparities between men and women under the changing wage and employment systems). *http://www.mhlw.go.jp/stf/houdou/2r985200000057do.html.*
Kraus, V., Schild, E. O., and Hodge, R. W. (1978). Occupational prestige in the collective conscience. *Social Forces,* 56(3), 900–918.
Kumagai, T. (2009). Does fair government engender inter-national conflict? The ironical relationship between intra-national justice and inter-national justice. Paper presented at The 3rd CICA-STR international conference, 5 September 2009, Belfast, UK.
Kumagai, T., Cakal, H., and Hewstone, M. (2010). Social identity and collective action: The effects of patriotism and nationalism on intergroup contact and endorsement of collective action to benefit the out-group. Poster session presented at British Psychology Society Social Psychology Section annual

conference 'Social psychology in action: Theoretical debate and social impact', 9 September 2010, Winchester, UK.

Kumagai, T., and Crisp, R. (2010). The effect of imagined contact and high ingroup identification on intercultural communication in home and out-group territory. Unpublished manuscript.

Kumagai, T., and Ohbuchi, K. (2009). Hi-tōjisha kōgeki ni taisuru shūdandōitsushi to higaino kōhēsa no kōka (The effects of group identification and the unfairness of harm on third party aggression). *Shakai Shinrigaku Kenkū* (Japanese Journal of Social Psychology), 24, 200–207.

Kumagai, T., Kawashima, N., Asai, N. (2009). The effects of intranational justice on the sense of international injustice. Paper presented at 22nd annual conference of International Association for Conflict Management, 16 June, 2009, Kyoto, Japan.

Kurasawa, S., and Akimoto, R. (1990). *Chōnaikai to chiiki shūdan* (Neighborhood association and local groups). Tokyo: Minerva Shobō.

Kuriyama, T. (2010). *Okinawa henkan, Nicchū kokkō seijōka, Nichibei "mitsuyaku"* (Okinawa's reversion, normalization of diplomatic relations between Japan and China and "secret agreement" between Japan and the US). Iwanami Shoten.

Lam, S. P. (2006). Predicting intention to save water: Theory of planned behavior, response efficacy, vulnerability, and perceived efficiency of alternative solutions. *Journal of Applied Social Psychology*, 36(11), 2801–2824.

Lavelle, J. J., Brockner, J., Konovsky, M. A., Price, K. H., Henley, A. B., Taneja, A., and Vinekar, V. (2009). Commitment, procedural fairness, and organizational citizenship behavior: A multifoci analysis. *Journal of Organizational Behavior*, 30, 337–357.

Leary, M. R., Tambor, E. S., Terdal, S. K., and Downs, D. L (1995). Self-esteem as an interpersonal monitor: The sociometer hypothesis. *Journal of Personality and Social Psychology*, 68, 518–530.

Lerner, M. J. (1980). *The belief in a just world.* New York: Plenum.

Leventhal, G. S. (1980). What should be done with equity theory?: New approaches to the study of fairness in social relationships. In K. J. Gergen, M. S. Greenberg and R. H. Willis (Eds). *Social Exchange: Advances in Theory and Research* (pp. 27–55). New York: Plenum Press.

Lewicka, M. (2005). Ways to make people active: The role of place attachment, cultural capital, and neighborhood ties. *Journal of Environmental Psychology*, 25, 381–395.

Lewicka, M. (2008). Place attachment, place identity, and place memory: Restoring the forgotten city past. *Journal of Environmental Psychology*, 28, 209–231.

Lewicka, M. (2010). What makes neighborhood different from home and city? Effects of place scale on place attachment. *Journal of Environmental Psychology*, 30, 35–51.

Lickel, B., Miller, N., Stenstrom, D. M., Denson, T. F., and Schmader, T. (2006). Vicarious retribution: The role of collective blame in intergroup aggression. *Personality and Social Psychology Bulletin*, 10, 372–390.

Lind, E. A. (2001). Fairness heuristic theory: Justice judgments as pivotal cognitions in organizational relations. In J. Greenberg and R. Cropanzano

(Eds). *Advances in organizational justice* (pp. 56–88). Palo Alto, CA: Stanford University Press.

Lind, E. A., Erickson, B. E., Friedland, N., and Dickenberger, M. (1978). Reactions to procedural models for adjudicative conflict resolution: A cross-national study. *Journal of Conflict Resolution*, 22, 318–341

Lind, E. A., Greenberg, J., Scott, K. S., and Welchans, T. D. (2000). The winding road from employee to complainant: Situational and psychological determinants of wrongful termination lawsuits. *Administrative Science Quarterly*, 45, 557–590.

Lind, E. A., Kray, L. J., and Thompson, L. (2001). Primacy effects in justice judgments: Testing predictions from fairness heuristic theory. *Organizational Behavior and Human Decision Processes*, 85, 189–210.

Lind, E. A., Thibaut, J., and Walker, L. (1976). A cross-cultural comparison of the effect of adversary and nonadversary processes on bias in legal decision making. *Virginia Law Review*, 62, 271–283.

Lind, E. A., and Tyler, T. R. (1988). *The social psychology of procedural justice*. New York: Plenum.

Lind, E. A., Tyler, T. R., and Huo, Y. (1997). Procedural context and culture: Variation in the antecedents of procedural justice judgments. *Journal of Personality and Social Psychology*, 73, 767–780.

Lindeman, M. (1997). Ingroup bias, self-enhancement and group identification. *European Journal of Social Psychology*, 27, 337–355.

Lubell, M., Zahran, S., and Vedlitz, A. (2007). Collective action and citizen responses to global warming. *Political Behavior*, 29, 391–413.

Lyon, F. (2006). Managing co-operation: Trust and power in Ghanaian associations. *Organization Studies*, 27(1), 31–52.

Mabuchi, R. (1996). Zenpan teki fukōheikan to ryōiki betsu fukōheikan (Social evaluation and the perception of justice in Japan). In Chūō Daigaku Shakaikagaku Kenkyūjo (Ed.). *Nihonjin no kōseikan* (Perception of justice in Japan) (Vol. 7, 79–101). Chūō Daigaku Shakai Kagaku Kenkyūjo Kenkyū Hōkokusho.

Mabuchi, R. (2000). Fukōheikan ga takamaru shakai jōkyō toha nani ka: Kōseikan to fukōheikan no rekishi (Under what social conditions does a sense of unfairness grow?: The history of the perception of fairness and the sense of unfairness). In M. Umino (Ed.). *Nihon shakai no kaisō shisutemu 2: Kōheikan to seiji ishiki* (Stratification system in Japan 2: A sense of fairness and political consciousness) (pp.151–170). Tokyo: Tokyo Daigaku Shuppankai.

Mackie, D. M., and Smith, E. R. (2002). Intergroup emotions and the social self: Prejudice reconceptualized as differentiated reactions to outgroup. In J. P. Forgas, and K. D. Williams (Eds). *The social self: Cognitive, interpersonal, and intergroup perspectives* (pp. 309–326). New York: Psychology Press.

Mackie, D. M., Devos, T., and Smith, E. R. (2000). Intergroup emotions: Explaining of offensive action tendencies in an intergroup context. *Journal of Personality and Social Psychology*, 79, 602–616.

Maeda, H., and Hirose, Y. (2009). Shimin sankagata kaigi ni okeru empawāmento hyōka (Volunteers' empowerment as the determinant of citizen participation in making a waste management plan). *Japanese Psychological Research*, 51(1), 24–34.

Maekawa, H., Takayama, J., and Rachi, M. (2002). Dōro keikaku ni okeru PI shuhō no katsuyō ni kansuru kenkyū (A study of the utilization of public involvement for road planning). *JSCE Infrastructure Planning Review*, 19(2), 213–220.

Maekawa, H., Takayama, J., and Rachi, M. (2003). PI wo mochiita dōro keikaku ni okeru gōi keisei no jittai to kadai (Study on actual condition and problems of the agreement formation in road planning by public involvement method). *Doboku keikakugaku kenkyū kōen shū* (Proceedings of infrastructure planning), 28, CD-ROM.

Major, B., Kaiser, C. R., and McCoy, S. K. (2003). It's not my fault: When and why attributions to prejudice protect self-esteem. *Personality and Social Psychology Bulletin*, 29, 772–781.

Major, B., Quinton, W. J., and McCoy, S. K. (2002). Antecedents and consequences of attributions to discrimination: Theoretical and empirical advances. In M. P. Zanna (Ed.). *Advances in experimental social psychology* (Vol.34, pp. 251–330). San Diego: Academic Press.

Major, B., Quinton, W. J., and Schmader, T. (2003). Attributions to discrimination and self-esteem: Impact of group identification and situational ambiguity. *Journal of Experimental Social Psychology*, 39, 220–231.

Manabe, T. (1996). Chiiki aichaku shin no kitei yōin: Chiiki seikatsu kankyō hyōka wo chūshin to shite (Community attachment and local life environmental evaluation). *Ningen Bunka Kenkyūka Nenpō* (Annual reports of Graduate School of Human Culture), 12, 115–124.

Manzo, L. C., and Weinstein, N. D. (1987). Behavioral commitment to environmental protection: A study of active and nonactive members of the Sierra club, *Environment and Behavior*, 19, 673–694.

Manzo, L. C., and Perkins, D. D. (2006). Finding common ground: The importance of place attachment to community participation and planning. *Journal of Planning Literature*, 20, 335–350.

Markus, H. R., and Kitayama, S. (1991). Culture and the self: Implications for cognition, emotion and motivation. *Psychological Review*, 98, 224–253.

Marshall, G., Rose, D., Newby, H., and Vogler, C. (1988). *Social class in modern Britain*. London: Hutchinson.

Maslow, A. H. (1954). *Motivation and personality*. New York: Harper & Brothers.

Maslow, A. H. (1971) *Ningensei no shinrigaku: Mochibēshon ando pāsonaritī* (Psychology of personality: Motivation and personality). T. Oguchi (Trans.). Tokyo: Sannōdai Shuppanbu.

Matsuda, M., and Ishida, H. (2002). Toshi keikaku masutā puran ni okeru PI purosesu no arikata ni kansuru kōsatsu: Ibaraki ken Ushiki shi o taishō toshite (A study for effective public involvement in the Ushiku city master plan process). *JSCE Infrastructure Planning Review*, 19(3), 129–136.

Matsui, A. (1999). Syakai shisutemu no rinrigaku: syoyū, fukushi, byōdō (Ethics of social systems: ownership, well-being and equality). In A. Takamasu and A. Matsui (Eds) (1999). *Anaritikaru Marukishizumu* (Analytical Marxism, pp. 131–151). Nakanishiya Shuppan.

McCoy, S. K., and Major, B. (2003). Group identification moderates emotional responses to perceived prejudice. *Personality and Social Psychology Bulletin,* 29, 1005–1017.

Mendoza-Denton, R., Shaw-Taylor, L., Chen, S., and Chang, E. (2009). Ironic effects of explicit gender prejudice on women's test performance. *Journal of Experimental Social Psychology,* 45, 275–278.

Mesch, G. S., and Manor, O. (1998). Social ties, environmental perception, and local attachment. *Environment and Behavior,* 30(4), 504–519.

Mikula, G. (1993). On the experience of injustice. In W. Strobe and M. Hewstone (Eds). *European review of social psychology* (Vol. 4, pp. 223–244). New York: Wiley.

Ministry of Education, Culture, Sports, Science and Technology (2009). *Gakkō kihon chōsa: Nenji tōkei* (School Basic Survey: Annual report). Retrieved 31 Jury 2010, from http://www.e-stat.go.jp/SG1/estat/List.do?bid=000001015843&cycode=0

Ministry of Foreign Affairs of Japan (2010) Share of expenses for United Nation, 2008–2010. (2008–10 nen Kokuren tsūjō yosan buntan ritsu / buntan kin). Retrieved 8 November 2010, from http://www.mofa.go.jp/mofaj/gaiko/jp_un/yosan.html.

Miyano, M. (1998). Kachikan, shakaitcki ninchi, makuro kōsei rinen (Values, social cognition, macro justice). In M. Miyano (Ed.). *Kōheikan to shakai kaisō: 1995-nen SSM chōsa shirīzu 8* (Sense of fairness and social strata) (pp.95–110), 1995 SSM Chōsa Kenkyūkai Hōkokusho.

Miyano, M. (2000). Kōhei rinen wa dono yō ni keisei sareru no ka: Gainen no seiri to Nihon no ichizuke (How is a philosophy of fairness formed: A consolidation of concepts and the Japanese position). In M. Umino (Ed.). *Nihon no kaisō shisutemu 2: Kōheikan to seiji ishiki* (Stratification system in Japan 2: A sense of fairness and political consciousness) (pp. 85–102). Tokyo: Tokyo Daigaku Shuppan Kai.

Morris, M., and Leung, K. (2000). Justice for all? Progress in research on cultural variation in the psychology of distributive and procedural justice. *Applied Psychology,* 49, 100–132.

Moya, M., Exposito, F., and Casado, P. (1999). Women's reaction to hostile and benevolent sexist situations. Paper presented at the 22nd General Meeting of the European Association of Experimental Social Psychology, Oxford, England.

Moya, M., Glick, P., Exposito, F., de Lemus, S., and Hart, J. (2007). It's for your own good: Benevolent sexism and women's reactions to protectively justified restrictions. *Personality and Social Psychology Bulletin,* 33, 1421–1434.

Mummendey, A., Klink, A., and Brown, R. (2001). Nationalism and patriotism: National identification and out-group rejection. *British Journal of Social Psychology,* 40, 159–172.

Muramoto, Y. (2009). Kojin shugi to shūdan shugi (Individualism and collectivism). The Japanese Society of Social Psychology (Ed.). *Shakai shinrigaku jiten.* (Social psychology dictionary) (pp. 474–475). Tokyo: Maruzen.

Nagamatsu, N. (2004). Zenpanteki fukōheikan no hassei jōken: Danjo kan no kitei kōzō no sai ni chūmoku shite (Conditions for the occurrence of a general sense of unfairness: Focusing on male-female difference in the determinant structure). In Y. Naoi and H. Tarōmaru (Eds). *Jōhōka shakai ni kansuru zenkoku chōsa chūkan hōkoku* (Interim report of the Japan survey on information society) (pp. 158–170).

Nakagawa, T. (1980). *Chōnaikai: Nihonjin no jichi kankaku* (Neighborhood association: Sense of self-government of the Japanese). Tokyo: Chūkō Shinsho.

Nakane, C. (1970). *Japanese society*. Berkeley, CA: University of California Press.

Nakao, K. (2000). Occupational prestige. In E. F. Borgatta, and R. J. V. Montgomery (Eds). *Encyclopedia of Sociology*. Revised edition (pp. 1996–2002). New York: MacMillan.

Nakao, K., and Treas, J. (1994). Updating occupational prestige and socioeconomic scores: How the new measures measure up. *Sociological Methodology*, 24, 1–72.

Nakayachi, K., and Watabe, M. (2005). Hitojichi teikyō ga shinraisei hyōka ni oyobosu eikyō: Jihatsuteki kyōshutsu to kōi jisseki no kōka (Influence of hostage posting on estimation of trustworthiness: The efficacy of voluntary posting). *The Japanese Journal of Psychology*, 76(3), 235–243.

Naoi, A. (1978). Shokugyō no bunrui to shakudo (Classification and scales of occupations). In 1975 Nen SSM Zenkoku Chōsa Iinkai (The 1975 SSM National Survey Committee). *Shakai kaisō to shakai idō 1975 nen SSM zenkoku chōsa hōkoku* (Social strata and social mobility: Report of the 1975 SSM National Survey) (pp. 270–288).

Naoi, A. (1979). Shokugyō teki chii shakudo no kōsei (The construction of an occupational status scale). In K. Tominaga (Ed.). *Nihon no kaisō kōzō* (Japan's stratum structure) (pp. 434–472). Tokyo: University of Tokyo Press.

Naoi, A., and Suzuki, T. (1978). Shokugyō no shakai teki hyōka no bunseki: shokugyō ishin sukoa no kentō (An analysis of social evaluations of occupations: A study on the occupational prestige score). In 1975 Nen SSM Zenkoku Chōsa Iinkai (The 1975 SSM National Survey Committee). *Shakai kaisō to shakai idō 1975 nen SSM zenkoku chōsa hōkoku* (Social strata and social mobility: Report of the 1975 SSM National Survey) (pp. 235–258).

Naoi, Y., and Sugano, T. (2004). Jōhōka shakai ni kansuru zenkoku chōsa gaiyō (JIS2001, JIS2002) (Brief summary of the Japan survey on information society (JIS2001, JIS2002)). In Y. Naoi and H. Tarōmaru (Eds). *Jōhōka shakai ni kansuru zenkoku chōsa chūkan hōkoku* (Interim report of the Japan survey on information society) (pp. 1–10).

National Institute of Labor Administration (1998). Kikai no byodo to kakusa no koseisa wo: Kobetsuka no shinten to roshikankei (Toward equal opportunity and fair disparity: Indivualization in industrial relations). Japan Productivity Center (Eds). *Sogo Shiryo M&L* (Integrated Data M&L) 243, p. 42–53.

NHK Broadcasting Culture Research Institute (1984). *Nihonjin no shūkyō ishiki* (Japanese religious attitude). Tokyo: Japan Broadcast Publishing Co., Ltd.

NHK Broadcasting Culture Research Institute (2010). *Gendai Nihonjin no ishiki kōzō* (Attitude structure of contemporary Japanese people), 7th edition. Tokyo: Japan Broadcast Publishing Co., Ltd.

Nietz, J. A. (1935). The depression and the social status of occupations. *Elementary School Journal*, 35, 434–472.

Nishihira, S. (1964). Shakai teki hyōka ni motozuku shokugyō bunrui no kokoromi (An attempt to classify occupations based on social evaluations). *Journal of Research on Social and Economic Life*, 3(10), 1–6.

Nonami, H., Katō, J., Ikeuchi, H., and Kosugi, K. (2002). Kyōyū zai to shiteno kasen ni taisuru kankyō dantaiin to ippan jūmin no shūgō kōi: Kojin kōdō to shūdan kōdō no kiteiin (Environmental volunteer and average resident collective action toward rivers as public goods: Determinants of personal and group behavior). *Shakai shinrigaku kenkyū* (Japanese journal of social psychology), 17, 123–135.

NORC (National Opinion Research Center) (1947). Jobs and occupations: A popular evaluation. *Opinion News*, 11, 3–13. Reprinted (1953) in R. Bendix, and S. M. Lipset (Eds). *Class, Status, and Power: A reader in social stratification* (pp. 411–426). New York: Free Press.

Nussbaum, M. (2005). *Josei to ningen kaihatsu: Senzai nōryoku apurōchi* (Women and human development: The capabilities approach). Y. Ikemoto, S. Taguchi, and H. Tsuboi (Trans.). Tokyo: Iwanami Shoten.

Obana, K., and Hirose, Y. (2008). Kōkyōjigyō keikaku no tetsuzukiteki kōseisa ga jigyō shutai no shinrai ni oyobosu eikyō to jiyū sairyō no chōsei kōka (The influence of procedural fairness in public project planning on trust in the project and its effectiveness in creating latitude). *JSCE Journal of Infrastructure Planning and Management D*, 64(4), 557–566.

Oda, T., and Abe, K. (2000). Fukōhei kan ha dono yō ni shite shōjiru noka: seisei mekanizumu no kaimei (How is a sense of unfairness formed?: An analysis of the formation mechanism). In M. Umino (Ed.). *Nihon shakai no kaisō shisutemu 2: Kōheikan to seiji ishiki* (Stratification system in Japan 2: A sense of fairness and political consciousness) (pp. 103–125). Tokyo: Tokyo Daigaku Shuppankai.

OECD (2006). *Policy brief: Economic survey of Japan*. Retrieved 9 October 2010, from http://www.oecd.org/dataoecd/50/23/37148463.pdf

Ohbuchi, K. (1998). Conflict management in Japan. In K. Leung and D. Tjosvold (Eds). *Conflict management in the Asian Pacific* (pp. 49–72). New York: Wiley & Sons.

Ohbuchi, K. (2001). Tasuijun no kōsei hyōka to kuni ni taisuru taido (Multi-level evaluation of fairness and attitudes towards the state). *Tōhoku Daigaku Bungaku Kenkyūka Nenpō* (The annual of the Graduate School of Arts and Letters, Tōhoku University), 51, 150–172.

Ohbuchi, K. (2004). Kuni ni taisuru kōsei handan no tagensei to kōsei no kizuna (Diversity in evaluation of fairness towards the state and a justice-bond). In K. Ohbuchi (Ed.). *Nihonjin no kōseikan: Kōsei ha kojin to shakai wo musubu kizuna ka?* (Japanese perceptions of fairness: Is fairness the bond that binds individuals and society?) (pp. 127–163) Sagamihara: Gendai Tosho.

Ohbuchi, K. (2007a). The social bonds of justice: Theory and research. In K. Ohbuchi (Ed.). *Social justice in Japan: Concepts, theories and paradigms* (pp. 3–33). Melbourne: Trans Pacific Press.

Ohbuchi, K. (2007b). The structure of justice: Theoretical considerations. In K. Ohbuchi (Ed.). *Social justice in Japan: Concepts, theories and paradigms* (pp. 72–92). Melbourne: Trans Pacific Press.

Ohbuchi, K. (2008a) Kōsei na shakai wo mezashite. (Toward a fair society). In J. Hara, T. Sato, and K. Ohbuchi (Eds). *Shakai kaisō to fubyōdō* (Social stratification and inequality) (pp. 222–234). Tokyo: Hōsō Daigaku Kyōiku Shinkōkai.

Ohbuchi, K. (2008b). Fubyodō to kōsei (Inequality and justice). In J. Hara., Y. Sato., and K. Ohbuchi (Eds). *Shakai kaisō to fubyōdō* (Social stratification and inequality) (pp. 209–221). Hōsōdaigaku Kyōiku Shinkōkai.

Ohbuchi, K. (2008c). Japanese conflict on justice: Fairness principles and social ideals. Working paper presented in the 2007 Annual Report of the Center for the Study of Social Stratification and Inequity, Tohoku University.

Ohbuchi, K. (2010). Nihon ni okeru shakai kaiso to kachikan (Social class and values in Japan). *The Annual Reports of Graduate School of Arts and Letters Tohoku University*, Vol. 60.

Ohbuchi, K., and Fukuno, M. (2003). Shakaiteki kōsei to kuni ni taisuru taido no kizuna kasetsu: Tasuijun kōsei hyōka, bunpai oyobi tetsuzukiteki kōsei (A justice-bond hypothesis on the relationship between social justice and attitudes towards the state: Multi-level evaluation of distributive and procedural fairness). *Shakai Shinrigaku Kenkyū* (Japanese Journal of Social Psychology), 18, 204–212.

Ohbuchi, K., and Kawashima, N. (2009a). Nihon no dentōteki kachi shakudo no sakusei: Bukkyō, Jukyō, Shintō, kokugaku shisō ni motozuite (Development of a scale of Japanese traditional values: Buddhism, Confucianism, and ancient Japanese thoughts). *Bunka*, 73(1, 2), 110–140.

Ohbuchi, K., and Kawashima, N. (2009b). Gendai Nihonjin ni yoru dentōteki kachi no juyō: Shakai zokusei to no kanren (How do the contemporary Japanese people accept Japanese traditional values? Differences across social groups). *Bunka*, 73(3, 4), 21–46.

Ohbuchi, K., Atsumi, E., and Takaku, S. (2008). Cross-cultural study on victim's responses to apology in interpersonal and intergroup conflicts. *Tōhoku Psychologica Folia*, 76, 53–60.

Ohbuchi, K., Kawashima, N., and Aoki, T. (2008). Shakai shihon seibi ni okeru kōkyōjuyō no yōin: Seisaku hyōka jigen to demogurafikku hensū ni yoru bunseki (Factors in the public acceptance of infrastructure development: Analysis of dimensions of policy evaluation and demographic variables). *JSCE Journal of Infrastructure Planning and Management D*, 64(3), 325–339.

Ohbuchi, K., Sato, S., and Tedeschi, J. (1999). Nationality, individualism-collectivism, and power distance in conflict management. *Tohoku Psychologica Folia*, 58, 36–49.

Ohbuchi, K., Satoh, H., and Miura, Y. (2008). Gendai Nihonjin no kachikan to dentōteki shisō: Bukkyō, Jukyō, Shintō, kokugaku no shisō naiyō to chōsa kōmoku no sakusei (How are Japanese contemporary social values affected by traditional thoughts? Investigation of thoughts of Buddhism, Confucianism, and Shinto of Japan and construction of items of them for social survey). *The Annual Reports of Graduate School of Arts and Letters Tohoku University*, 58, 154–180.

Ohbuchi, K., Teshigahara, K., Imazai, K., and Sugawara, I. (2005). Procedural justice and the assessment of civil justice in Japan. *Law and Society Review*, 39, 875–892.

Ohtsuka, K. (2008). *Nihon no seiji bunka* (Japanese political culture). Tokyo: Keisō Shobō.

Olson, J. M., Roese, N. J., Meen, J., and Robertson, D. J. (1994). The reconditions and consequences of relative deprivation: Two field studies. *Journal of Applied Social Psychology*, 25, 944–964.

Oyserman, D. (1993). The lens of personhood: Viewing the self and others in a multicultural society. *Journal of Personality and Social Psychology*, 65, 993–1009.

Pattanaik, P. K., and Xu, Y. (1990). On ranking opportunity sets in terms of freedom of choice. *Recherches Economiques de Louvain*, 56, 383–390.

Petty, R. E., and Cacioppo, J. T. (1986). The elaboration likelihood model of persuasion. *Advances in Experimental Social Psychology*, 19, 123–205.

Phan, M. B. (2008). We're all in this together: Context, contacts, and social trust in Canada. *Analysis of Social Issues and Public Policy*, 8(1), 23–51.

Porter, B. E., Leeming, F. C., and Dwyer, W. O. (1995). Solid waste recovery: A review of behavioral programs to increase recycling. *Environment and Behavior*, 27(2), 122–152.

Porter, L. W., Steers, R. M., Mowday, R. T., and Boulian, P. V. (1974). Organizational commitment, job satisfaction, and turnover among psychiatric technicians. *Journal of Applied Psychology*, 59, 603–609.

Pratto, F., Stallworth, L. M., Sidanius, J., and Siers, B. (1997). The gender gap in occupational role attainment: A social dominance approach. *Journal of Personality and Social Psychology*, 72, 37–53.

Proshansky, H. M. (1978). The city and self-identity. *Environment and Behavior*, 10, 147–169.

Randall, D. M. (1990). The consequences of organizational commitment: Methodological investigation. *Journal of Organizational Behavior*, 11, 361–378.

Rawls, J. (1971). *A theory of justice*. Cambridge, MA: Harvard University Press.

Rawls, J. (2010). *Seigiron: kaiteiban* (A theory of justice: revised edition). T. Kawamoto, S. Fukuma, and Y. Kamishima (Trans.). Tokyo: Kinokuniya Shoten.

Reicher, S. D. (1984). Social influence in the crowd: Attitudinal and behavioral effects of de-individuation in conditions of high and low group salience. *The British Journal of Social Psychology*, 23, 341–350.

Robbins, L. (1932). *An essay on the nature and significance of economic science*. London: George Allen and Unwin.

Roemer, J. E. (1996). *Theory of Distributive Justice*. Cambridge: Harvard University Press.

Rosenberg, S., Nelson, C., and Vivekananthan, P. S. (1968). A multidimensional approach to the structure of personality impressions. *Journal of Personality and Social Psychology*, 9, 283–294.

Rubin, Z., and Peplau, L. A. (1975). Who believes in a just world? *Journal of Social Issues*, 31, 65–90.

Rudman, L. A., and Heppen, J. (2003). Implicit romantic fantasies and women's interest in personal power: A glass slipper effect? *Personality and Social Psychology Bulletin*, 29, 1357–1370.

Rudman, L. A., Greenwald, A. G., and McGhee, D. E. (2001). Implicit self-concept and evaluative implicit gender stereotypes: Self and ingroup share desirable traits. *Personality and Social Psychology Bulletin*, 27, 1164–1178.

Ruggiero, K. M., and Taylor, D. M. (1997). Why minority group members perceive or not perceive the discrimination that confronts them: The role of self-esteem and perceived control. *Journal of Personality and Social Psychology*, 72, 373–389.

Saitō, Y., and Yamagishi, T. (2000). Nihonjin no fukōheikan wa tokushu ka: Hikaku shakaironteki shiten de (Is the Japanese sense of unfairness unique?: From the perspective of comparative social theory). In M. Umino (Ed.). *Nihon shakai no kaisō shisutemu 2: Kōheikan to seiji ishiki* (Stratification system in Japan 2: A sense of fairness and political consciousness) (pp.127–49). Tokyo: Tokyo Daigaku Shuppankai.

Sakakibara, H., Kidera, K., Kirishima, K., and Takahashi, D. (2006). Seisaku konfurikuto ni okeru komyunikeishon sokushin no kōka ni kansuru kenkyū (A study of the effects of communication between stakeholders in policy conflicts). *JSCE Infrastructure Planning Review*, 23(1), 79–89.

Satō, T. (2005). Sakushu, bunpai teki seigi, shoyūken: Orutanatibu shakai wo motomete (Exploitation, distributive justice, ownership: In pursuit of an alternative society). *Kikan Keizai Riron* (Economic Theory Quarterly), 41, 4.

Sato, T. (2000). *Fubyōdō shakai Japan: Sayōnara sōchūryū* (Unequal society Japan: Goodbye all middle-class). Chūkō Shinsho.

Schmitt, M. T., and Branscombe, N. R. (2002a). The meaning and consequences of perceived discrimination in disadvantaged and privileged social groups. *European Review of Social Psychology*, 12, 167–199.

Schmitt, M. T., and Branscombe, N. R. (2002b). The internal and external causal loci of attributions to prejudice. *Personality and Social Psychology Bulletin*. 28, 620–628.

Schmitt, M. T., Branscombe, N. R., Kobrynowicz, D., and Owen, S. (2002). Perceiving discrimination against one's gender-group has different implications for well-being in women and men. *Personality and Social Psychology Bulletin*, 28, 197–210.

Schwartz, S. H. (1977). Normative influence on altruism. In L. Berkowitz (Ed.). *Advances in experimental psychology*, 10, 221–279. New York: Academic Press.

Seiyama, K. (2004). Fukushi ni totte no byōdō riron: Sekinin byōdō shugi hihan (Theories of equality in relation to social welfare: A critique of egalitarianism). In Y. Shionoya, K. Suzumura and R. Gotoh (Eds) (2004). *Fukushi no kōkyō tetsugaku* (A public philosophy of welfare), (pp. 179–195). Tokyo: Tokyo Daigaku Shuppankai.

Seligman, M. E. P. (1975). *Helplessness: On depression, development, and death*. San Francisco, California: W.H. Freeman & Co., Publishers.

Sen, A. K. (1979a). Utilitarianism and welfarism. *The Journal of Philosophy*, 76, 463–489.
Sen, A. K. (1979b). Personal utilities and public judgements: Or what's wrong with welfare. *The Economic Journal*, 89, 537–558.
Sen, A. K. (1980). Equality of what? In A. K. Sen (1982). *Choice, welfare and measurement* (pp. 353–369). Cambridge: MIT Press.
Sen, A. K. (1982). *Choice, welfare and measurement*. Cambridge: MIT Press.
Sen, A. K. (1985a). *Fukushi no keizaigaku: Zai to senzai nōryoku* (Commodities and capabilities). K. Suzumura (Trans.). Tokyo: Iwanami Shoten.
Sen, A. K. (1985b). Well-being, agency and freedom: The Dewey Lectures 1984, *The Journal of Philosophy*, 82, 169–221.
Sen, A. K. (1989). *Gōritekina orokamono: Keizaigaku = rinrigaku teki tankyū* (Choice, welfare and measurement), T. Ōba and T. Kawamoto (Trans.). Tokyo: Keisō Shobō.
Sen, A. K. (1992). *Fubyōdō no saikentō* (Inequality re-examined). Y. Ikemoto, H. Nogami and J. Sato (Trans.). Tokyo: Iwanami Shoten.
Sen, A. K. (1999). *Jiyū to keizai kaihatsu* (Development as freedom). M. Ishizuka (Trans.). Tokyo: Tōyō Keizai Shinpōsha.
Sen, A. K. (2004). Elements of a theory of human rights. *Philosophy and Public Affairs*, 32, 315–356.
Sewell, W. H., Haller, A. O., and Ohlendorf, G. W. (1970). The educational and early occupational status attainment process. *American Sociological Review*, 35, 1014–1027.
Shelton, J. N., Richeson, J. A., and Salvatore, J. (2005). Expecting to be the target of prejudice: Implications for interethnic interactions. *Personality and Social Psychology Bulletin*, 31, 1189–1202.
Shionoya, Y. (2002). *Keizai to rinri* (Economics and ethics). Tokyo: Tokyo Daigaku Shuppankai.
Shionoya, Y., Suzumura, K., and Gotoh, R. (Eds) (2004). *Fukushi no kōkyō tetsugaku* (A public philosophy of welfare). Tokyo: Tokyo Daigaku Shuppankai.
Shiotani, Y. (2010). Shokugyō teki chii no kōsei imēgi to chii shikō: shokugyō no shakai teki chii no zentaizō ni kansuru kojin no ninchi ni chakumoku shite (Structural image of occupational status and status orientation: Focusing on individual perception about the overall picture of the social status of occupations). *Sociological Theory and Methods*, 25(1), 65–80.
Shōgai Gakushū Kyoku. (2008). *Gakkō kyōin tōkei chōsa heisei 19 nendoban* (Statistics of school teachers: 2007 edition). Ministry of Education, Culture, Sports, Science and Technology, Japan.
Siegel, P. M. (1971). *Prestige in the American occupational structure*. Ph.D. Dissertation. Department of Sociology, University of Chicago.
Skarlicki, D. P., and Folger, R. (1997). Retaliation in the workplace: The roles of distributive, procedural, and interactional justice. *Journal of Applied Psychology*, 82, 434–443.
Skitka, L. J. (2002). Do the means always justify the ends, or do the ends sometimes justify the means? A value protection model of justice reasoning. *Personality and Social Psychology Bulletin*, 28, 588–597.

Smith, H., Spears, R., and Oyen, M. (1994). The influence of personal deprivation and salience of group membership on justice evaluations. *Journal of Experimental Social Psychology*, 30, 277–299.

Smith, M. (1935). Proposals for making a scale of status of occupations. *Sociology and Social Research*, 20, 40–49.

Sōmu Shō (Ministry of Internal Affairs and Communications) (2009). *Heisei 21 nen rōdōryoku chōsa* (2009 workforce survey). http://www.stat.go.jp/data/roudou/index.htm.

Stathi, S., and Crisp, R. J. (2008). Imagining intergroup contact promotes projection to outgroups. *Journal of Experimental Social Psychology*, 44, 943–957.

Statistics Bureau and Director-General for Policy Planning (2007). *Employment Status Survey (2007)*. Ministry of Internal Affairs and Communications.

Statistics Bureau, Director-General for Policy Planning and Statistical Research and Training Institute (2001). *Special Survey of the Labour Force*. Ministry of Internal Affairs and Communications.

Stehr, N. (1974). Consensus and dissensus in occupational prestige. *British Journal of Sociology*, 25, 410–427.

Stevens, L., and Jones, E. E. (1976). Defensive attribution and the Kelly Cube. *Journal of Personality and Social Psychology*, 34, 809–820.

Stevens, S. S. (1975). *Psychophysics: Introduction to its Perceptual, Neural and Social Prospects*. New York: Wiley.

Stewart, A., and Blackburn, R. M. (1975). The stability of structural inequality. *Sociological Review*, 23, 481–508.

Stouffer, S. A., Suchman, E. A., DeVinney, L. C., Star, S. A., and Williams, R.A., Jr. (1949). *The American soldier: Adjustments during army life* (Vol. 1). Princeton: Princeton University Press.

Struch, N., and Schwartz, S. H. (1989). Intergroup aggression: Its predictors and distinctness from in-group bias. *Journal of Personality and Social Psychology*, 56, 364–373.

Sugimoto, Y., and Mouer, R. (1995). *Nihonjinron no hōteishiki* (The Nihonjinron formula). Tokyo: Chikuma Gakugei Bunko.

Sugimoto, Y., Narumi, K., Sawaki, M., and Oka, E. (2003). Daitoshi shigaichi nai shūraku ni okeru shinrai kyojūsha no kyūrai komyunitī he no sanka kanōsei ni kansuru kenkyū: Dentō teki matsuri he no sanka jittai to ishiki wo tsūjite (The study on the possibility of newcomer-residents' participation in old village's community in urban area: Through the participation in and consciousness of a conventional festival). *Kankyō jōhō kagaku ronbunshū* (Papers on environmental information science), 17, 183–188.

Suminaga, T., Hatori, T., and Fujii, S. (2009). Machizukuri ni okeru 'Chiiki karisuma' no chō ritateki dōki no kitē yōin ni kansuru kenkyu (An empirical study on determinants of super altruistic motivation in a local community development by 'regional charismas'). *Doboku keikakugaku kenkyū kōen shū* (Proceedings of infrastructure planning), 40, CD-ROM.

Supreme Court (2010). *Justice Statistics*, http://www.courts.go.jp/sihotokei/nenpo/pdf/B21DMIN1-1.pdf (accessed on 19 November 2010).

Suzuki, A. (2008). Kyaria, jendā to fubyōdo (Career, gender and inequality).

In J. Hara, Y. Sato and K. Ohbuchi (Eds). *Shakai kaisō to fubyōdou* (Social stratification and inequality) (pp.177–191).
Suzumura, K., and Gotoh, R. (2001). *Amartia Sen: Keizaigaku to rinrigaku* (Amartya Sen: Economics and ethics). Tokyo: Jikkyō Shuppan.
Swim, J. K., and Hyers, L. L. (1999). Excuse me—What did you just say?!: Women's public and private responses to sexist remarks. *Journal of Experimental Social Psychology*, 35, 68–88.
Tachibanaki, T. (1998). *Nihon no keizai kakusa: Shotoku to shisan kara kangaeru* (Economic disparities in Japan: Income and assets). Iwanami Shoten.
Tachibanaki, T. (2006). *Kakusa shakai: Nani ga mondai nano ka* (Social disparities: What is the problem?). Iwanami Shoten.
Tachibanaki, T., and Urakawa, K. (2006). *Nihon no hinkon kenkyū* (A study of poverty in Japan). Tokyo: Tokyo Daigaku Shuppankai.
Tajfel, H. (1982). Social psychology of intergroup relations. *Annual Review of Psychology*, 33, 1–39.
Tajfel, H., and Turner, J. (1979). An integrative theory of intergroup conflict. In W. G. Austin and S. Worschel (Eds). *The social psychology of intergroup relations.* (pp. 33–47). Pacific Grove, CA: Brooks/Cole Publishing.
Tajfel, H., and Turner, J. (1986). The social identity theory of intergroup behavior. In S. Worchel, and W. G. Austin (Eds). *Psychology of intergroup relations* (pp. 7–24). Chicago: Nelson.
Tajfel, H., Billig, M., Bundy, R., and Flament, C. (1971). Social categorization and intergroup behaviour. *European Journal of Social Psychology*, 1, 149–178.
Takahashi, J. (1982). Komyunitī senchimento ni kansuru ichi kōsatsu: Chiiki he no aichaku ishiki wo chūshin ni (A study on community sentiment: With special reference to community attachment). *Shōtoku Daigaku Kenkyū Kiyō* (Memoirs of Shukutoku College), 16, 45–63.
Takamasu, A., and Matsui, A. (Eds) (1999). *Anaritikaru Marukishizumu* (Analytical Marxism). Nakanishiya Shuppan.
Takano, Y. (2008). *Shudanshugi toiu sakkaku* ('Collectivism' as an illusion). Tokyo: Shinyosha.
Tanaka, K. (1996). Kōsei sekai no sinpōsha ha kōsei na hyōka ni oite jiko chūshin teki ni nariyasui ka (Are just-world-believers apt to be egocentric in fairness judgments?). *Kokusai Keizai Ron Shū* (Journal of International Economics, Hamamatsu University), 3, 69–75.
Tanaka, K. (2008). *Kōhai suru shokuba/ hangyaku suru jūgyōin: Shokuba ni okeru jūgyōin no han shakaiteki kōdō ni kansuru shinrigaku teki kenkyū* (Decaying workplaces/rebellious employees: A psychological study on antisocial behavior of employees at workplaces). Nakanishiya Shoten.
Tanaka, N., Todoroki, O., Nakajima, N., and Tawada, M. (2008). Fūdo ni nezashita infurasutorakuchā keisei ni kansuru kenkyū: Kakinosawa chiku no michi bushin wo jirei toshite (Infrastructure management rooted in a cultural climate: Case study on the 'pass construction' in Kakinosawa area). *Doboku gakkai ronbun shū* (Journal of infrastructure planning and management), D-64, 218–227.

Tanishita, M. (2001). Shakai shihon seibi no keikaku sakutei tetsuzuki ni okeru shimin sanka (Citizen participation in infrastructure planning procedure). *Doboku gakkai ronbun shū* (Journal of infrastructure planning and management), D-52, 37–49.

Tarohmaru, H. (1998a). Shokugyō hyōteichi oyobi shokugyō ishin sukoa no kihonteki tokusei (The basic characteristics of occupational rating value and occupational prestige score). In 1995 Nen SSM Chōsa Iinkai (1995 SSM Survey Committee), *1995 nen SSM chōsa shirīzu 5: Shokugyō hyōka no kōzō to shokugyō ishin sukoa* (1995 SSM Survey series vol. 5: System of occupational evaluation and occupational prestige score), 31–44.

Tarohmaru, H. (1998b). Shokugyō hyōtei no icchido to kanshukan teki kaisō kōzō (The degree of consensus on the occupational prestige rating and intersubjective structure of social stratification). In 1995 Nen SSM Chōsa Iinkai (1995 SSM Survey Committee), *1995 nen SSM chōsa shirīzu 5: Shokugyō hyōka no kōzō to shokugyō ishin sukoa* (1995 SSM Survey series vol. 5: System of occupational evaluation and occupational prestige score), 15–29.

Tarohmaru, H. (1998c). Shokugyō ishin to shakai kaisō: han jyunjyo kankei toshiteno shakai kaisō (Occupational Prestige and Social Stratification: Social Stratification as Partial Order). In 1995 Nen SSM Chōsa Iinkai (1995 SSM Survey Committee), *1995 nen SSM chōsa shirīzu 5: Shokugyō hyōka no kōzō to shokugyō ishin sukoa* (1995 SSM Survey series vol. 5: System of occupational evaluation and occupational prestige score), 1–14.

Taylor, D. M., Wright, S. C., Moghaddam, F. M., and Lalonde, R. N. (1990). The personal/group discrimination discrepancy: Perceiving my group, but not myself, to be a target of discrimination. *Personality and Social Psychology Bulletin*, 16, 254–262.

Taylor, R. B., Gottfredson, S. D., and Brower, S. (1985). Attachment to place: Discriminant validity, and impacts of disorder and diversity. *American Journal of Community Psychology*, 13(5), 525–542.

Taylor, S., and Brown, J. D. (1988). Illusion and well-being: A social psychological perspective on mental health. *Psychological Bulletin*, 103, 211–222.

Thibaut, J., and Walker, L. (1975). *Procedural justice: A psychological analysis*. Hillsdale, NJ: Lawrence Erlbaum.

Thibaut, J., and Walker, L. (1978). A theory of procedure. *California Law Review*, 66, 541–566.

Thøgersen, J. (1994). A model of recycling behavior, with evidence from Danish source separation programmes. *Journal of Research in Marketing*, 11, 145–163.

Thøgersen, J. (1996). Recycling and morality: A critical review of the literature. *Environment and Behavior*, 28(4), 536–558.

Tominaga, K. (1979). Shakai kaisō to shakai idō eno apurōchi (An approach to social strata and social mobility). In K. Tominaga (Ed.). *Nihon no kaisō kōzō* (Japan's stratum structure) (pp. 3–29). Tokyo: University of Tokyo Press.

Tost, L. P, and Lind, E. A. (2010). Sounding the alarm: Moving from system justification to system condemnation in the justice judgment process. In E. A. Mannix, M. A. Neale, and E. Mullen (Eds). *Research on Managing Groups and Teams* (Vol. 13). Greenwich, CT: Elsevier Science Press.

Townsend, P. (1993). *The International Analysis of Poverty*. New York and London: Harvester Wheatsheaf.
Treas, J., and Tyree, A. (1979). Prestige versus socioeconomic status in the attainment process of American men and women. *Social Science Research*, 8, 201–221.
Treiman, D. J. (1977). *Occupational Prestige in Comparative Perspective*. New York: Academic Press.
Triandis, H. C., and Gelfand, M. J. (1998). Converging measurement of horizontal and vertical individualism and collectivism. *Journal of Personality and Social Psychology*, 74, 118–128.
Troppe, L. R., and Wright, S. C. (1999). Ingroup identification and relative deprivation: An examination across multiple social comparisons. *European Journal of Social Psychology*, 29, 707–724.
Tsuzuki, K. (2000). Hito wa nani ni naritai noka: Shokugyō miryoku no kōzō (What do people want to become?: The structure of attractiveness of occupations). In M. Umino (Ed.). *Nihon no kaisō system 2: kōheikan to seiji ishiki* (Stratification system in Japan 2: A sense of fairness and political consciousness) (pp. 37–60). Tokyo: University of Tokyo Press.
Turner, J. C., and Onorato, R. S. (1999). Social identity, personality, and the self-concept: A self-categorizing perspective. In T. R. Tyler, R. M. Kramer, and O. P. John (Eds). *The psychology of the social self* (pp. 11–46). Mahwah, NJ: Lawrence Erlbaum Associates.
Turner, J. C., Hogg, M. A., Oakes, P. J., Reicher, S. D., and Wetherell, M. (1995). Shakai shūdan no sai hakken. Jiko kategorīka riron (*Rediscovering the social group: A self-categorization theory* [Oxford: Blackwell (1987)]). C. Araragi, M. Isozaki, T. Naito, and Y. Endo (Trans.). Kyoto: Kitaōji Shobō.
Turner, J. C., Oakes, P. J., Haslam, S. A., and MacGarty, C. (1994). Self and collective: Cognition and social context. *Personality and Social Psychology Bulletin*, 20, 454–463.
Twigger-Ross, C. L., and Uzzell, D. L. (1996). Place and identity processes. *Journal of Environmental Psychology*, 16, 205–220.
Tyler, T. R. (1989). The psychology of procedural justice: A test of the group-value model. *Journal of Personality and Social Psychology*, 57(5), 830–838.
Tyler, T. R., and Lind, E. A. (1992). A relational model of authority in groups. In M. P. Zanna (Ed.). *Advances in experimental social psychology* (Vol. 25, pp. 115–191). New York: Academic Press.
Tyler, T. R., Boeckmann, R. J., Smith, H. J., and Huo, Y. J. (1997). *Tagen shakai ni okeru seigi to kōsei* (Social justice in a diverse society). K. Ohbuchi and I. Sugahara (Trans.). Tokyo: Brain Sha.
Tyler, T. R., Degoey, P., and Smith, H. (1996). Understanding why the justice of group procedures matters: A test of the psychological dynamics of the group-value model. *Journal of Personality and Social Psychology*, 70, 913–930.
Tyler, T. R., and Blader, S. L. (2003). The group engagement model: Procedural justice, social identity, and cooperative behavior. *Personality and Social Psychology Review*, 7, 349–361.

Tyler, T. R., and Smith, H. J. (1998). Social justice and social movements. In D. T. Gilbert, S. T. Fiske, and G. Lindzey (Eds) *The handbook of social psychology* (4th ed., pp. 595–642), Boston: McGraw-Hill.

Uchida, Y., Kitayama, S., Mesquita, B., Reyes, J. A. S., and Morling, B. (2008). Is perceived emotional support beneficial? Well-being and health in independent and interdependent cultures. *Personality and Social Psychology Bulletin*, 34, 741–754.

Umino, M., and Saitō, Y. (1990). Kōheikan to manzokukan: Shakai hyōka no kōzō to shakaiteki chii (Senses of fairness and satisfaction: The structure of social evaluation and social position). In M. Umino (Ed.). *Nihon shakai no kaisō shisutemu 2: Kōheikan to seiji ishiki* (Stratification system in Japan 2: A sense of fairness and political consciousness) (pp.97–123). Tokyo: Tokyo Daigaku Shuppankai.

United Nations Committee on the Elimination of Racial Discrimination (2001). *Concluding Observations of the Committee on the Elimination of Racial Discrimination.* http://www.mofa.go.jp/mofaj/gaiko/jinshu/index.html.

Urmson, J. O. (1998). *Arisutoteresu rinrigaku nyūmon* (Aristotle's Ethics). T. Amemiya (Trans.). Tokyo: Iwanami Shoten.

Usuda, Y., Fujimoto, A., Yamashita, T., Aoki, T., and Matsuda, C. (2000). PI prosesu ni okeru jikan seiyaku no eikyō (Effect of time constraints on behavior of participants in public involvement processes). *JSCE Journal of Construction Management*, 8, 37–44.

Van den Bos, K. (2001). Uncertainty management: The influence of uncertainty salience on reactions to perceived procedural fairness. *Journal of Personality and Social Psychology*, 80, 931–941.

Van den Bos, K., and Lind, E. A. (2002). Uncertainty management by means of fairness judgments. In M. P. Zanna (Ed.). *Advances in experimental social psychology* (Vol. 34, pp. 1–60). San Diego, CA: Academic Press.

Van den Bos, K., and Lind, E. A. (2009). The social psychology of fairness and the regulation of personal uncertainty. In R. M. Arkin, K. C. Oleson, and P. J. Carroll (Eds). *Handbook of the uncertain self* (pp. 122–141). New York: Psychology Press.

Van den Bos, K., Brockner, J., Stein, J. H., Steiner, D. D., Van Yperen, N. W., and Dekker, D. M. (2010). The psychology of voice and performance capabilities in masculine and feminine cultures and contexts. *Journal of Personality and Social Psychology*, 99, 638–648.

Van den Bos, K., Ham, J., Lind, E. A., Simonis, M., van Essen, W. J., Rijpkema, M. (2008). Justice and the human alarm system: The impact of exclamation points and flashing lights on the justice judgment process. *Journal of Experimental Social Psychology*, 44, 201–219.

Van den Bos, K., Heuven, E., Burger, E., and Fernández Van Veldhuizen, M. (2006). Uncertainty management after reorganizations: The ameliorative effect of outcome fairness on job uncertainty. *International Review of Social Psychology*, 19, 75–86.

Van den Bos, K., Lind, E. A., and Wilke, H. (2001). The psychology of procedural justice and distributive justice viewed from the perspective of fairness heuristic theory. In R. Cropanzano (Ed.). *Justice in the workplace:*

Volume II—From theory to practice (pp. 49–66). Mahwah, NJ: Lawrence Erlbaum and Associates.
van den Bos, K., Lind, E. A., Vermunt, R., and Wilke, H. A. M. (1997). How do I judge my outcome when I do not know the outcome of others? The psychology of the fair process effect. *Journal of Personality and Social Psychology*, 72, 1034–1046.
Van Prooijen, J. W. (2006). Retributive reactions to suspected offenders: The importance of social categorizations and guilt probability. *Personality and Social Psychology Bulletin*, 32, 715–726.
Vescio, T. K., Gervais, S. J., Snyder, M., and Hoover, A. (2005). Power and the creation of patronizing environments: The stereotype-based behaviors of the powerful and their effects on female performance in masculine domains. *Journal of Personality and Social Psychology*, 88, 658–672.
Viki, G. T., Abrams, D., and Hutchison, P. (2003). The "true" romantic: Benevolent sexism and paternalistic chivalry. *Sex Role*, 49, 533–537.
Vorauer, J., and Kumhyr, S. M. (2001). Is this about you or me? Self- versus other-directed judgments and feelings in response to intergroup interaction. *Personality and Social Psychology Bulletin*, 27, 706—719.
Walster, E., Walster, G. W., and Berscheid, E. (1978). *Equity: Theory and research*. Boston: Allyn and Bacon.
Watanabe, T. (2006). Chiiki ni taisuru kōteikan no kiteiin: Aichakudo, sumiyasusa, chiiki imēji ni kansuru bunseki (The factors which determine an affirmative consciousness about living area: An analysis of attachment to a local area, ease of living and acceptance of a local image). *Chiiki burando kenkyū* (Local brand research), 2, 99–129.
Wegener, B. (1990). Equity, relative deprivation, and the value consensus paradox. *Social Justice Research*, 42, 278–284.
Wegener, B. (1992). Concepts and measurement of prestige. *Annual Review of Sociology*, 18, 253–280.
Weiner, B. (1979). A theory of motivation for some classroom experiences. *Journal of Educational Psychology*, 71, 3–25.
Wicklund, R. A., and Brehm, J. W. (1976). *Perspectives on cognitive dissonance*. Hillsdale, NJ: Erlbaum.
Williams, D. R., Patterson, M. E., and Roggenbuck, J. W. (1992). Beyond the commodity metaphor: Examining emotional and symbolic attachment to place. *Leisure Science*, 14, 29–46.
Yai, T. (2006). Tetsuzukiteki datōsei gainen o mochiita shimin sankakugata keikaku purosesu no rironteki wakugumi (A theoretical framework of citizen participatory planning processes using a concept of procedural validity). *JSCE Journal of Infrastructure Planning and Management D*, 62(4), 621–637.
Yai, T., and Terabe, T. (1996). Beikoku ni okeru kōtsū keikaku e no paburikku inborubumento (A Public Involvement process for transportation planning and project development in the US). *Papers on City Planning*, (31, pp. 430–408). The City Planning Institute of Japan.
Yai, T., Terabe, T., and Seki, K. (2000). Kōiki kōtsūkeikaku ni okeru paburikku inborubumento no hōhō ni kansuru kenkyū (A study of methods

for involving the public in transportation planning). *JSCE Journal of Infrastructure Planning and Management*, 653(IV-48), 105–115.
Yamaguchi, K., and Wang, Y. (2002). Class identification of married employed women and men in America. *American Journal of Sociology*, 108, 440–475.
Yamamoto, T., and Ohbuchi, K. (2010). Jihiteki seisabetu no teikyō ni taisuru kitai to fubyōdō no seitōka (Expectations for offering benevolent gender discrimination and justifications for inequality). Poster session presented at the 51st Annual Meeting of the Japanese Society of Social Psychology. Osaka University, Japan.
Yamamoto, T., and Ohbuchi, K. (2011). The effect of women's social status on the attitude toward benevolent sexism. Poster session presented at the 12th Annual Conference of Society for Personality and Social Psychology, San Antonio, TX. USA.
Yamashige, S. (1998). Kazoku oyobi chiiki kyōdōtai no kinō to seifu no yakuwari (Functions of families and communities, and roles of governments: Economic analysis of Japanese-style welfare society). *Hitotsubashi Ronsō* (The Hitotsubashi Review), 120, 826–850.
Yomiuri Shimbun (2009). *Keizai teki na yutakasa ga kōhei ni yukiwatatte iru ka* (Is the economic wealth fairly distributed?). Morning newspaper, 22 September.
Yoshihara, N. (2003). Bunpai teki seigi no keizai riron: Sekinin to hoshō apurōchi (Theories of distributive justice: Responsibility and compensation), *Keizaigaku Kenkyū* (Economic Resarch), Hokkaidō University, 53, 3.
Yoshihara, N. (2004). Amartia Sen to syakai sentakuron (Amartya Sen's social choice theory). In H. Esyo and K. Yamazaki (Eds.). *Amartia Sen no sekai* (The World of Amartya Sen) (pp. 51–82). Tokyo: Kōyō Shobō
Young, M., and Willmott, P. (1956). Social gradings by manual workers. *British Journal of Sociology,* 7, 337–345.
Zuckerman, M. (1979). Attribution of success and failure revisited, or: The motivational bias is alive and well in attribution theory. *Journal of Personality*, 47, 245–287.

Index

Aboriginal Canadian 139
African-American 104, 107, 132
alarm activation 11, 13, 15–18, 20
altruistic behavior 164
ambiguous 130
American 6–7, 14, 16–17, 20, 37–8, 44, 48–9, 54, 77, 79, 83, 104, 106–7, 128, 132, 141
animism 56
antisocial behavior 23
anxiety 35–6, 38, 132, 138–9
attribution
  to discrimination 135, 137–40, 142–5, 147, 181
  to prejudice 135, 13–9
atypical job 45, 129

Belgium 73
beliefs in a just world 24
Benedict, Ruth 49–50
benevolent sexism 115–30 see also hostile sexism
big-class schema 66, 85–6
BJW 24, 36–9
  general 24
  personal 24
blue-collar 72, 74, 76
Bonferroni test 47
bubble economy 6, 45, 47
Buddhism/Buddhist 54–9, 61–3

Canada 73–4
capability approach 87, 90, 92, 96, 98–100

causal attribution 131, 133, 135, 142–4, 147–8, 181 see also attribution
  strategy 131, 133, 135, 142, 144, 147
causality 13–14
census 69
Central America 48
child abuse 150
China/Chinese 44, 111–12
Christianity/Christian 55–6
class 17, 41–2, 45–7, 50–2, 57, 59–61, 63–4, 66, 68, 71, 74, 76, 81, 85–6, 119, 121–2, 126, 170
cognitive dissonance 36
cognitive error hypothesis 78–80
cohesiveness 156
collectivism 41, 48–54, 58–60, 63–4
  horizontal 51–4, 58, 60
  vertical 51–4, 58–9, 63
commitment 36, 103, 108, 145, 155–61, 170
  community commitment 155–61
  organizational 155–6
conflict 114
Confucianism/Confucian 56–9, 61, 63
consensus building 163, 166–74
consequentialism 99, 180
cooperative action 8
cross-cultural psychology 3–4, 6
cultural fairness dynamic 8

cultural self 48
cultural style 49
cultural value dimensions 4
culture 3–10, 12–14, 16, 18–19, 21, 31, 49, 62, 74, 108, 141, 146
  American 7, 16
  Japanese 49
cyber homeless 33

decision-making 42, 154
defensive psychological mechanism 127
Democratic Party 41, 169
deservedness 23, 42–3
deviant remonstrative behavior 23
disability 91–5
disadvantage 25, 35–9, 61, 89, 91, 97, 127, 129–48
discount hypothesis 133–137, 139
discrepancy ratio 80
discrimination 104–5, 109, 115–18, 127–28, 130–48, 180–1
distributive
  equality 31
  fairness 7, 29–31, 33–4, 39, 42–3, 170–2, 176
  justice 87–91, 94, 96, 100, 103, 177, 180
Dutch 110
Dworkin, R. 89–90, 94–5, 100, 180–1

East Asia 48
economic
  bubble 22, 45
  disparities 65
  downturn 5–6, 11, 15
  inequality 29

  recession 14, 45
  theory 87
  wealth 23
  welfare 14
educational background 22, 25–8, 34, 37, 157
educational credentials 72
efficiency 180
egalitarian 73, 88–9, 92, 94–7, 115–16, 129, 181
egalitarianism 88, 92, 94–7, 181
ego threat 104, 106
egocentrism 75–6
egotism 165
Elaboration Likelihood Model 168
Emperor 50
employee 22, 50, 53, 68, 70, 104, 153, 155–6
employment status 22, 25, 65, 75
enlightenment effect hypothesis 28
environmental factors 156, 158–9
environmental psychology 163, 178
equal distribution 30, 34, 42–7, 63, 92, 94, 110
Equal Employment Opportunity Law 116, 141
equality 12, 28–31, 32–4, 38, 42–7, 63–4, 89–90, 92, 94–6, 117, 120, 126–8, 130, 180–1
  orientation 45
  principle 38
equitable distribution 19, 30, 34, 42, 44–6, 63
equitable treatment 30

equity orientation 31
equity principle 31–5, 38
equity theory 9, 103
Europe 38, 48, 120, 163
fairness 3–47, 63, 87–8, 103–13,
    162–3, 168–72, 174, 176–80
  intergroup 103
  intragroup 103
  macro 23–30, 34–5, 37–9
  micro 23–8, 30, 34–5, 38–40
  procedural 7, 9–10, 16, 42, 170,
    172, 174, 176–7
  psychology of 3–5, 7–8, 16,
    20–1
  sense of 22–9, 31–5, 37, 39–40,
    42, 44,–5, 63
  theory 9, 170, 178
Fairness Heuristic Model/
    Theory 8, 10–12, 15, 17,
    19–20, 171, 176
fairness-oriented information
    processing model 168, 174
family 42, 51, 56, 100, 149–50,
    154, 177, 180
filial piety 60
folk religion 56
foreigner 111–12
France 44
freedom 43, 90–1, 94, 97–9
functionalism/functionalist 84–5

game theory 169
gender 22, 34, 111–12, 115, 117,
    119–22, 124–26, 128–30,
    138, 140
  gap 22, 115–17, 120, 124, 128
  stereotypes 115, 119
  traditional gender roles 117,
    119–22, 125–6, 128–9
Germany/German 44, 73, 76,
    110

global values survey 44
global warming 152
globalization 149
gradational schema 66–7, 86
group 5, 7–9, 12–13, 19, 23,
    29–33, 36, 40, 42–4, 47–51,
    53–4, 57, 59–63, 67, 69, 72,
    74–5, 77–9, 81, 84, 103–14,
    124, 126–7, 131–49, 151–6,
    163, 165, 167, 169–71, 173–4,
    177
  achievement 50
  engagement model 9
  identification 107–12
  norms 50, 155
  objectives 48
  utilitarianism 57, 59–61
  value model 29, 104, 165, 171,
    177

Hamaguchi Eshun 48, 50
happiness 48, 88
health 16, 23, 40, 88–9, 149 *see
    also* mental health
  care reform 16
high school 32, 47, 51, 53, 69, 83
Hofstede, G. 4–5, 48, 179
hostile sexism 115–16, 125–7,
    130 *see also* benevolent
    sexism
human diversity 91

IBM 48
Iceland 120
identity
  group 105, 106, 155, 165, 171
  individual 105
  Japanese 108, 109, 121
  national 107, 109, 112, 113
  social 103, 105, 106, 109,135,
    137, 138, 140

identification 105, 106–12, 156, 171
ideology 13, 38, 73, 116, 124
income 7, 22, 25–8, 30, 32, 34, 39, 43–6, 51–4, 59–62, 66, 72, 75, 78, 82–3, 88, 90–1, 95, 98, 100, 128–9, 132, 150, 160, 181
  inequality 7, 25
  satisfaction level 28
individual objectives 48
individualism 48–51, 62
  horizontal 51
  vertical 51
industrialization 72, 74, 149
inequality 7, 22–5, 27, 29–33, 35, 38–9, 65–6, 88–91, 94, 117, 129–30
  of opportunity 22
information quantity hypothesis 28
injustice 7, 12, 15, 24, 42, 111
instrumental model 171
intergenerational mobility 66–7, 84–5
intergroup unfairness 103, 105–8, 111, 113 *see also* fairness
intra-cultural differences 20
Isawa Dam 168, 172–3, 177–8
Islam 55–6
Israel 81, 110

judgment phase 10, 13, 15–18
jury verdicts 42
justice 3, 6–7, 9, 12, 15, 18, 20–1, 23–4, 42, 87–91, 94, 96, 100, 103, 111, 177
  macrojustice/microjustice 23
  psychology of 3, 20–1
Justice-Bond Theory 9

kindness perception 33, 34, 35
Koizumi Shinichiro 22
Korea 48, 71

Latino 107
Liberal Democratic Party 41, 169
Lind, E. A. 3, 5–6, 8–15, 18, 20, 29, 104, 171, 177
luck egalitarianism 94–6

malice 115, 121, 126–7
managerial 66, 68, 72–3, 141
marginal utility 92–3, 95
mental health 131–7, 139–40, 142, 144–8
meritocratic belief 38
minimizing hypothesis 135, 139
multiple linear regression analysis 26
mutual aid 149–50
Nakane Chie 48, 50
nation 14, 23, 50, 108, 120
national identity 105, 107, 109, 112–13
nationalism 108–9, 111–14
necessity principle 38
NEET 33
net cafe refugee 33
Netherlands 4–5, 19
New zealand 73
NHK 54–6
Nihonjinron 48–9
Norm Activation Model 164
normative behavior 23

occupation 22, 28, 34, 40, 48, 52–4, 61, 65–86, 119–20, 130
occupational prestige 65–74, 76, 78–86

scores 65, 70, 74
studies 65–7, 69, 76, 78, 84, 86
OECD 32
Ohbuchi Ken-ichi 3, 5–6, 9, 12, 17, 19–21, 23, 25, 27–9, 31, 34, 37–8, 41–2, 45, 49, 56–9, 104–5, 115, 125, 129–30, 135, 157–8, 165, 169, 179
OPS 65–75, 77–86, 152
organizational psychology 4
Oyserman scale 49

paternalism 124
patriot 108–9, 111–14
patriotism 108–9, 111–14
perception 13–4, 22, 24, 29–36, 38–40, 72, 75–9, 84, 103, 107–9, 112–13, 124, 126, 133, 136, 139–40, 142–6, 148, 152, 154
personal attributes 156, 160
personal liberty 7
personal uncertainty 5–8, 10–11, 13–16
physical diversity 91
polytheism 63
poverty 32, 62, 73, 88–9, 100, 149
prejudice 109–10, 113, 127–8, 131, 134–9, 145–8
procedural justice theory 9
professional occupations 53, 68, 76
pro-social behavior 10, 17, 162, 164, 178
Protestant work ethic 38
psychological dynamic 14, 18
psychological repression 13
psycho-social mechanism 64
public involvement 152, 167

quality of life 16, 99–100, 170

rationalization mechanism 22, 38
rationalization of status quo 36, 38
reality diversity hypothesis 78–80
recession 7, 14–16, 22, 45, 161, 170
reciprocity perception 33–5
regulatory reform 22
relative deprivation 39, 100, 103, 106–7, 160–1
relative poverty 32
relativism 58
religion 12, 41, 54–6, 59, 63
remuneration 31, 46–7, 124
  distribution 46
responsibility 61, 82, 90, 94–8, 100, 125, 133–4, 137, 164
rights 16, 19, 42–3, 90, 104, 106, 141
Russian 106

safety net 33, 45
schooling 46–7, 51–2, 54, 61–3
Second World War 49, 113, 149
SEI 67, 69, 83–4, 86
self-concept 48, 132, 135, 139, 141
self-esteem 24, 29, 33, 35, 38, 48, 61, 118, 127, 132–4, 137–9, 142, 144, 158, 177
self-interest 24–6, 35, 37–9, 58, 63, 121, 150, 153, 155, 168, 171
Sen, A. K. 88–9, 90, 91–4, 96–100, 180
sexism 115–30

Shinto 55–9, 61, 63
social attitude 44
social benefit 162, 166
social bond 13
social class 41–2, 45–7, 51–2, 59–60, 63–4
social decision 42
social dilemma 8, 150–3, 162–3
social disparity 22
social environment 20, 137, 145, 158–9, 162, 173, 178
social factors 156
social harmony 12, 30–1, 42, 44, 49, 57–60
social ideal realization 29–30, 32–3, 35, 39
social identity theory 105
social inequality 22, 24–5, 29, 32, 39, 65
social insecurity 45, 47
social institutions 7
social justice 12, 21, 103
social mobility 28, 66, 68–9, 84–7
social networks 154, 156
social psychologist 3
social psychology of justice 21
social psychology 4, 7, 20–1, 23, 132, 134, 167
social security 31, 33–4, 41, 88
social status 22, 66–9, 75–7, 79–80, 82, 84–5, 117–23, 126, 132, 137, 141, 158
social strata 12, 80, 160
social stratification 67–8
social structure 12, 18, 30, 32, 79, 117–21, 129
social values 41, 45, 56
social welfare 12, 89, 169–70, 180
socialization 12, 119

socioeconomic index 66–7, 69, 83
socio-economic status 22, 25, 26–8, 36–40, 82–3, 117, 121, 129
Soviet Union 73
SSM Survey 26–8, 68, 70–1, 80, 82, 179–80
standard international occupational prestige score 74
status attainment process 66–7, 83–4, 86
stratification model 28, 36
stratification 28, 36, 67–8, 8–1
subjective norms 154, 164
survey data 7, 28, 57
syncretism 56, 63
system justification
  process 14, 18
  theory 7, 36, 179

Taiwan 48
theory of Japanese 49, 50, 63
  see also Nihonjinron
threat 6–7, 12–14, 24, 35, 49, 104–6, 111–13, 122, 136–9, 141, 145–6
traditional Japanese values 57
  see also culture, Japanese
treatment 8, 11, 15–20, 23–6, 29–30, 37, 39, 41–2, 44, 95, 103–5, 107, 109, 111, 113, 116, 124, 128, 132–9, 142, 144–8, 165, 171, 174, 176–7, 179
Triandis and Gelfand score/scale 51, 54
trust 10, 41, 50, 58, 111–12, 153–4, 168–9, 171, 173–6, 178

UK 22–3, 58, 66, 68, 71, 75, 84, 131, 149, 160
UN Security Council 107
uncertainty management theory 8, 10–11, 13, 15
United States 3–6, 8, 163, 167 *see also* USA
universal health care 16
university 20, 32, 47, 51, 53, 60, 68–70, 76–7, 79, 122, 179
USA 13–14, 43–44, 48, 62, 128–29, 131, 133, 135, 138, 142,–4, 147–8, 160, 181 *see also* United States
use phase 10–13, 16, 18
utilitarian motives 164, 167, 176
utilitarianism 57, 59–61, 89, 165, 180
utility/utilities 88–95, 164, 181
utilization function 93

Van den Bos, K. 3–6, 8, 10, 12–13, 15, 19–20, 171, 179
vendetta effect 18

welfarism 88–9, 91–2, 94–5, 100, 180
well-being 24, 90–1, 97, 132, 136, 170
  individual 90
  personal 24
  psychological 136
  subjective 24
World Values Survey 30, 54–5